A Rat Is a Pig Is a Dog Is a Boy

A Rat Is a Pig
Is a Dog
Is a Boy

The Human Cost
of the Animal Rights Movement

Wesley J. Smith

ENCOUNTER BOOKS
NEW YORK · LONDON

First American edition published in 2009 by Encounter Books, an activity of Encounter for Culture and Education, Inc., a nonprofit, tax exempt corporation. Encounter Books website address: www.encounterbooks.com

Manufactured in the United States and printed on acid-free paper. The paper used in this publication meets the minimum requirements of ANSI/NISO Z39.48-1992 (R 1997) (Permanence of Paper).

FIRST AMERICAN EDITION

LIBRARY OF CONGRESS CATALOGING-IN-PUBLICATION DATA

Smith, Wesley J.
    A rat is a pig is a dog is a boy : the human cost of the animal rights movement / Wesley J. Smith.
    p. cm.
    Includes bibliographical references and index.
    ISBN-13: 978-1-59403-346-9 (hardcover : alk. paper)
    ISBN-10: 1-59403-346-3 (hardcover : alk. paper)
    1. Animal rights.   2. Human-animal relationships.   3. Animal welfare.   I. Title.
HV4708.S623 2009
179.3—dc22

                                                              2009018977

To Bruce Chapman, in deep appreciation of his leadership, personal support, and abiding friendship

Other Books by Wesley J. Smith

The Lawyer Book: A Nuts and Bolts Guide to Client Survival

The Doctor Book: A Nuts and Bolts Guide to Patient Power

The Senior Citizens Handbook: A Nuts and Bolts Guide to More Comfortable Living

Winning the Insurance Game (co-authored with Ralph Nader)

The Frugal Shopper (co-authored with Ralph Nader)

Collision Course: The Truth about Airline Safety (co-authored with Ralph Nader)

No Contest: Corporate Lawyers and the Perversion of Justice in America (co-authored with Ralph Nader)

Forced Exit: Euthanasia, Assisted Suicide, and the New Duty to Die

Culture of Death: The Assault on Medical Ethics in America

Power over Pain: How to Get the Pain Control You Need (co-authored with Eric Chevlen, MD)

Consumer's Guide to a Brave New World

Contents

Foreword

This is a world of infinite layers and of insoluble enigmas. Our five senses bring us considerably more information than we are able to comprehend. Because we human beings often pride ourselves on the certainty of our knowledge and our opinions, a failure to comprehend disquiets us. Consequently, we lie to ourselves about the nature of the world. We resist inferring the Truth that is implicit in every moment of every day. We want a simple world, but it is instead thrillingly complex. Complexity disquiets us because it implies meaning, and we are afraid of meaning except as we craft it to suit ourselves.

Truth is what it is. The small truth of any mundane event and the ultimate Truth, which is the meaning and the way of the world, cannot be crafted. Intuition is our truthfinder. All profound truths are intuitive, neither derived from experience nor limited by it, but they are also fortified by reasoned observation: our born understanding of space and time, our born awareness that the whole is greater than any of its parts and that two things which are equal to a third are also equal to each other, our recognition of design in nature, our sense that dimensions exist beyond the material.

We can be educated—or argued—out of our intuitive knowledge, but then we become irrational and are unaware of our irrationality. We thereafter comprehend the world through a narrow theory or ideology that reduces complexity to simplicity. We are comforted by this crafted simplicity, this fiction, and we call it Truth, at which point we cross a line into a functional madness. By embracing fiction as truth, we surrender our connection with the transcendental and therefore with nature in all its layered mystery.

Truth is always stranger than fiction because we craft fiction to fit our preferences, but we have no control of the truth. The universe does not exist to fulfill our cherished expectations, and therefore truth frequently surprises us, bursting into our lives from the least expected source. Such as from a dog.

A golden retriever changed my heart, my life, and my writing. Her name was Trixie, and I sometimes say that I learned more from her than from all my years in school. That is not a cute quip but the truth. She encouraged in me a tenderness that I didn't know I possessed, restored my sense of wonder to the brightness it had in my youth, and renewed my awareness of the mystical nature of life. She gave and received love in abundance, was innocent and direct—and yet mysterious. Losing her was the hardest loss of my life, and the intensity of my grief did not begin to diminish for weeks.

Because of my experiences with Trixie, I believe that, like us, a few species among the higher animals must have souls, although of a different kind from ours. This simple soul is an aspect of their being that provides them an awareness of death and of an unseen dimension of existence, the preternatural. My dog seemed to have not only instinct but also that more exalted form of knowledge called intuition.

Having for years been involved with assistance-dog organizations, I know scores of people who work daily with dogs, and most will say not only that these animals have intuition—in addition to base instinct—but also that just as human beings are born with a Tao, a sense of right and wrong, so are dogs. The canine Tao is akin to—but simpler than—the human Tao; and more important, dogs largely live according to it, perhaps because they lack the free will that gives human beings the capacity to rebel against natural law.

Some denominations of Judaism believe that an animal spirit, something like our soul, may survive death if the animal, by the comfort and affection it gives to its human companion, inspires that companion to perform a great many mitzvahs—good and praiseworthy deeds—during his life. My intuition tells me this must be true: as faith and charity are the pillars of the bridge that allows a good person to cross the void between this world and eternity, so each of us is the bridge by which a beloved dog may follow us.

The committed animal rights activist must deny the existence of any kind of animal soul, for to acknowledge it would be to admit the existence of a human soul. And the game here is less about protecting animals than about denying the existence of the sacred.

I, on the other hand, recognizing the sacredness of all creation, must believe ardently in animal welfare. Every creature is the work of my own Creator, and therefore worthy of respect and mercy.

But recognizing a vertical of sacred order, I must also believe that rights do not come from men or courts, or from governments, but only from God. Rights granted by men, courts, and governments are not rights but merely privileges that can be modified or denied according to the whims of those in power. This is why the founders of our country specified that "life, liberty, and the pursuit of happiness" were rights of divine origin, beyond the power of moral leaders to limit unreasonably or to abrogate.

Therefore, not being God, we cannot grant rights to animals any more than we can grant ourselves the right to take our neighbors' property or their lives. Under a corrupt political regime, much property and many lives might be taken from one group for the benefit and the satisfaction of others, but this can never be a *right* of the takers; it is merely their exercise of raw power in the service of their avarice and hatred. A society might legalize slavery, which makes some men the property of others, but the power to own slaves is not the same as the *right* to own them.

For thousands of years, the intuition of countless generations in many cultures has been that humankind is exceptional among all the species of this world. This born knowledge is fortified—and one might argue is confirmed—by reasoned observation. Recognition and acceptance of human exceptionalism gives rise to a sense of duty and a moral obligation to a higher power that, when fulfilled, leads to a better world for everyone. History shows that slavery is eliminated, the number of the impoverished is reduced, pollution is curbed, and all the other ills of humankind are best addressed by people with a sense of a merciful divine imperative, not by those whose motivation is a concept as imprecise as "justice." *God* means one thing supreme; but *justice* has infinite definitions, as when Hitler dealt "justice" to the Jews, and Stalin to anyone who did not submit to his boot.

Ironically, the movement to deny human exceptionalism has arisen primarily if not exclusively in the Christian West. Its roots are in the desire to deny the roundness of creation and to force upon society a simple and intellectually hollow materialism that reduces nature to a machine lacking in mystery and reduces all the splendid, diverse creatures on the earth to one and the same thing: meat. It is a denial of the world's profound depth, of meaning and sacred order.

Like every antidemocratic ideology, this one is by definition antihuman, and like any antihuman ideology, it ultimately deteriorates into a nihilistic bitterness that is anti-*life*. That's why animal shelters run by animal rights advocates can justify the wholesale killing of cats and dogs instead of finding them homes, why the most radicalized ideologues can justify killing human beings, and why someone can write a book about how wonderful the world would be without humankind and apparently give no thought to the fact that some will read it as a call for mass murder.

When we blind ourselves to the Truth of the world's magnificent complexity and mystery—of which we are a fundamental part—we do not only cut a thin wedge from the roundness of existence and convince ourselves that this one theory or ideology is the whole Truth. In our narcissism, we also insist that those who refuse to wear our blinders are villainous and depraved and corrupt. In this regard, an ideologue is no different from a member of a religious cult who has carved a sliver off the body of Christian theology and has made it his be-all and end-all. But the entire truth of a vast forest is not embodied in a single leaf.

A recognition of the world's complexity requires an acceptance of the truth that intentions and nuance matter. Puppy mills are an outrage and should be shut down because they horribly abuse breeder dogs for no purpose but profit. This isn't the same as a scientist, following merciful protocols (as most do), using lab rats in search of cures for disabling diseases. A sound argument might be made for the cruelty of denying a wide-ranging and undomesticable animal like an elephant the freedom to roam, keeping it chained to a stake for no purpose but to entertain us with clever tricks in the circus; though a well-designed zoo park might not be cruel at all. Training a dog to do tricks is not cruel, because dogs are pack animals and consider us members of their pack, because they would rather be with us than elsewhere, and because their natural inclination to play makes learning tricks a joy for them.

Among other things, this book is a rational, reasonable argument for the need to accept the nuanced complexity of the world and to resist the dangerous simplifications of antihuman ideologies. Wesley J. Smith knows too well that if the activists ever succeeded in their goals, if they established through culture or law that human beings have no intrinsic dignity greater than that of any animal, the world would not be a better place for either humankind or animals. Instead, it would be a utilitarian nightmare in which the strong would destroy the weak, in which power-crazed leaders would destroy everyone who loved peace, in which the wealth of the world would be concentrated in the hands of a murderous few, in which mercy would be unknown and the only virtue would be the ability to survive, in which the only right would be the right to die.

Dean Koontz
April 2009

Introduction

The Walt Disney Company used to advertise Disneyland as the happiest place on earth. But for my money the Assistance Dog Institute of Santa Rosa, California—"helping dogs help people"—is more joyful.[1] The Space Mountain and Pirates of the Caribbean rides are certainly fun, but for pure bliss, nothing beats being surrounded by friendly and happy dogs!

Assistance dogs are remarkable canines specially bred and trained to help people with physical and developmental disabilities lead happier and more independent lives. As I walked into ADI's offices in preparation for writing this book, I suddenly found myself awash in beautiful and energetic golden and Labrador retrievers. I stuck my head into the office of Bonnie Bergin, president of ADI and creator of the assistance-dog concept, and saw four or five eager dogs leaning forward for a scritch. I walked down a short hall and a big golden put his front paws on the closed bottom half of a Dutch door, looking for a quick chin chuck and a hand to lick. Then, I was told to be very quiet as I watched a specially trained volunteer "puppy petter" softly stroke a tiny days-old puppy whose mother was nursing the puppy's siblings nearby. Finally, in the large training room, I laughed as a rambunctious puppy named Trixie opened a refrigerator door on command by biting on a cloth attached to the door and pulling. Hearing an enthusiastic "Good Girl!" she leaped into her trainer's arms for more praise and a good snuggle.

By the time they are six months old, assistance dogs in training like Trixie have learned obedience and gross retrieval skills. As they mature, their training intensifies and they acquire astonishingly sophisticated abilities. By the time they "graduate" at about eighteen months, assistance dogs can respond to no fewer than ninety-four commands, such as "closer," "tug," "drop it," "hold," and "release." The next step is to pair a disabled person with the dog that will become a loving assistant and companion. The two will bond intensely as they learn how to work together, so the dog can perform everyday tasks that may be of urgent concern for people with disabilities: opening and closing doors, retrieving dropped items (phone or keys, e.g.), turning lights on and off.

The practical benefits of service dogs are obvious. But they can also provide an even more valuable service, as "Frank" the service dog did for Kip, a young man disabled in an accident. Kip's mother, Lisa, wrote:

> There is no doubt in my mind that Frank's most critical job is to open the door socially [for Kip]. Prior to Kip's injury, he was a strong, healthy, active, physically fit young 18 year-old. To go from being the high school athlete to being in a chair, there is not a person who did not approach him differently, if they even approached him. Most people would tend to just ignore Kip's presence, looking right over him.... What Frank has done is open the door for people so they can communicate directly with Kip. Frank's presence helps people get over their fears about approaching Kip. The conversation usually begins with, "What a beautiful dog," or "What's your dog's name?" or, "May I pet your dog?" To have people acknowledge Kip's presence through Frank has been life-changing for Kip.[2]

One would think that the Assistance Dog Institute—and other organizations like it throughout the United States, such as Canine Companions for Independence[3]—would be uncontroversial: The dogs are happy and well cared for; the students at the institutes are happy; those receiving the canine services are overjoyed. But if animal rights activists had their way, ADI would not exist. They believe that all instrumental uses of animals are immoral, no matter how benign to the animals or how beneficial to humans. And so for the past three-plus decades they have mounted an increasingly radical campaign aimed at the eventual "liberation" of animals from humans—a campaign that has left virtually no animal use untouched.

It is not my purpose in this book to act as a defender of animal industries. Rather, my goals are primarily to expose the antihuman ideology of the animal rights/liberation movement,* expose its many deceptions, and

---

*Some movement activists distinguish "animal rights" from "animal liberation." In this view, the former term describes the beliefs of the movement, while the latter refers to direct actions taken in furtherance of those beliefs, such as releasing mink from their

warn against its sometimes violent tactics. I will also defend the use of animals as necessary and appropriate to promote human welfare, prosperity, and happiness. Finally, I will mount an unequivocal defense of the belief that human beings stand uniquely at the pinnacle of moral worth, a concept sometimes called "human exceptionalism."

I am very well aware that these positions, once almost universally accepted, have become controversial in recent years. Few issues generate such intense emotionalism or fervent support by their adherents as does "animal rights." Thus, I want to make it very clear at the outset—as I will throughout the book—that I love animals and, like most people, I wince when I see them in pain. Moreover, I believe strongly that we as enlightened people have a profound moral and ethical obligation to treat animals humanely and respectfully—a core obligation of human exceptionalism—and by all means never to cause them to suffer for frivolous reasons. I also strongly support laws against cruelty to animals and I favor strengthening them when appropriate. In fact, I believe that animal abuse is a terrible wrong, not only because it causes the victimized animal to suffer, but also because cruelty to animals diminishes our own humanity.

Now, consider why I felt it necessary to make such an unusual disclaimer: Over the past thirty years, the concept of "animal rights" has seeped into the bone marrow of Western culture. (This is especially true among the young.) Part of the reason is that "animal rights" is used so loosely it is often taken to mean little more than being nicer to animals. But this isn't true. Although animal rights groups do sometimes engage in animal welfare–type activism, the term "animal rights" actually denotes a *belief system*, an ideology, even a quasi religion, which both implicitly and explicitly seeks to create a moral equivalence between the value of human lives and those of animals. This belief was succinctly expressed in 1986 when Ingrid Newkirk, the head of the animal rights absolutist organization People for the Ethical Treatment of Animals (PETA), told the *Washingtonian* magazine, "A rat is a pig is a dog is a boy. They are all mammals."[4]

---

cages into the wild. But we need not concern ourselves here with such arcane distinctions, and thus, unless otherwise noted, the terms will be used interchangeably.

Animal rights ideologues embrace their beliefs with a fervency that is remarkably intense and sustained, to the point that some dedicate their entire lives to "speaking for those who cannot speak for themselves." Some believe their cause to be so righteous that they are entitled to cross the line from legitimate advocacy to terroristic attempts at coercion. Indeed, what other than "true belief" can possibly explain the vicious campaign—of harassment and vandalism, criminal attacks, bombings, and even threats of murder—that has been launched in recent years against medical researchers, the fur and food industries, and others accused of "animal abuse"?

Our Love Affair with Animals

Perhaps we should not be surprised at the growth of the animal rights movement. Americans *love* animals. We coddle our cats and dogs as if they were human children. We paste "Save the Whales" bumper stickers on our cars. We flock to national parks to catch fleeting glimpses of bear, elk, and antelope—remnants of a wild America. We anthropomorphize the animal world with movies like *Bambi* and *Babe*. We want our cheese to come from "happy cows." At the same time, as primarily urbanites, we disassociate ourselves emotionally from the fact that meat comes from killing animals and that our stylish leather jackets were first worn by cows or sheep.

This love affair with animals can be charming, if a bit loopy at times. It is also a potent indicator of our prosperity and cultural success. Most people in the West have become so removed from the struggle for daily survival that we have the luxury of caring deeply about animals and their suffering—*which is a good thing*. Moreover, our care for animals reflects our empathy, one of the great human virtues.

Our deep affinity with animals begins very early in life. I was reminded of this a few years ago while on a family vacation to Ireland. In the western coastal town of Dingle there is a unique tourist attraction: "Fungi" the lone dolphin. Tourist boats advertise trips into the harbor to see Fungi, with no fee charged unless he makes an appearance. Liking dolphins and wanting to see one up close, my wife Debra, niece Jennifer, and I eagerly bought tickets, and along with about twenty other tourists we were soon on a boat slowly cruising toward the mouth of Dingle's small picturesque harbor.

As if on cue, Fungi arrived, swimming almost within reach on the starboard side. We all pressed eagerly up against the railing to get a good look. I was standing behind a little boy who couldn't have been older than four, and who was very excited about being so close to the magnificent animal. Suddenly, he sighed in ecstasy, held his arms out as wide as he could, and with all the love in his innocent heart, crooned, "Ah, Fungi!"

It was a touching moment. Fungi was utterly indifferent to the child, no doubt swimming alongside the boat knowing he would be fed by a deck hand as his usual cut of the day's profits for making an appearance. But to the little boy, Fungi epitomized the joy and hope of life itself.

On the same vacation, Debra had been enjoying a biography of the great French novelist Alexandre Dumas—until, that is, she came across a disturbing section. It seems that Dumas was traveling across the English Channel when dolphins began swimming by his ship, jumping, squeaking, and riding the ship's bow wave as is their wont. Dumas apparently fancied himself to be a great hunter. He had never killed a dolphin, so he went to his stateroom, got his gun, and killed an "ancestor" of Fungi—just for the fun of it.

"Why did you read us that?" Jennifer and I moaned in unison, our splendid moods of the moment ruined at the thought of such gratuitous cruelty against an innocent animal. The fact that the incident had occurred more than one hundred years ago did nothing to soothe our feelings.

And yet: Killing animals has always been and remains inextricably bound with human thriving. We do so for food and leather, in medical research, in sport, and to ensure environmental balance when necessary. More to the point, there is a lot at stake in this debate. Pause a moment and ponder the consequences if we were prevented from domesticating animals, as animal rights/liberationists advocate. Medical research would be materially impeded. There would be no more fishing fleets, cattle ranches, leather shoes, steak barbeques, animal parks, bomb-sniffing or Seeing Eye dogs, wool coats, fish farms, horseback riding, pet stores, perhaps not even attractions like Fungi. Millions of people would be thrown out of work, our enjoyment of life would be substantially diminished, our welfare and prosperity reduced.

How We Shall Proceed

To understand why animal rights/liberation is such a serious threat to human well-being, we must begin at the level of core ideas and fundamental beliefs. We will first look into the basic differences between animal welfare or animal protection on the one hand, and animal rights on the other. Here too we will examine the common belief that unites the disparate animal rights/liberation philosophical approaches: the belief that it is wrong to treat human beings differently from animals—to practice what is known as "speciesism," which many consider to be as odious as racism or other forms of bigotry against particular categories of people.

Next we will examine the utilitarian philosophy of the Princeton bioethicist Peter Singer. Contrary to popular understanding, Singer does not believe in animal rights per se. But his call to grant animals "equal consideration" with people in judging the morality of actions and public policies revolutionized thinking in this area and jump-started what became the animal rights/liberation movement.

We will then explore the purist animal rights ideology as articulated by the most prominent thinkers in the field. Included here are the preaching of People for the Ethical Treatment of Animals (PETA), the abolitionist philosophy of Gary Francione, and the influential Tom Regan's call to treat animals equally with people as the "subjects of a life."

From abstract ideas, we move into the various advocacy campaigns playing out in the public square. First up will be the Great Ape Project, the explicit purpose of which is to demote human beings from the exceptional species into members of a "community of equals" that also includes great apes—an idea that, alarmingly, has already achieved some success. We will also review the true story of the notorious "Silver Spring monkey case," a successful political and legal attack that helped make PETA a political force as it nearly destroyed the life and work of a prominent medical researcher who was targeted because he used monkeys in important experiments aimed at developing a new treatment for victims of stroke.

Among other disclosures, you will learn that pregnant pigs have been given certain constitutional rights under the Florida Constitution, how and why the Australian wool industry is under threat of international boycott because of a method for protecting sheep against a terrible maggot infestation, and the manner in which your children are being proselytized by animal rightists, often in the schools.

Everyone has the right to advocate for his or her beliefs in a free society, of course, no matter how ill-advised their goals. Alas, some animal rights activists aren't content merely to persuade but increasingly seek to impose their views by threats of violence and acts of outright criminality. Loose groups like ALF (Animal Liberation Front), ELF (Environmental Liberation Front), SHAC (Stop Huntingdon Animal Cruelty), and other anarchists attack and threaten scientists, labs, animal-processing plants, fur ranches, and other places where animals are used for human benefit. Like all terrorism, these activities have two purposes: to harm the specific person or group targeted, and more broadly to scare other similarly situated people into thinking of themselves as potential targets. We will name names and go into details about these more extreme animal rights radicals—and show that rather than being separate and apart, the terrorists within the movement are, if not mainstream, certainly not outcasts among co-believers.

One of the primary threats posed by the animal rights movement to society is its unremitting campaign to thwart the advance of science and medicine by means of animal research. We will explore this area in detail, exposing the patently false argument made by many liberationists that using animals in research is both scientifically unnecessary and harmful to human health. We will also discuss why animal research is necessary—for example, as a way of protecting human research subjects—as well as the efforts being made by researchers to minimize the use of animals and the harm caused to them in experiments.

From there, we will turn to some of the other areas in which humans benefit from the proper and humane use of animals. Here we will focus primarily on animals as food. Animal rightists promote veganism and vegetarianism as a matter of both ethics and human health. But human beings are biologically omnivores, and meat is a natural part of our diet. Still, our raising of food animals does entail important animal welfare issues, particularly regarding the acceptability of industrial farming and the best practices for slaughtering food animals. And while it is impossible to examine every controversy involving the use of animals, we will also look into the debates over fur, zoos, and hunting.

Our concluding chapter returns to the realm of ideas. The great philosophical question of the twenty-first century, it seems to me, is whether we will knock human beings off the pedestal of moral distinctiveness, or move forward to create a better world for people and animals alike from the position of human moral responsibility. This goal, I argue, requires not the relinquishing of human exceptionalism, but rather its wholehearted embrace.

The stakes in the animal rights controversy are larger than the sum of its parts. It is my hope that after finishing this book, readers will agree that it is a distinctly human and noble calling to continually improve our ways of raising and caring for animals. But this effort must not and cannot include granting rights to animals as if they were people. I hope this book will convincingly demonstrate that the very concept of animal rights should be rejected because by seeking to destroy the principle of human exceptionalism, the movement subverts human rights as it undermines our ability to promote human health, prosperity, and well-being.

Wesley J. Smith
May 2009

PART ONE

"For the Animals"

1

Animal Advocacy Isn't What It Used to Be

When Arthur Rosenbaum, a pediatric ophthalmologist at UCLA, found a deadly explosive device planted underneath his car, only a defective fuse prevented the bomb from going off and killing him. Dr. Rosenbaum was not surprised to have been targeted. Like other researchers, he had been the victim of a sustained and vicious campaign of harassment and intimidation, subjected to vandalism, threats of harm to himself and his family, and now, a potentially deadly assault.

Why would someone want to kill or badly scare the scientist and his colleagues? He and the police knew precisely whom to blame. Nor were the perpetrators shy about their crime: A communiqué from the Animal Liberation Front (ALF)—the name used by decentralized terrorist cells of animal rights fanatics—acknowledged the attack, stating in part, "Rosenbaum, you need to watch your back because next time you are in the operating room or walking to your office, you just might be facing injections into your eyes like the primates [upon which you experiment], you sick twisted f—k."[1] Yes, the researcher faced possible murder because—and only because—he conducts animal experiments.

The failed pipe-bomb attack on Rosenbaum was merely one skirmish in a years-long war waged by ALF against UCLA scientists. Another target was Dr. Edythe London, a lab administrator involved with the study of the biology of addiction. In October 2007, animal rights fanatics flooded her home, and ALF, as in other cases, claimed responsibility in an anonymous press release:

> Edythe London, your job as administrator of the UCLA Center that addicts primates to methamphetamines is despicable. You appear to make all of the sick perverted vivisectors who addict primates to meth possible. . . . You may have the privilege of coordinating all of this pain and suffering from a slight distance, but as people who act out of conscience we will not allow you to simply lurk in the shadows of UCLA's labs of torture.

After disclosing London's home address for other liberationists' information, the "communiqué" continued:

> Here's how we got started. We found your million dollar house in Beverly Hills on the windy night of October 20, we discovered you weren't home so we snuck into your backyard. First, we effectively clogged the intake drain of your pool pump. It probably ran dry for a couple of hours and burned itself out. . . . Next we smashed a window and inserted your garden hose, turned it on to full blast of course. Bet you were surprised when you came home. Edythe, do you have flood insurance?

Then came the unveiled threat:

> One more thing Edythe, water was our second choice. Fire was our first. We compromised because we in the ALF don't risk harming animals human and non human and we don't risk starting brush fires. It would have been just as easy to burn your house down Edythe. As you slosh around your flooded house consider yourself fortunate this time. We will not stop until UCLA discontinues its primate vivisection programe [sic]. We are ALF.[2]

These were not empty threats. In February 2008, the ALF ratcheted up its terrorism, setting fire to Dr. London's house by exploding an incendiary device. She was not home when the blaze was ignited and fortunately nobody was hurt. But the fire could easily have turned into a conflagration, destroying London's and other homes and perhaps killing firefighters.[3] And just as before, the ALF bragged about its criminality in a press release.[4]

At about the same time, a similar intimidation campaign was also being waged against a UCLA scientist named Dario Ringach, who had been experimenting with monkeys to find ways to allow the blind to see through an optical implant in the brain. But helping the blind wasn't worth the lives of monkeys to the ALF terrorists. When Ringach began to fear for the safety of his children, he decided the time had come to capitulate and buy some peace. According to "Throwing in the Towel," a story published in *Inside Higher Ed,*

> The constant calls, the people frightening his children, and the demonstrations in front of his home apparently became a little too much. Dario Ringach, an associate neurobiology professor at the University of California at Los Angeles, decided this month to give up his research on primates because of pressure put on him, his neighborhood, and his family by the UCLA Primate Freedom Project, which seeks to stop research that harms animals.... In an e-mail this month to several anti-animal research groups, Ringach wrote that "you win," and asked that the groups "please don't bother my family anymore."[5]

Whether Ringach would have succeeded in helping the blind to see cannot be known. But this much is sure: a talented scientist was driven from legitimate work by terrorists who cared more about monkeys than about people suffering from visual impairments.

Animal rights terrorism is an international phenomenon that if anything has been waged even more ruthlessly overseas, especially in the United Kingdom. Consider the plight of David and Christopher Hall, owners of the Darley Oaks Farm and targets of a nasty campaign of threats and vandalism by animal rights radicals because they raised guinea pigs for use in medical research. An incendiary device was left on the porch of John Hall's daughter. Other family members "were accused of being pedophiles and banned from their local pub and golf course."[6] As the *Telegraph* reported,

> For years the gang tormented the Halls.... Petrol bombs, death threats, voodoo dolls, graffiti, slander, vandalism to cars and houses, they stopped at nothing as they reveled in their reputation as untouchable sophisticated terrorists. The Halls were, in fact, terrorized: Chris Hall said, "We were under siege. We might as well have been in prison for six years."[7]

And the terrorism was not restricted to the Hall family either. According to the *Guardian*, "Almost 100 people connected to the farm were targeted. Explosive devices were sent to some, mail threatening to kill and maim to others. There were attacks on homes, cars and businesses."[8]

For years the Halls stood fast. But then, the liberationists escalated their war to a macabre extreme: They *robbed the grave* of Gladys Hammond, the mother-in-law of Christopher Hall, and refused to give her body back until the family stopped raising guinea pigs. Finally, the exhausted Halls could take no more. They promised to cease raising guinea pigs, issuing a statement saying: "We hope that, as a result of this announcement, those responsible for removing Gladys's body will return her so she can lie once again in her rightful resting place."[9]

Four animal liberationists eventually were arrested and pleaded guilty to conspiracy to blackmail, receiving sentences ranging between four and twelve years.[10] The perpetrators were an odd lot to have engaged in such cruelty, coming from the bedrock of respectable society—including a former teacher, the son of an Anglican vicar, and a psychiatric nurse. Gladys Hammond's body was eventually returned to her grave, when a few days prior to sentencing one of the criminals told police where it could be found in the hope of getting an easier deal.[11]

What source of disdain and loathing could drive people to plant bombs, terrify children, disrupt neighborhoods, destroy property, commit arson, intimidate families, harass entire villages, rob graves, and as we shall see later, even justify murder? It comes down to a fervently held belief that borders on religious dogma: animal rights/liberationists hold that what is done to an animal is morally equivalent to the same action done to a human being. Because humans have the right to life, so do animals. Since we are entitled not to be enslaved, animals too have the right not to be owned.

So fervently do animal rights adherents hold their beliefs that thousands of activists dedicate their lives to impeding the humane use of animals through means fair—demonstrations, political activism, properly brought litigation—or foul, including frivolous lawsuits and mendacious advocacy, while the more radical fringe presumes the right to prevent animal "exploitation" through criminal actions and even thinly veiled threats of murder.

"Animal Welfare" versus "Animal Rights"

It wasn't always like this. Animal protection advocacy has a noble history, such as the many societies for the prevention of cruelty to animals and the local humane societies that shelter stray dogs and cats and operate neutering clinics. Today's animal rights movement is often conflated with such "animal welfare" activities, but it grows from a dramatically different concept. Both movements are concerned with the way people treat animals, but that is where the similarity ends. In fact, animal welfare and animal rights represent incompatible moral principles and mutually exclusive goals.

The first difference between the animal rights and animal welfare philosophies is that the latter doesn't regard animals as being entitled to human-type "rights." As we shall discuss more fully in the last chapter, only moral beings possess rights, since that entitlement assumes concomitant duties. But animals are amoral and cannot conceive of honoring the rights of others or of bearing obligations.

The only true moral species is *Homo sapiens*. We understand the concepts of right and wrong, good and bad. Hence, in free societies at least (and even tyrannies give mouth service to the notion), we are deemed each to be born with fundamental rights such as those mentioned in the Declaration of Independence—the rights to "life, liberty, and the pursuit of happiness."

But that isn't the end of the story. Human exceptionalism also imposes responsibilities upon us—*one of which is to treat animals humanely*. And here is another difference between animal welfare and animal rights: As they call upon us to seek ever-improving methods of animal husbandry, welfarists also acknowledge that, assuming appropriate practices, we are entitled to benefit from animals in furtherance of human interests.

Perhaps the most important difference between the two belief systems is that unlike animal rights advocates, proponents of animal welfare do not seek to create a moral equivalence between human beings and animals. As Michael Schau, an attorney in the emerging field of animal law, wrote in a law review article on the issue:

Animal welfare is rooted in the principles of humane care and treatment. Welfare positions are founded on the basic premise that animals can and will be used to benefit humans, and the responsibilities created by this carry certain obligations for humans to the animals. These responsibilities include appropriate husbandry, provision of essential food, water and shelter, health care and maintenance, alleviation of pain and suffering, and other needs. Some animal advocates assert that there are essential uses of animals such as biomedical research and nonessential uses of animals such as entertainment. These advocates will ardently support animal use practices that are perceived to produce widespread benefits to society, thus justifying the required use of animals, but reject support for nonessential use.[12]

Animal rights activists, on the other hand, deny that human beings have the right to use animals to further any human purpose—no matter how beneficial. Knowing that most of society disagrees with this proposition, animal rights organizations often hide their radical ultimate agenda (to end all human use of animals) behind a façade of animal welfare–style activism. But in reality, the animal rightist disdains the animal welfare approach precisely because animal welfarism accepts that human beings have greater value than animals, and more centrally, that we have the right to own and use animals for our benefit. True animal rights activists reject the idea that animals can ever properly be considered property. As one of the world's leading animal rights advocates, Professor Gary L. Francione of Rutgers University's Animal Rights Law Center, explained:

> Recent scholarship on the human/animal relationship contends that the modern animal "rights" movement is fundamentally different from its historical predecessor, the animal welfare movement, or the humane movement. These differences reflect the rejection by rights advocates of a central tenet of animal welfare: that non-humans are the property of humans and human obligations to non-humans are limited to a prohibition against the unnecessary infliction of pain or death on non-humans. Rights advocates generally hold that at least some non-humans possess moral rights that protect certain interests in a more absolute way, just as human rights protect certain human interests.[13]

Co-opting the Welfare Approach:[14]

Disdaining animal welfare as a philosophy doesn't mean, however, that animal rights activists are not more than happy to co-opt the abundant goodwill earned by the animal welfare movement to further their own agendas. The advocacy of Henry Spira, an early animal rights activist, is a prime example. As Peter Singer describes it in his biography *Ethics into Action*,[15] after embracing the ideology of animal rights in the early days of the movement, Spira understood that claiming human-type rights for animals would not go down well with a general public that loved animals but still considered them less important than people. So, instead of pursuing his actual agenda openly, Spira organized a campaign to stop the American Museum of Natural History in New York from conducting experiments in which cats were surgically altered so that they could not feel sexual sensations. Singer writes:

> The fact that the experimental subjects were cats was significant. Ethically, in Henry's view, it does not make any difference whether an experiment is done on a cat, a hamster, or a rat: They are all sensitive creatures capable of feeling pain. But he knew that it would be easier to arouse members of the public to protest against experiments on animals to which they could easily relate. Since dogs and cats are by far the most commonly kept companion animals, experiments on them made the ideal target.[16]

In other words, Spira knew that if he attempted to rouse the public against the use of rats in medical experiments, or cattle for making leather shoes, or horses to pull Amish buggies—activities that he and his fellow animal rights radicals want eliminated—it would be a protest to which nobody came. So, he hit upon a wolf-in-sheep's-clothing strategy: incite a cat-loving public to rage against the use of felines in medical experiments, while disguising the ultimate animal rights agenda behind the benign façade of animal welfare—an approach, according to Singer, that Spira actually believed to be outdated and fundamentally immoral.

After Spira's campaign against the museum succeeded, he continued his work, again often in the guise of an animal welfare advocate. He incorporated Animal Rights International—essentially, his alter ego—as a nonprofit corporation, which, Singer chortled, allowed Spira to receive grant money from traditional animal welfare organizations such as the American Society for the Prevention of Cruelty to Animals. Singer writes, "The collaboration between Henry and these [animal welfare] leaders helped to draw this long-established side of the movement closer to the newer animal rights movement, with its more far-reaching goals."[17]

This disingenuous approach continues to this day. As Kathy Guillermo, an authorized spokeswoman for People for the Ethical Treatment of Animals (PETA), told me several years ago when I was researching another book, "There are a lot of people who support PETA because they see that animals are suffering and they want to do something about it." These are people, Guillermo admits, who would not agree with "everything PETA says."[18] Thus, by partially camouflaging its true face, animal rights organizations such as PETA benefit enormously from the substantial goodwill built up over the decades by animal welfare organizations.

Such duplicity permits these organizations to have their cake and eat it too: By publicizing welfare activities they vacuum up substantial financial and moral support from animal lovers who believe they are promoting animal welfare, which also gives these organizations the resources to pursue their far more radical purposes.

Ironically, this may work to the detriment of some animals. According to Frederick K. Goodwin, a former director of the National Institute for Mental Health who has long tangled with the animal rights movement, "Many traditional animal welfare organizations are now entirely co-opted [by the animal rights agenda]. The cruel irony is that they have drained funds from traditional welfare activities, programs such as neutering pets and stopping cruelty. All of the things which have really helped animals historically are now run on shoe strings."[19] Indeed, according to a thorough investigative report about the animal rights movement published by the *Washingtonian* in 1990, "The once diverse animal-protection movement is now dominated by a single goal: to stop exploitation of animals for any purpose and, in particular, to abolish animal experimentation altogether."[20]

"Speciesism"

Before describing the differing ideological premises that drive the animal liberation rebellion, we need to focus briefly on the subversive concept around which all real believers in animal rights unite: that treating animals as having less value than human beings is a form of discrimination just as morally odious as racism. A primary goal of animal rights/liberation is to eradicate this discrimination—known as "speciesism"—from our culture and public policies, root and branch.

Speciesism was conceived in 1970 by the British psychologist Richard D. Ryder, who recalled, "The word speciesism came to me while I was lying in a bath in Oxford some 35 years ago. It was like racism or sexism—a prejudice based upon morally irrelevant physical differences."[21] But the concept was actually popularized a few years later by the Australian moral philosopher, and now Princeton University professor, Peter Singer. In his 1976 book, *Animal Liberation*, Singer defined the term as "a prejudice or attitude of bias in favor of the interests of members of one's own species and against those of members of other species."[22]

To demonstrate why speciesism is supposedly immoral, Singer took a giant leap into the land of the bad analogy:

> It should be obvious that the fundamental objections to racism and sexism made by Thomas Jefferson [in writing against the slavery of African Americans] and Sojourner Truth [advocating for women's rights as well as abolition] apply equally to speciesism. If possessing a higher degree of intelligence does not entitle one human to use another for his or her own ends, how can it entitle humans to exploit non humans for the same purposes?[23]

But this is all wrong. Opposing slavery and sexism has nothing to do with intelligence, but rather with the wrongness of invidious discrimination by the powerful against their moral equals. In other words, antebellum slavery was evil *precisely because the victims were fellow human beings who were treated like animals.* That is not at all akin to treating a cow like a cow instead of like a human, since bovines and *Homo sapiens* are not moral equals.

Be that as it may, the concept of speciesism found ready acceptance not only among members of the nascent animal rights movement, but also among many in the intelligentsia. Avoiding the odor of speciesism soon became the mainstream view in secular bioethics, philosophical materialism, environmentalism, and even among some scientists. Thus, the evolutionary biologist Richard Dawkins bought into the odious moral equivalence of comparing bigotry against fellow humans, a true evil, to the perfectly rational distinction that people make between themselves and animals:

> Nowadays, we are immensely conscious of the danger of racism and sexism, discrimination on the basis of race or sex. A couple of centuries ago, racism would have been taken absolutely for granted, and now we've grown out of that. Today we live in a speciesist world. We automatically, without question, without even thinking about it, assume that there is one law for Homo sapiens and one law for the rest of the animal kingdom. That is speciesism.[24]

Dawkins—who is, after all, a biologist—and other proponents of speciesism are so caught up in their own ideology that they ignore the ingrained speciesism of all other creatures. In nature, what animal would ever object to putting the needs of its own kind first, and usually, exclusively? Elephants certainly don't. They will protect their calves, but couldn't care less when wild dogs hunt gazelle or when their own foraging destroys the nests of birds. Chimpanzees carefully watch over members of their own group, and yet are indifferent to the fate of the monkeys they hunt and eat. The same is true of rhinoceroses, whales, field mice, and any other wild animal you could mention. In fact, speciesism is essential to most animals' very survival.

So, we now know some of the practices that animal rights activists oppose. But what exactly do they believe? In a sense, that is like asking what Christians or Muslims believe. Like those religions, the animal rights/liberation movement is not a rigid monolith. Yet just as all practicing Christians and Muslims have certain core beliefs that are universally accepted among the truly faithful, so too the many factions that make up the animal rights/ liberation movement generally agree about the fundamentals—that speciesism is always wrong, that most (or all) animals should not be deemed property, and that the lives and suffering of animals should be regarded in the same way that we view the lives and suffering of people.

Within these broad areas of accord, there are important nuances that distinguish liberationist ideologies and affect their advocacy tactics. Having covered enough preliminary ground, we are now prepared to dive into the deep end of the pool and plunge into the topsy-turvy world of animal rights/liberation ideology.

2

"All Animals Are Equal"

"All Animals Are Equal," Peter Singer asserted in the title of the first chapter of his epochal 1975 book, *Animal Liberation*.[1] Singer did not mean that horses are equal to cows or chickens to squirrels. Rather, he meant that the "interests" of animals should be accorded "equal consideration" with those of people—an all but unheard of notion when Singer broke into public awareness.

The publication of *Animal Liberation* was a watershed moment, unleashing passionate social forces that continue to shake much of the developed world. As Singer boasted in the preface to the 1990 revised edition, when *Animal Liberation* was originally published, "there was no Animal Liberation movement," but now, "Animal Liberation is . . . a worldwide movement, and it will be on the agenda for a long time to come."[2]

He was not exaggerating. In the intervening thirty-plus years, the animal rights/liberation movement has grown geometrically in size, visibility, and influence through activities ranging from "rescuing" farm animals and impeding animal research, to proselytizing for veganism, seeking to have animals granted legal standing as named litigants in lawsuits, and most disturbingly, engaging in coercion, criminality, and violence "for the animals." The advocacy phrase "animal rights" has burrowed deeply into the popular lexicon to become the catchall term for virtually any effort to protect animals. In fact, the movement has become such a fixture of modern life that Singer's opening statement from the first chapter—"'Animal

Liberation' may sound more like a parody of other liberation movements than a serious objective"—now seems quaintly obsolete.[3]

Not only is animal liberation a serious objective for millions of people around the world, but the movement has become something of a runaway train. Despite Singer's guru-like status among most animal rights aficionados, the movement's uncompromisingly radical spirit has passed him by, to the point that he is now viewed by some prominent liberationists as something of a conservative and even, of all things, a speciesist. Thus Gary Francione, a leading intellectual in the animal rights movement, decries Singer because he "explicitly rejects animal rights and the abolition of animal exploitation; he does not regard eating animals or animal products as per se morally wrong; he maintains we can be 'conscientious omnivores.'"[4] Moreover, as we shall see, Singer's assertion that all animals are equal is now embraced far more literally by most animal rights dogmatists than even Singer intended.

"Personhood" Theory and the "Quality of Life" Ethic

Peter Singer is undoubtedly the most famous and influential advocate for erasing what he has called the "species boundary" between humans and animals.[5] This is ironic because Singer doesn't actually believe that animals have intrinsic rights. In fact, as a utilitarian philosopher, the godfather of animal liberation and internationally known bioethicist doesn't really accept the concept of "rights" at all, whether animal or human.

In Singer's view, the morality of every action should be judged not by unchanging principles of right and wrong, but rather by an informed analysis of likely or actual outcomes. That which promotes happiness or reduces suffering the most, while serving the preferences or interests of those with the highest "quality of life" be they human or animal, is ethical. Thus Singer believes that not only may animals in rare instances be killed or used instrumentally—a view that separates him from most others in the animal rights/liberation movement—but so too may the weakest and most vulnerable humans.

Utilitarianism has been around for a long time, of course; but prior to Singer, believers in the philosophy restricted their moral analyses to the interests and well-being of people. The late Joseph Fletcher, perhaps the most influential American utilitarian philosopher of the post–World War II period, did not pause to consider the suffering of animals in promoting what he considered the human good.[6] In his last book, *The Ethics of Genetic Control,* he suggested that we learn how to genetically alter and breed animals to do our dirty work:

> A sensible policy [toward obtaining a subhuman class of menial workers] is to breed animals for special purposes instead of humans, where possible, if the specialization delimits human capacities. Dolphins, fish, pigeons, primates are even now being used to do dull and dangerous work for us. We could even design species from scratch. There is no need to drag humans down genetically to do special or menial jobs; we can bring animals *up* to them.[7]

Fletcher took his logic to an extreme when he advocated creating human/ape chimeras to perform "dangerous or demeaning jobs" (with my emphasis):

> Hybrids could be designed by sexual reproduction, as between apes and humans. If interspecific coitus is too distasteful, then laboratory fertilization and implant could do it. If women were unwilling to gestate hybrids, animal females could.... *What counts is human need and wellbeing.*[8]

I bring up Fletcher's lunatic proposal both because it illustrates the ultimate peril of stark utilitarianism, but more relevantly to the subject of this book, because the sentence I italicized presumed human moral primacy. Joseph Fletcher may have been intensely controversial in his lifetime, but there was general agreement with his emphasis on promoting human good, with its concomitant implication that human beings stand alone on the pedestal of highest moral worth.

My, how times have changed! Today, among many of the intelligentsia—and certainly in animal rights circles—the presumption that humans occupy the apex of moral worth is anathema. Considering that Fletcher's book was released barely over twenty years ago, some might ask how so many traveled so quickly from accepting that animals may properly be used to promote human thriving, to the far shore of decrying speciesism, sometimes at a substantial cost to human well-being. The answer: They traveled over the intellectual bridge that Peter Singer built.

The planks of that bridge were simple but subversive. First came the idea that catapulted Singer into international prominence: His belief that animals should be granted "equal consideration" in determining utilitarian harms and benefits, and his popularizing of speciesism as a moral wrong, akin to racism or anti-Semitism. As a consequence of these new moral imperatives, Singer wrote in his *Animal Liberation*, human beings should no longer be viewed as having greater value than animals, nor should distinctly human needs receive priority over those of animals in determining the morality of actions. In Singer's view (with his emphasis):

> Equality is a moral idea, not an assertion of fact. There is no logically compelling reason for assuming that a factual difference in ability between two people justifies any difference in the amount of consideration we give their needs and interests. *The principle of equality of human beings is not a description of an alleged actual equality among humans: it is a prescription of how we should treat human beings....*
>
> It is an implication of this principle of equality that our concern for others and our readiness to consider their interests ought not to depend on what they are like or on what abilities they possess. Precisely what our concern or consideration requires us to do may vary according to the characteristics of those affected by what we do: concern for wellbeing of children growing up in America would require that we teach them to read; concern for the wellbeing of pigs may require no more than that we leave them with other pigs where there is adequate food and room to run freely. But the basic element— the taking into account of the interests of the being, whatever those interests may be—must according to the principle of equality, be extended to all beings, black or white, masculine or feminine, human or non human.[9]

The language of equality is seductive and compelling. It is a value that we in the West have paid a great price to attain over hundreds of years. But once we accept Singer's thesis that species membership is irrelevant to moral value and the protection of interests, we become like the snake eating its own tail: Universal human rights—which, after all, depend on accepting that all humans are equal simply because they are human— become untenable. Why? Because equality ceases to be an objective trait intrinsic to all members of the species *Homo sapiens*.

Once intrinsic value is jettisoned, a question must be asked: If being human is not what grants the highest moral value, what does? For Singer, the answer is found by measuring the cognitive capacities of "individuals" —meaning both animals and humans. Those individuals with higher capacities, whether human or animal, are deemed to have greater value than individuals with lower capacities, again whether human or animal. Specifically, Singer wrote:

> To avoid speciesism we must allow that beings who are similar in all relevant respects have a similar right to life—and mere membership in our own biological species cannot be a morally relevant criterion for this right.... We may legitimately hold that there are some features of certain beings that make their lives more valuable than those of other beings; but there will surely be some nonhuman animals, whose lives, by any standards, are more valuable than the lives of some humans. A chimpanzee, dog, or pig, for instance, will have a higher degree of self-awareness and a greater capacity for meaningful relations with others than a severely retarded infant or someone in a state of senility. So, if we base the right to life on these characteristics we must grant these animals a right to life as good as, or better than, such retarded or senile human beings.[10]

Singer is proposing a radical departure in human morality: Those organisms with higher cognitive capacities or abilities have greater moral worth than those with lower acumen. (Writing elsewhere, Singer has called this the "quality of life" ethic.)[11] If this view were ever accepted as the moral foundation of society and the basis for our public policies, it would mean an end to human rights, and ironically it would preclude establishing a regime of animal rights, since an individual's value and the protection of his or her interests and preferences would be subject to change over time with increases or decreases in capabilities.

In order to distinguish those individuals that are owed the highest consideration, Singer asserts that society should primarily protect the lives and freedoms of "persons." To this end, he redefines the word "person" to include any being that exhibits "two crucial characteristics," specifically, "rationality and self consciousness."[12] Most humans are still persons under this theory, of course, but since species membership is irrelevant, Singer also claims that some animals are persons, including "whales, dolphins, monkeys, dogs, cats, pigs, seals, bears, cattle, sheep, and so on, perhaps even to the point where it may include all mammals."[13]

Meanwhile, tens of millions of human beings would be stripped of legal personhood, including newborn human infants, people with advanced Alzheimer's disease, or other severe cognitive disabilities—since Singer claims they are not self-conscious or rational—along with animals that do not exhibit sufficient cognitive capacity to earn the highest value, such as fish and birds. This has led Singer to create an explicit moral equivalency between some people and a mackerel, writing, for example, "Since neither a newborn infant nor a fish is a person the wrongness of killing such beings is not as great as the wrongness of killing a person."[14]

Speciesism and Bioethics

Singer is not alone in these misanthropic views. Some of the world's most prominent bioethicists agree that speciesism is odious and must be avoided in crafting medical ethics and public policies. Thus, John Harris, an influential bioethicist from the United Kingdom, wrote in the *Kennedy Institute of Ethics Journal* (arguing that the capacity to value life should be the prime indicator of personhood):

> Personhood provides a species neutral way of grouping creatures that have lives that it would be wrong to end by killing or by letting die. These may include animals, machines, extra-terrestrials, gods, angels or devils. . . .
>
> Persons who want to live are wronged by being killed because they are thereby deprived of something they value. . . . Nonpersons or potential persons [meaning human embryos, fetuses, and infants] cannot be wronged in this way because death does not deprive them of anything they can value. If they cannot wish to live, they cannot have that wish frustrated by being [painlessly] killed.[15]

Accepting speciesism as a legitimate concern—the avoidance of which is the primary purpose for seeking to supplant human rights with personhood theory—not only endangers the lives of so-called human nonpersons but exposes the weakest among us to instrumental exploitation as if they were mere natural resources. Georgetown University's bioethics bigwig Thomas Beauchamp, also writing in the *Kennedy Institute of Ethics Journal*, illustrated the implications of accepting personhood as the essential criterion in according rights:

> Much has been made of the potential breakdown of the lines that have traditionally distinguished human and nonhuman animals. If nonhumans turn out to possess significantly more advanced capacities than customarily envisioned, their moral standing would be upgraded to a more human level. However, this possibility remains speculative and may be less important than the thesis that because many humans lack the properties of personhood or are less than full persons, they are thereby rendered equal or inferior in moral standing to some nonhumans. If this conclusion is defensible, we will need to rethink our traditional view that these unlucky humans cannot be treated in the ways we treat relevantly similar nonhumans. For example, they might be aggressively used as human research subjects and sources of organs.
>
> Perhaps we can find some justification of our traditional practices other than a justification based on status as persons or non persons. However, if we cannot find a compelling alternative justification, we either should not be using animals as we do, or we should be using humans as we do not.[16]

This belief that profoundly cognitively disabled or undeveloped human beings—now reduced in moral status to nonpersonhood in order to avoid speciesism—could ethically be used along with, or in place of, animals in medical research has been discussed respectfully at the highest levels of professional discourse, in books, journals, public media, and at symposia. For example, writing in the philosophical journal *Between the Species*, the self-described utilitarian bioethicist R. G. Frey of Bowling Green University wrote:

> I know of nothing that cedes human life of any quality, however low, greater value than animal life of any quality, however high. If, therefore, we are going to justify medical/scientific uses of animals by appeal to the value of their lives, we open up directly the possibility of our having to envisage the use of humans of lower quality of life in preference to animals of higher quality of life.[17]

Frey's writing vividly reveals the consequences of accepting Singer-style utilitarianism and the concept of speciesism, both of which are destructive to the very basis of human rights. Frey, in fact, concedes that these concepts would extract a "severe cost":

> If ... not all human life has the same value, then the possibility arises that the quality of life of a perfectly healthy baboon can exceed that of a human. So, if one is going to appeal to human benefit to justify animal research, and if the benefit in this case can be realized either through experimenting on the baboon or the human, then why use the baboon in preference to the human? A quality-of-life view of the value of a life gives a consistent answer over taking a life and saving a life; so, if either the baboon or the human has to be used in order to realize the benefit, the human must, all other things being equal, be used. Clearly, my view on the value of life is not speciesist.[18]

Note that in the quality-of-life view, not only could humans be used in place of animals to save human lives, but so too could some humans, denigrated as having a low quality of life, be sacrificed to save the lives of animals with a putatively higher quality of life. And indeed, such an atrocity has already been proposed, although certainly not implemented, as the disability rights author Joseph Shapiro reports in *No Pity*:

> [I]n 1991, David Larson, the co-director of the Center for Christian Ethics at Loma Linda University, suggested taking the hearts of disabled children to keep monkeys alive. Asked about the ethics of the Baby Fae case, the first human to receive a heart transplant from a baboon, Larson replied, "If a primate's capability was higher than that of the human—say a severely mentally handicapped child—I think it would be appropriate to support the opposite approach of a Baby Fae, a transplant from a child to save the life of a healthy baboon or chimpanzee."[19]

Unsurprisingly, Peter Singer has also suggested that his quality-of-life ethic would permit profoundly disabled human beings to be experimented upon in place of animals. Thus, in a question-and-answer interview in the February 1999 *Psychology Today*, Singer was asked about using chimpanzees in the development of the hepatitis vaccine—which has been an undeniable boon to human health:

PT: Let's take a specific case. Research on chimpanzees led to the hepatitis B vaccine, which has saved many human lives. Let's pretend it's the moment before the research is to begin. Would you stop it?

SINGER: I'm not comfortable with any invasive research on chimps. I would ask, is there no other way? And I think there are other ways. I would say, What about getting the consent of relatives of people in vegetative states?

PT: That would cause a riot!

SINGER: Well, if you could really confidently determine that this person will never recover consciousness, it's a lot better to use them than a chimp.[20]

But this doesn't mean that Singer believes in animal rights. Remember, he doesn't believe in the intrinsic value of either human or animal life, and moreover, he rejects the very concept of rights. Thus, unlike the broad animal rights/liberation movement that he inspired, Singer is not categorically opposed to animal experimentation or eating meat.

This became clear when Singer publicly supported using monkeys in lethal medical experiments designed to find treatments for Parkinson's disease. His endorsement of primate experimentation, part of a BBC documentary on medical research, was reported in the *Sunday Times* and other British papers, which quoted Singer's exchange with a neurosurgeon and primate researcher named Tipu Aziz:

During the exchange Aziz tells Singer, "I am a surgeon and also a scientist, and part of my work has been to induce Parkinsonism in primates. I was one of a group internationally that showed that an area in the brain that was never associated with Parkinsonism ... was overactive, and by operating on it, reducing its activity, one can significantly—very significantly—improve Parkinson's. To date 40,000 people have been made better with this, and worldwide at the time, I would guess only 100 monkeys were used at a few laboratories."

Singer replies, "Well, I think if you put a case like that, clearly I would have to agree that was a justifiable experiment. I do not think you should reproach yourself for doing it, provided ... there was no other way of discovering this knowledge. I could see that as justifiable research."[21]

Singer's comments caused outrage among animal rights purists, who deny absolutely that humans have the right to use animals to improve our lives and reduce our suffering. Thus, an animal rights blogger known as "Arkangel" denied that the monkey experiments led to the Parkinson's treatment and castigated Singer for his utilitarian views:

> Incredibly, Peter Singer seems to have fallen foul of the lies propagated by the vivisectionists and many in the animal rights movement are now expressing their disgust at the naivety of a philosopher who believes not in animal rights but in "Utilitarianism"—the belief that anything can be justified as long as it can be shown to be for the greater good. This doctrine, which, in a nutshell states that the greatest happiness of the greatest number should be the end and aim of all social and political institutions, has been adopted and transformed from its pure form to be applied to humans only, effectively shoving aside ethical and utilitarian consideration for animals, some of which (such as the mice and rats in laboratories) can far outnumber the human population and would therefore qualify as "the greatest number."[22]

Gary Francione angrily followed a similar line in his blog:

> If you read what Peter Singer has been writing for 30 years now, it is absolutely clear that he regards the use of nonhumans—and humans—in vivisection as morally permissible. Indeed, Singer explicitly rejects animal rights and the abolition of animal exploitation; he does not regard eating animals or animal products as per se morally wrong; he maintains we can be "conscientious omnivores"; he claims that we can have "mutually satisfying" sexual relationships with animals; and he claims that it is morally permissible to kill disabled infants.*

---

*Singer is the world's foremost proponent of permitting infanticide, based on his philosophical contention that infants are not "persons." For more details of this disturbing aspect of Singer's work, see my *Culture of Death: The Assault on Medical Ethics in America* (San Francisco: Encounter Books, 2000). Francione's allusion to Singer's approval of human/animal sex is a reference to an admiring review of a book about bestiality that Singer wrote for an online erotica site in which he asserted, "We are animals, indeed more specifically, we are great apes. This does not make sex across the species barrier normal, or natural, whatever those much-misused words may mean, but it does imply that it ceases to be an offense to our status and dignity as human beings." Peter Singer, "Heavy Petting," *Nerve*, March 2001.

In short, rather than asking "can you believe what Singer has said?" it is more appropriate to ask: Can someone please explain how Singer got to be the "father of the modern animal rights movement"?[23]

The answer to Francione's question is that although Singer is not a purist and is not technically an animal rights advocate, he unquestionably paved the way for the absolutist thinking that dominates animal protection advocacy today. Singer's insistence that the interests of animals deserve equal consideration to those of people was groundbreaking. His popularization of speciesism, alas, continues to reverberate throughout bioethics, philosophy, culture, and politics. His theories of personhood have influenced medical decisions and public policies, and as we shall see later, have already led Spain to the brink of granting human-type rights to great apes. Indeed, accepting Singer's subversion of human exceptionalism and of the intrinsic sanctity of human life is *the precondition* for animal rights/liberation advocacy.

One can—as I do—profoundly disagree with Peter Singer. But no one can deny that he is one of the most influential thinkers in the world today.

3

Animals Are People Too

As we have seen, Peter Singer does not believe in true animal rights. But his call to grant animals "equal consideration" with people in determining ethical outcomes sparked an even more radical ideology that left Singer's utilitarianism in the dust.

True animal rights ideology rejects both human exceptionalism and the quality-of-life ethic that distinguishes between persons and nonpersons. Instead, animal rights ideology is absolutist: it posits a moral equality between humans and animals, as a consequence of which it declares that it is immoral for humans to make any instrumental use of animals—no matter the benefit we might receive. The movement's apologetics primarily support this dogma from three distinct intellectual justifications: the ability to feel pain, sentience, and being "the subject of a life." In the end, these are differences with little distinction because the goal is the same—the eradication of all domestication of animals, perhaps even as pets.

"Painience" and the Capacity to Suffer

The philosophy of the animal rights activist Richard D. Ryder—who, we saw earlier, originated the concept of speciesism that so influenced Singer's thinking—epitomizes how animal rightists create an explicit human/animal moral equality. Ryder takes egalitarianism to a surreal extreme by claiming that since all vertebrates—mammals, fish, and birds—experience the sensation of pain, all are equal members in the moral community. Writing in the *Guardian*, he explained his concept of "painience" as the basis for rights:

> Our concern for the pain and distress of others should be extended to any "painient"—pain feeling—being regardless of his or her sex, class, race, religion, nationality or species. Indeed, if aliens from outer space turn out to be painient, or if we ever manufacture machines who are painient, then we must widen the moral circle to include them. Painience is the only convincing basis for attributing rights or, indeed, interests to others.[1]

Ryder's concept of pain is extremely plastic. It includes not only unpleasant sensation, but also "all forms of suffering including fear, boredom and distress."[2] Any being capable of experiencing pain or suffering, according to Ryder, must be brought "into the same moral and legal circle as ourselves" so that "we will not be able to exploit them as our slaves."[3]

Accepting painience as the basis for bearing rights would be disastrous. Taking literally the belief that the ability to feel pain is what establishes moral value—which is precisely how it is meant to be taken—would subvert the importance of being human and tie society up in a Gordian knot. Think about it: Since a cow or a rat can feel pain, then whatever might be done to them would be construed as if *the same actions were being done with or to a human.*

In this view, killing a cow might be considered akin to murder, and experimenting on lab rats judged as heinous as Mengele's notorious experiments on identical twins in the German death camps. Thus, Alex Pacheco, a cofounder with Ingrid Newkirk of PETA, an organization that follows the Ryder view, once stated, "The time will come when we will look upon the murder of animals as we now look on the murder of men."[4] Along these same lines, when Newkirk, the current head of PETA (Pacheco is no longer with the group) was asked whether she would object to "experiments on five thousand rats, or even five thousand chimpanzees, if it was required to cure AIDS," she said she would, asking rhetorically, "Would you be opposed to experiments on your daughter if you knew it would save fifty million people?"[5]

Holocaust on Your Plate

The twisted mindset of the PETA world can best be seen in the organization's now defunct pro-vegetarian campaign called "Holocaust on Your Plate," which compared eating meat to the genocide perpetrated by the Nazis against Jews. Launched in February 2003, Holocaust on Your Plate did not preach this odious moral equivalence subtly or imply it between the lines. Rather, it was the central point of the entire campaign.

First, there were the outrageous juxtapositions of unrelated photographs: In brochures, on posters brought to university campuses, and on its website, PETA presented historic photos of emaciated concentration camp inmates in their tight-packed wooden bunks alongside pictures of chickens in cages. Worse, in a truly despicable comparison (on several levels), a gruesome photograph of the piled bodies of emaciated Jewish Holocaust victims was matched with the picture of a pile of dead *pigs*. The message in these and other equally objectionable photographic juxtapositions was clear: killing pigs and caging chickens is Auschwitz all over again.[6]

The text accompanying the campaign was even worse. PETA explicitly equated the experience of Jews in torture camps like Buchenwald and Dachau with the meat and leather industries:

> Like the Jews murdered in concentration camps, animals are terrorized when they are housed in huge filthy warehouses and rounded up for shipment to slaughter. The leather sofa and handbag are the moral equivalent of the lampshades made from the skins of people killed in the death camps.[7]

Other animal rights activists added their supportive statements. For example, Alex Hershaft, founder and president of the Farm Animal Reform Movement, said that "biomedical research laboratories, factory farms, and slaughterhouses ... are our Dachaus, our Buchenwalds, our Birkenaus. Like the good German burghers, we have a fair idea of what goes on there, but we don't want any reality check."[8]

Not surprisingly, Holocaust on Your Plate was roundly condemned by the Anti-Defamation League, among many others. Abraham H. Foxman, ADL's national director and a Holocaust survivor, asserted that preventing another genocide depends on acknowledging humanity's unique status:

Rather than deepen our revulsion against what the Nazis did to the Jews, the project will undermine the struggle to understand the Holocaust and to find ways to make sure such catastrophes never happen again.

Abusive treatment of animals should be opposed, but cannot and must not be compared to the Holocaust. The uniqueness of human life is the moral underpinning for those who resisted the hatred of Nazis and others ready to commit genocide even today.[9]

PETA was undeterred and unrepentant. For two years, the organization took the Holocaust on Your Plate campaign throughout the United States and much of the world. Then suddenly, on May 5, 2005, Ingrid Newkirk issued an "apology for a tasteless comparison."[10] But it was a classic nonapology apology that never really said, "We are sorry. We were wrong." In fact, Newkirk took pains to justify PETA's approach:

The "Holocaust on Your Plate" Campaign was designed to sensitize to different forms of systematic degradation and exploitation, and the logic and methods employed in factory farms and slaughterhouses are analogous to those used in concentration camps. We understand both systems to be based on a moral equation indicating that "might makes right" and premised on a concept of other cultures or other species as deficient and thus disposable.[11]

Not only did Newkirk's statement lack true repentance, but her pseudo *mea culpa* pointedly emphasized PETA's ongoing support for the message of a book titled *Eternal Treblinka: Our Treatment of Animals and the Holocaust*, by Charles Patterson, which had inspired PETA to launch the Holocaust on Your Plate campaign in the first place. (Treblinka was a notorious Nazi death camp.)

The entire substance of *Eternal Treblinka* is the same as the Holocaust on Your Plate argument, stated at greater length. Patterson puts his premise succinctly in the book's forward:

In *Eternal Treblinka*, not only are we shown the common roots of Nazi genocide and modern society's enslavement and slaughter of non-human animals in unprecedented detail, but for the first time we are presented with extensive evidence of the profoundly troubling connection between animal exploitation in the United States and Hitler's Final Solution.[12]

And that is just the opening page! Throughout the book, Patterson draws obnoxious moral comparisons, such as likening animal husbandry to the evil of eugenics. "The road to Auschwitz begins at the slaughterhouse,"[13] he contends, because "breeding the most desirable [animals] and castrating and killing the rest—led to compulsory sterilization in the United States and to compulsory sterilization, euthanasia killings, and genocide in Nazi Germany."[14]

Patterson makes an extraordinary—and frankly nutty—leap into illogic by claiming that because Henry Ford was inspired by slaughterhouses in developing the automobile assembly line, the meat packing industry bears responsibility for Ford's anti-Semitism—and hence deserves to share history's opprobrium with Hitler for the Final Solution.[15] Patterson also strongly implies that meat eating played a role in the Holocaust:

> Judging from letters and diaries of the killers in the camps, eating animals was one of their greatest pleasures. In a letter to his wife (September 27, 1942), SS-Obersturmfuhrer Karl Kretschmer ... complains about nearly everything except the food. After grumbling about the "Jewish war" he has to fight and about how he is feeling down ("I am in a very gloomy mood. I must pull myself out of it. The sight of the dead—including women and children—is not very cheering") his tone suddenly shifts. "Once the cold weather sets in you'll be getting a goose now and again when somebody goes on leave. There are over 200 chattering around here, as well as cows, calves, pigs, hens and turkeys. We live like princes. Today Sunday, we had roast goose (1/4 each). This evening we are having pigeon."[16]

Get it? Kretschmer ate meat and it so degraded him morally that he was able to murder Jews.

By agreeing with and supporting the message of *Eternal Treblinka*— even as it "apologized" for Holocaust on Your Plate—PETA made it abundantly clear that it still believes "the leather sofa and handbag are the moral equivalent of the lampshades made from the skins of people killed in the death camps." The apology was thus merely a cynical tactical maneuver by PETA to extricate itself from what threatened to become a public relations debacle; merely a way to avoid having to defend itself for the indefensible in media interviews and during debates.

But the leopard had not changed its spots. Soon after Holocaust on Your Plate was hauled down from the PETA website, a strikingly similar "education campaign" took its place. In the "Animal Liberation Project" (ALP), PETA yet again employed odious photographic juxtapositions that in other hands would be considered explicitly racist—such as a lynched African American, murdered during Jim Crow, alongside a dead cow being hoisted by a rope for butchering. Adding to the speciesism-equals-racism mindset, the ALP also asserted a moral equivalence between the Tuskegee Institute outrage—in which scientists allowed African American men with syphilis to go untreated in order to study how the disease progresses—to contemporary medical experimentation with animals.[17]

As one would expect, the ALP was roundly condemned by civil rights organizations and other people who resented the pain of African American slaves being compared to the killing of cows. When the campaign reached Connecticut, as reported by the New Haven Register, it caused an uproar:

> "I am a black man! I can't compare the suffering of these black human beings to the suffering of this cow," said Michael Perkins, 47, of New Haven. He stood in front of a photo of butchered livestock hung next to the photo of two lynched black men dangling before a white mob. "You can't compare me to a freaking cow," shouted John Darryl Thompson, 46, of New Haven, inches from Carr's face. "We don't care about PETA. You are playing a dangerous game."[18]

In the face of such protests, PETA quickly suspended the Animal Liberation Project in 2005.

PETA's Holocaust on Your Plate campaign and its Animal Liberation Project vividly illustrate the twisted reasoning at the heart of the animal rights/liberation movement. If one truly believes that moral value comes from the capacity to feel pain and suffer—as broadly defined by Richard Ryder—then PETA's advocacy is logical. But it is deeply wrong and subversive. Animals are not people. Any movement that seriously believes eating meat and raising domestic animals are equivalent to our most potent examples of barbarism and evil has no business preaching morality to anyone.

"The Right Not to Be Property"

Professor Gary L. Francione of the Rutgers School of Law is one of the most candid leaders of the animal rights movement. Borrowing language used by the movement to end slavery, Francione argues in favor of what he calls "abolition," that is, the utter cessation of any and all human uses of animals. And, while recognizing that such a dramatic cultural change would take time, he urges that the full goal be continually pursued with all possible dispatch.

Toward this end, Francione dismisses both "painience" and "personhood" theory as inadequate bases for determining the rights of any living being because they would leave some animals out. Rather, he asserts that mere "sentience is the only characteristic that should be required for personhood status and for having a right not to be treated as a thing."[19] This means that all mammals, fish, and birds—perhaps even insects, since even a fly will try to escape a swatter—have an absolute right not to be owned as property, Francione fervently insists; and this would require a total end to the domestication of any animals. In an interview published on the animal rights advocacy website Abolitionist-Online, Francione said:

> I am very clear that the right not to be property is another way of talking about the right to equal inherent value, the right not to be a human resource. If we were to recognize such a right (initially as a moral/social matter and later protected by law), we would stop bringing domestic animals into existence altogether and we would thus eliminate 99.99% of the "conflicts" that exist between humans and nonhumans. There may be conflicts between humans and non-domesticated animals living in the wild, but our recognition that nonhumans have inherent value would require that we give equal consideration to their interests.[20]

This kind of thinking leads Francione, like most of his fellow believers in animal rights/liberation, into making crassly relativistic moral comparisons between evil done to men and women and the ordinary practices of animal husbandry. Thus, when Peter Singer and Jim Mason (who, with Singer, co-authored *The Way We Eat*, a book on making ethical food choices that could include being a "conscientious omnivore")[21] spent a day artificially inseminating turkeys to see what the experience was like, Francione blew a gasket:

It is deeply disturbing that Singer and Mason regard it as morally acceptable
to engage in violence against nonhumans for any purpose, particularly to satisfy their curiosity about what "this work really involved." I suggest that there
is no non-speciesist way to justify what Singer and Mason claim to have done
without also justifying the rape of a woman, or the molestation of a child, in
order to see what those acts of violence "really involved."²²

Francione also disagrees with PETA and the Humane Society of the
United States on their strategy of advancing the animal rights agenda by
bringing animal welfare–type protests or lawsuits to improve the care of
animals in industry—actions often intended, as a tactical matter, to
impede the use of animals or make it more expensive, but not end it
entirely. In the same article in which he castigated Singer and Mason,
Francione criticized Bruce Friedrich, PETA's vice president of International Grassroots Campaigns, for promoting the idea (Francione claimed)
that improving the humane slaughter of animals and other welfare
improvements benefit the cause of animal rights. Francione believes that
such actions actually *betray* the animals whose well-being they are meant
to serve. "The message that this approach sends is quite clear," he wrote,
"and if Singer and Friedrich really think that it does not encourage the
consumption of animal products, they are deluded. Moreover, welfare
reforms may increase demand and increase net animal suffering."²³

Instead of acting incrementally, Francione urges animal rightists to
engage in a campaign of total noncooperation with animal users and to
show individual leadership by example. Thus, instead of complimenting
animal users when they institute improved methods of animal husbandry—as PETA sometimes does when one of its varied and ubiquitous
protests succeeds—he urges instead that all animal rights/liberationists
lead strict vegan lifestyles, meaning no meat, cheese, or egg consumption,
no leather shoes, no use of anything that contains animal products.²⁴

As a committed leftist, Francione—and he is far from alone in this—
believes that the animal rights/liberation cause is an extension of the
"international peace movement." And here Francione outshines most of
the other leaders of the movement—many of whom wink at violence and
other lawless tactics followed by groups such as the Animal Liberation

Front—by forcefully advocating exclusively *peaceful* tactics of resistance, including legal demonstrations and boycotts:

> [I]n my view, the animal rights position is the ultimate rejection of violence. It is the ultimate affirmation of peace. I see the animal rights movement as the logical progression of the peace movement, which seeks to end conflict between humans. The animal rights movement ideally seeks to take that a step further and to end conflict between humans and nonhumans.[25]

Gary Francione is a principled radical who believes unequivocally in ending all animal domestication. He told me, "We have a moral obligation to care for the domesticated nonhumans that we have brought into existence but we should not produce more." He also acts on his beliefs, as he explained: "We [Francione and his wife] share our home with four dogs. We had seven, but three died in the past year or so. We take only those dogs who will otherwise be killed because they are considered as 'not adoptable.' We consider them to be refugees in a world in which they really do not belong."[26]

Caring for dogs that few others will take in is admirable. But consider this: In a world of Francione's devising, there would eventually be no meat-eating by humans, no leather shoes, no sushi, fishing fleets, medical advances that involve animal research, pets, guide or assistance dogs, wool clothing, steak dinners, or any other use of animals by humans for any reason no matter the extent of the benefit to be derived. Not only that, when wild animals and humans came into conflict, the perceived needs and desires of the beasts of the field would have to be given equal consideration to the thriving and well-being of humans.

"The Subject of a Life"[27]

Tom Regan, a philosopher at North Carolina State University, has long exerted substantial influence over the animal rights movement. Like Singer, Francione, Newkirk, and Friedrich, Regan denies that human lives have greater value than those of animals, a belief he opposes as "arbitrary" and "speciesism." Unlike Singer's utilitarian thinking, but in accord with most other animal rights advocates, Regan accepts the existence of inherent "rights" to the extent that he makes the dubious claim that "the animal rights movement is part of, not opposed to, the human rights movement."[28]

Like Singer and most other bioethicists, Regan does not believe that rights apply equally to all people. Rather, he asserts that humans and animals have rights only if they are the "subject of a life." By this term, Regan means that a being must be either a "moral agent" or a "moral patient." Moral agents can make moral judgments and thus are capable of acting in ways that are good or bad. "Normal humans" fall into this category. Moral patients, whether human or animal, have equal value to Regan. While they do not make moral judgments and can never be said to be morally accountable, they are "conscious and sentient," and they have mental lives, "desires and goals; they perceive and remember, and they have the ability to form and apply general beliefs."[29] This makes them moral patients who "may be on the receiving end, so to speak, of the right and wrong acts performed by others."[30] Regan claims that a being has a right not to be harmed if it has "inherent value," which is determined by whether the human or animal in question is the "subject of a life."

Implicitly acknowledging that humans *are* morally different from animals, Regan, unlike Singer, argues *against* infanticide and the abortion of viable fetuses, asserting that they should be treated "*as if* they are the subjects-of-a-life, *as if* they have basic moral rights, even while conceding that, in viewing them in these ways, we may be giving them more than their due." (Regan's emphasis.)[31] He asserts that the subjects-of-a-life, whether animal or human, have "basic moral rights" that are "universal, and possessed equally."[32] This includes the right to "respectful treatment," which means they cannot be treated as "receptacles," that is, they have a "prima facie basic moral right not to be harmed."[33]

Regan sounds more reasonable than Singer because at least he shows concern for helpless humans whom Singer would haughtily dismiss as nonpersons. But Regan careens off the rails by charging those participating in normal and proper animal industries with engaging in a "vast evil." In *The Animal Rights Debate*, he promiscuously applies the pejorative against those engaged in animal husbandry, calling the treatment of animals in the food, research, and fashion industries "a magnitude of evil so vast that, like light-years in astronomy, it is all but incomprehensible."[34] To

Regan, eating a crispy chicken leg at your local fast food restaurant is something out of the bowels of hell:

> From the perspective of the rights view ... the magnitude of the evil in the world is not represented only by the evil done to animals when their rights are violated, it includes as well the innumerable human preferences that are satisfied by doing so. That the majority of people who act on such preferences (e.g., people who earn a living in the fur industry or those who frequent KFC) do not recognize the preferences that motivate them as evil—indeed, that some will adamantly assert that nothing could be further from the truth—settles nothing. Whether the preferences we act on are evil is not something to be established by asking how strenuously we deny that they are; their moral status depends on whether by acting on them we are party to or complicit in the violation of someone's rights.[35]

It is important in understanding animal rights ideology that when Regan referred to "someone," he wasn't writing about people, but chickens and mink.

As we shall see, promoting animal rights leads directly to inflicting wrongs on humans. Indeed, how could it be otherwise? Animal rights/liberation embraces a morally subversive premise that we and animals are equal, to the point that normal and logical species distinctions are condemned as akin to racism, anti-Semitism, and every other act of bigotry by man against his brothers and sisters. Such views are not merely radical, they are profoundly antihuman.

4

Let It Begin with Apes

"**I** am an ape," declared Pedro Pozas, a Spanish animal rights activist, in 2006.[1] No, Pozas wasn't commenting on his appearance. He is the secretary general in Spain of the Great Ape Project (GAP), which seeks a United Nations declaration granting great apes—chimpanzees, bonobos, apes, and orangutans—full membership with human beings in a "community of equals,"[2] and his simian self-declaration was made in support of a proposal introduced in the Spanish Parliament to adopt the GAP into law.

The GAP was the brainchild of Peter Singer and the Italian philosopher Paola Cavalieri, editor of the journal *Etica & Animali*. Realizing that granting equal moral consideration to all animals will be a multigenerational project, Singer and Cavalieri decided to prime the pump by obtaining immediate equality for great apes, the animals that are genetically closest to and bear the most physical resemblance to human beings. Accordingly, in 1993, Cavalieri and Singer published a "Declaration on Great Apes" and supported the proposal in a book called *The Great Ape Project: Equality Beyond Humanity*, a collection of essays written by scientists, academics, and animal advocacy notables such as the primatologist Jane Goodall, the biologist Richard Dawkins, and PETA's director, Ingrid Newkirk, along with Singer and Cavalieri themselves.

The "Declaration on Great Apes" defines the "community of equals" as "the moral community with which we accept certain basic moral principles or rights as governing our relations with each other and enforceable at law."

In what could be construed as a parody of the Declaration of Independence (and even though Singer is a utilitarian who believes in satisfying interests rather than establishing fixed liberties), Cavalieri and Singer then identified three rights, not intended as an exclusive list, to which all members of the community of equals are entitled: the right to life, the protection of individual liberty, and the prohibition of torture.

Extending these human rights to apes is intended to—and would—have an earth-shattering impact on human society. For example, it could conceivably require that we treat the killing of a chimp as the same level of wrongdoing as a homicide. The right to liberty would prevent any domestication of chimps and gorillas, except in sanctuaries.

All animal abuse is wrong, of course, and should be prevented through rigorous enforcement of strict animal welfare laws. We should also concede that this is a special concern with chimpanzees, given their intelligence and the empathy we feel toward these magnificent animals. But by seeking to grant rights to apes, rather than generally promoting their improved care as a matter of human moral obligation, proponents of the Great Ape Project risk causing great harm to humans.

Take, as just one example, the purported right against torture. This seems reasonable until one reads the project's definition of torture as "the deliberate infliction of severe pain on a member of the community of equals, either wantonly or for an alleged benefit to others." Clearly, the proposed right isn't meant to stop beatings or to punish neglect—which current law already prohibits, as it should. The real aim, when combined with the liberty right and illustrated by the phrase "benefit to others," is to prevent apes from being used in medical research.

Chimps are not actually used much in research anymore, but occasionally—not often—it remains necessary. A 2005 commentary written by the primate researchers John VendeBerg and Stuart Zola in the science journal *Nature* demonstrated how a universal prohibition on such research could be deleterious to the project of ameliorating serious human illnesses.

Chimpanzees' genomic similarity to humans—a major rationale, as we shall see, behind the GAP—is precisely the biological attribute that makes these animals "invaluable" for use in some medical experiments. One exciting example involves the development of revolutionary bioengineered substances known as "monoclonal antibodies," which offer tremendous potential to treat a wide range of human maladies, including cancer, multiple sclerosis, and "virtually any disease caused by a viral infection." Chimpanzees are essential to this research because unlike other animals, their immune systems do not attack these genetically engineered antibodies. Consequently, the experimental substance remains in the chimps' blood for extended periods, permitting researchers to fully evaluate the safety and efficacy of such interventions before commencing human trials.

Chimpanzees also are occasionally necessary in drug testing because they "predict ... the time course of absorption, distribution, metabolism and excretion of [experimental] drugs in the body more accurately than other animal models, including rats, dogs and other non-human primates." But perhaps most compellingly, they are the only other animal capable of being infected with the human HIV-I virus, which for reasons not fully understood does not usually make them ill. Thus, VendeBerg and Zola write, chimpanzees are "important for testing vaccines aimed at preventing HIV-I infection or reducing the virus load in infected individuals."[3]

The GAP would prevent chimpanzees from being used in medical research, but the same purpose could be accomplished through animal welfare laws, as has been done in several European countries and New Zealand. Protecting apes isn't the real point of the GAP, however. The real intent is to set forces in motion that will materially alter our self-perception and restructure human society. At its core, the Great Ape Project is a frontal assault on the unique status of human beings, a point that Cavalieri and Singer readily acknowledge:

> Our request comes at a special moment in history. Never before has our dominion over other animals been so pervasive and systematic. Yet this is also the moment when, within that very Western civilization that has so inexorably extended this dominion, a rational ethic has emerged challenging the moral significance of membership of our own species. This challenge seeks equal consideration for the interests of all animals, human and nonhuman.[4]

The whole thing is absurd. Take, for example, Cavalieri and Singer's argument in favor of granting apes a putative right to individual liberty.

> Members of the community of equals [meaning apes and humans] are not to be arbitrarily deprived of their liberty; if they should be imprisoned without

due legal process, they have the right to immediate release. The detention of those who have not been convicted of any crime, or of those who are not criminally liable, should be allowed only where it can be shown to be for their own good, or necessary to protect the public from a member of the community who would clearly be a danger to others if at liberty. In such cases, members of the community of equals must have the right to appeal, either directly or, if they lack relevant capacity, through an advocate, to a judicial tribunal.[5]

But of course, *no ape is capable of committing a crime* because, as an amoral being, it does not distinguish right from wrong and hence cannot form the intent required to act criminally. Nor would any ape have the capacity to enforce its putative right to liberty—another concept it could not comprehend—before a judicial tribunal, the very existence of which would also be wholly beyond its ken. Hence, granting apes the right to individual liberty would actually be a backdoor scam intended to empower animal liberationists to bring lawsuits in pursuit of their ideological obsessions, using the ape "litigant" as their front men, er, apes.

Just Like Us

The arguments in favor of the GAP are long on emotionalism and anthropomorphism. Advocates seek to persuade us to include apes in the "community of equals" by convincing us that they are more like people than animals. Take, for example, the essay in *The Great Ape Project* written by Jane Goodall, a widely celebrated primatologist and novelist.

Novelist? But doesn't she write nonfiction books? Well, yes—but also no, as she admits explicitly in leading off the arguments in support of the GAP. First, she quotes her own work recounting her observations of chimpanzee bands (with my emphasis):

> She was too tired after their long, hot journey to set to on the delicious food, as her daughters did. She had one paralyzed arm, the aftermath of a bout of polio nine years ago, and walking was something of an effort. *And so, for the moment, she was content to rest and watch as her two daughters ate.* One was adult now, the other still caught in the contrariness of adolescence—grown

up one moment, childish the next. Minutes passed. *And then her eldest, the first pangs of hunger assuaged, glanced at the old lady, gathered food for both of them and took it to share with her mother.*[6]

Good writing, but much of it—the parts I italicized—is little more than Goodall's anthropomorphic projections. What she could report objectively and scientifically was that the old female chimp stopped short and did not partake of the food eaten by the rest of the animals. She watched the others eat. One of her two daughters was adult and the other an adolescent. One daughter eventually brought food over to her. The rest is a product of Goodall's imagination because she did not—and could not—know that the "old lady" (note the humanizing term) was "too tired" to eat or that she was "content" to rest and watch. That is putting human thoughts and emotions into the heads of animals that may not have really experienced them. Goodall can't even know if the daughter brought her mother food because her hunger was "assuaged," or if the chimps thought the food was "delicious."

Here's a more egregious example of Goodall's fictionalizing her expert observations to create an emotional impact on her readers. She watched as four chimps warily strayed into another band's territory. Note her use of humanizing terms such as "patrol," threats that appear "sinister," moving on without "a word," seeking "approval," feeling "exhilarated," and being "fascinated"—all intended to make the animals seem like us:

> The leader of the patrol, hearing the sudden sound, stopped and stared ahead. The three following froze in their tracks, alert to the danger that threatened *ever more sinister* as they penetrated further into neighboring territory. Then they relaxed: it was only a large bird that had landed in the tree ahead. The leader looked back, *as though seeking approval* for moving on again.

The chimpanzee band sits at a lookout place for an hour. Then:

> ... the leader rose, glanced at the others and moved on. One by one they followed him. *Only the youngest, a youth still in his teens, stayed on for a few minutes by himself, reluctant it seemed, to tear himself away from the prospect of violence. He was at that age when border skirmishes seemed exhilarating as well*

as challenging and dangerous. He couldn't help being fascinated, hoping for, yet fearing, a glimpse of the enemy. But clearly there would be no fighting that day and so he too followed his leader back to familiar haunts and safety.[7]

Once again I have italicized the portions that are pure figments of Goodall's imagination and classic examples of unscientific anthropomorphism—that is, "an interpretation of what is not human or personal in terms of human or personal characteristics."[8] Thus, in addition to being a dedicated research scientist who has unquestionably added invaluable knowledge to our understanding of chimpanzee behavior, Goodall is also a very talented storyteller. Indeed, her international fame is as much a consequence of her talent for the latter as her keen scientific abilities.

What is interesting—and I must say unexpected—is Goodall's admission that she intentionally anthropomorphized her subjects precisely to have an emotional impact on her readers:

Those anecdotes were recorded during our thirty-one years of observation of chimpanzees of Gombe, in Tanzania. Yet the characters could easily be mistaken for humans. This is partly because chimpanzees do behave so much like us, and partly because I deliberately wrote as though describing humans, and used words like "old lady," "youth," and "mannish."[9]

Goodall justifies her anthropomorphizing ways—and the GAP—on the basis of the genetic and behavioral similarities between humans and chimpanzees. And she falls back on the noxious relativistic comparison between the enslavement of African humans in prior centuries and our capture of chimpanzees. So intent on transforming chimpanzees into the moral equals of humans, she almost screeches as she anthropomorphizes away:

Now for a moment, let us imagine beings who, although they differ genetically from *Homo sapiens* by about 1 percent, lack speech, nevertheless behave similarly to ourselves, can feel pain, share our emotions and have sophisticated intellectual abilities. Would we condone the use of those beings as slaves? Tolerate their capture and export from Africa? Laugh at degrading performances, taught through cruelty, shown on television screens? Turn a blind eye to their imprisonment, in tiny barren cells, often in solitary confinement, even though they had committed no crimes? Buy products tested on them at the cost of their mental or physical torture? Those beings exist and we do condone their abuse. They are called chimpanzees.[10]

Never mind that chimps are not used to test products and are rarely used in medical research—although I'll bet Goodall, having traveled abroad, received the hepatitis vaccine that did require chimps for its development. And never mind that chimps can't be degraded because they don't share the human desire to be dignified and are oblivious to being on television. And forget the veiled moral equivalence she makes between chimps and human Africans being brought to America. We are supposed to overlook all that and be cowed by Goodall's righteous anger and hyperemotionalism.

But there is too much at stake to kowtow to Goodall's false equivalence. The question the GAP has placed before the house is *whether chimpanzees and other great apes should be deemed persons, akin to human beings,* as members of a "community of equals." Thus, Goodall asserts that "we should respect the individual ape just as we should respect the individual human; that we should recognize the right of each ape to live a life unmolested by humans, if necessary helped by humans, in the same way we should recognize these rights for individual human beings; and that the same ethical and moral attitudes should apply to ape beings and human beings alike."[11] Of course, the only ones recognizing such rights, or even understanding them, would be us. Chimpanzees would owe neither us nor each other any obligation to respect any right: Such attitudes and obligations lie exclusively within the human sphere—belying the assertion of moral equality.

Anthropomorphism—and one must say, insipid romanticism—permeates advocacy for the GAP, as it does much of the wider animal rights movement. Such moral and scientific confusion reaches surreal levels in an essay written by Barbara Noske, a philosopher from the University of Amsterdam. Noske urges that we apply the methods of anthropology— the study of human beings—to research on apes. Ignoring the fact that we are the only truly rational species, she proposes that *we try to find out what other species think of us!* "How about apes teaching humans *their* language?" she asks, as if apes could do any such thing.[12]

Learning the "language" of apes, and of other animals, would permit us, Noske claims loftily, to hear what animals think about their cruel human overlords. She writes:

> *Homo sapiens* is not exactly known for its fair treatment of the human other, let alone the animal other. But to get an idea of our own reputation throughout the animal kingdom, we would have to be taught an immense number of animal languages and world views. Let's start with great apes.[13]

Needless to say, this is utter nonsense. Are any wild animals "fair" in their treatment of other species? Is there any species other than our own that even understands the very concept of offering fair treatment? And of course, apes and other animals don't have language in the human sense, much less do they hold "world views."

"We Are Apes"

Another arrow in the GAP's advocacy quiver is to argue that since humans and chimps must each have a shared ancestry with a now-extinct intermediate species, apes should be ceded the same moral value as ourselves—because, in the biologist Richard Dawkins' words, not only are we "like apes" but "we *are* apes."[14]

This assertion is based on a theory—the details of which are still somewhat in flux—that places human beings, great apes, and gibbons within a "super family" known as "Hominoidea," all of which are believed to be descended from an as yet undiscovered distant common ancestor. Needless to say, there are great differences among all members of the putative Hominoidea super family—and while scientists generally accept the Hominoidea concept, we still stand out as a unique and unprecedented species. Moreover, at the time the *Great Ape Project* essays were written, scientists believed that *Homo sapiens* emerged from a common ancestor with chimpanzees about six million years ago. More recent research indicates that the purported "human-ape split" could easily have been twenty million years ago, perhaps even up to forty million.[15]

Regardless of how many tens of millions of years ago scientists conclude that humans and apes took their separate evolutionary paths, the "intermediate species" and "common ancestors" arguments are really appeals to a very distant past, ignoring the extensive biological differences that distinguish us today from chimpanzees and other great apes. For example, we often hear—as Goodall stated—that there is only a 1 or 2 percent genetic difference separating human beings from chimpanzees. But that statistic is highly misleading and factually wrong.

Genomic research conducted after the publication of *The Great Ape Project* has revealed some interesting facts that show the dramatic differences between humans and chimps, not our sameness. For example, according to an article published in *Science*, the actual percentage of genetic differences that account "for the anatomical and behavioral disparities between our knuckle-dragging cousins and us" may be higher than 6 percent.[16] Moreover, the purported similarity of somewhere between 94 and 99 percent—take your pick—is itself a big overstatement because it doesn't compare the total genetic makeup of chimps and humans, but only the DNA that "encodes proteins," that is, stimulates the production of the building blocks of our physical bodies. Such encoding DNA makes up only a small fraction of our total genome, perhaps 2 percent,[17] which is why the author of the *Science* article carefully referred to genes that explain "anatomical and behavioral disparities" rather than the entire genome of the two species. Skip past the small amount of our DNA that stimulates the production of proteins, to the bulk of our genes, known as "nonrepetitive" or "noncoding" DNA, and we find some congruence, but mostly a vast genomic gulf separating humans from chimpanzees.

So why hasn't this been brought up forcefully before? It was once thought that these significant genetic differences didn't really matter because noncoding DNA was considered a mere vestige of evolution that no longer served a purpose, hence their former nickname of "junk DNA." But recent studies conducted after the publication of *The Great Ape Project* have shown that this junk DNA isn't really junk: It has function.[18] Research continues as to its exact nature and purposes, but given the striking differences between human and ape noncoding DNA, even if the figure of 98 percent genetic similarity is true, it actually refers to only about 2 percent of our total genetic makeup.

Whether we share 94 or 98 percent of coding DNA, these numbers gloss over the great biological differences between humans and chimps

First, according to the physician William Hurlbut, a Stanford professor and a member of the President's Council on Bioethics, "Even where genes are similar, the timing and degree of gene expression can result in dramatically different adult body structures and functions."[19] This means that even those areas of genetic similarity between us and chimps do not necessarily produce the same physiological or anatomical outcomes. An article published in *Scientific American*, accepting the high end of the coding estimate, remarks: "The DNA sequences of humans and chimpanzees are 98 percent identical. Yet that 2 percent difference represents at least 15 million changes in our genome since the time of our common ancestor roughly six million years ago."[20]

Other scientists regard the figure of fifteen million for "changes in our genome" as a vast understatement. After the genome of the chimpanzee was fully mapped and compared with that of *Homo sapiens*, research published in *Nature* by an international research consortium found *forty million* identifiable basic biological distinctions between the two species at the DNA molecular level. The results were summarized in the *Harvard Gazette*:

> Among the 3 billion base pairs [DNA building blocks] in the DNA of both humans and chimpanzees, researchers found differences in 40 million sites. It is in those sites where the differences between the two species lie.
>
> "Just what makes us human? Now, in a sense, we can answer that question," said Tarjei Mikkelsen of the Broad Institute and the research paper's lead author. "We now have a nearly complete catalog of all genetic differences between humans and chimps and there's about 40 million of them. And any human-specific trait that's encoded in our DNA is caused by one or more of those 40 million changes."[21]

Forty million differences at the most fundamental biological level is not a mere crack in the pavement, as the likes of Goodall and Dawkins imply. No wonder that the geneticist Svante Paabo, a chimp consortium member based at the Max Planck Institute for Evolutionary Anthropology, told *Science*, "I don't think there's any way to calculate a number. In the end, it's a political and social and cultural thing about how we see our differences."[22]

Yes, that's the nub of the matter: politics, ideology, and a fervent desire to destroy traditional cultural values that explicitly uphold the highest moral worth of human beings. This philosophical and, one must say, antireligious antagonism is expressed most vividly in *The Great Ape Project* by the essay of Richard Dawkins, a biologist who may be best known for his bitter proselytizing for atheism. For Dawkins, the argument about "intermediate but extinct species" seems like mainly a pretext for supporting the GAP; what he cares about most is eroding the current moral order because it rests on Judeo-Christian moral philosophy, which upholds the overriding importance of humankind. Thus he yearns for the discovery or genetic creation of a living intermediate species or *human/chimp hybrid* that could interbreed with both species. The beauty of such a development, from Dawkins' perspective, is that it would upset our human-centric values:

> It is sheer luck that this handful of intermediates no longer exist. ("Luck" from some points of view; for myself, I should love to meet them.) But for this chance, our laws and our morals would be very different. We need only discover a single survivor, say a relict *Australopithecus* in the Budongo Forest, and our precious system of norms and ethics could come crashing about our ears. The boundaries with which we segregate our world would be shot to pieces. Racism would blur with speciesism in obdurate and vicious confusion. Apartheid, for those that believe in it, would assume a new and perhaps more urgent import.[23]

Dawkins then refers to a computer-generated photograph that is included as part of his essay—an imaginative rendering of what an intermediate species might look like, which appears to be a chimp's face altered to have humanlike eyes and mouth. He writes:

> This arresting picture is hypothetical. But I can assert without fear of contradiction, that if somebody succeeded in breeding a chimpanzee/human hybrid the news would be earth-shattering. Bishops would bleat, lawyers would gloat in anticipation, conservative politicians would thunder, socialists wouldn't know where to put the barricades. The scientist that achieved the feat would be drummed out of politically correct common-rooms; denounced in pulpit and gutter press; condemned, perhaps, by an Ayatollah's *fatwa*.[24]

To say the least, Dawkins' acidic prose betrays his desire to use the GAP not to advance science, but as a cudgel with which to bash human exceptionalism and other cultural norms of contemporary society.

That is also Singer and Cavalieri's ultimate motive. The GAP, they admit, is speciesist in that it would treat apes as having higher value than other animals simply because of their greater similarity to human beings. But leaving other animals behind is a temporary expedient, a necessity for beginning the incremental changes that will eventually lead to other animals being invited into the community of equals. By successfully elevating apes to the moral status of humans and granting them ancillary legal rights—such as the proposal to create "the first nonhuman independent territories," under United Nations auspices—the GAP would "have an immediate practical value for chimpanzees, gorillas and orangutans all over the world," and even more significantly, it would establish "a concrete representation of the first breach in the species barrier."[25] The first case is the hardest, as they say. After that, it would be all downhill.

GAP in the Law

The Great Ape Project has enjoyed remarkable success since its launch in 1993. New Zealand partially adopted some GAP precepts into its law. The Animal Welfare Act of 1999 forbids using nonhuman hominids in medical research, testing, or teaching unless approved by the director general of agriculture and only if the use is in the interests of the nonhuman hominid itself or its species.[26]

At least the New Zealand law maintains a focus on animal welfare. Not so in Spain. In March 2007, the Balearic Islands, an autonomous community of Spain, issued a declaration in support of the Great Age Project, equating the protection of apes with the protection of human children.[27] A little more than one year later, the Spanish parliament was poised to adopt the GAP formally into Spanish law and instruct its diplomats to push internationally for other countries to accept the GAP until the UN declaration can be achieved.[28]

So, it turned out that when Pedro Pozas said he was merely an ape, he wasn't speaking for himself, but for Spain. And Spain's leaders hope their declaring that people are apes and apes are people will make it easier to convince the rest of us to go along. By conceiving the Great Ape Project and moving it boldly into early acceptance, Peter Singer and Paola Cavalieri gave a big boost to the animal rights movement's ultimate goal of subverting the unique status of human life.

Here Comes the Judge

nimal liberationists understandably see the courts as a crucial tool for seizing control of the moral values that drive public policy. The thinking goes something like this: The law not only reflects our values, it molds them. In our morally polyglot society, if something is deemed legal that is akin to being declared "right."

The essence of this approach is the establishment of a right (for at least some animals) not to be considered "property." This school of animal rights advocacy returns to the question of personhood that was popularized by Peter Singer—but without the Princeton professor's utilitarian bent, which denies the very concept of rights and permits disabled humans, infants, and others to be used instrumentally.

Seeking a Declaration of "Personhood" for Animals in Courts

Steven M. Wise, a law professor and president of the Center for the Expansion of Fundamental Rights (CEFR), is one of the nation's most prominent proponents of the "right not to be property" approach. (According to its mission statement, the CEFR "seeks to expand such fundamental legal rights as bodily integrity and bodily liberty to nonhuman animals, beginning with chimpanzees and bonobos, through litigation and education.")[1] Wise understands that no animal has the capacity to demand rights. Rather, he argues that any animal exhibiting sufficient cognition to be considered a "person" is entitled to the protection of legal immunities. In *Drawing the Line: Science and the Case for Animal Rights*, Wise explains:

> I may kidnap you, but I can't enslave you because human bondage is prohibited under domestic and international law. Persons are simply *immune* from enslavement. Rational arguments cannot be made that someone must be smart enough to assert an immunity to have one as immunities don't need to be asserted. Such immunities as freedom from slavery and torture are the most basic kind of legal rights, and so it's these to which nonhuman animals, like human beings, are most strongly entitled.[2]

Wise asserts that all animals capable of exercising what he calls "practical autonomy" are entitled to "personhood and basic liberty rights," based on mere "consciousness" and "sentience." This is actually a very low threshold since it would apply to any animal that has: 1) the ability to "desire"; 2) the capacity to "intentionally try to fulfill her desires"; and 3) "a sense of self-sufficiency to allow her to understand, even dimly, that it is she who wants something and it is she who is trying to get it."[3] It is wrong, indeed "evil" in Wise's view, to deprive an animal possessing "practical autonomy" of liberty—because no person should be "enslaved"—and to use it as the subject of medical research, which he regards as torture.

Wise's advocacy seems more limited than that of PETA and other animal rights advocates because it would not encompass all animals that have the capacity to experience pain. But this ostensible limitation is only a form of Kabuki theater, intended to establish the principle that animals are entitled to rights just like humans—which would push the far bigger boulder rolling downhill with unstoppable momentum, leading to a very broad inclusion of animals as equals within the moral community.

This isn't a cynical conclusion on my part: Wise acknowledges that his argument does not reflect his personal views. "If I were Chief Justice of the Universe," he wrote, "I might make the simpler capacity to suffer [Ryder's and PETA's approach], rather than practical autonomy, sufficient for personhood and dignity-rights." Moreover, he sees practical personhood as a better argument to make in court when seeking legal rights for animals because the "capacity to suffer appears irrelevant to common-law judges in their consideration of who is entitled to basic rights."[4] And since Wise's purpose is to specially plead as a lawyer to gain formal legal recognition of animal rights, for tactical reasons he does not (at this time) demand that all animals be brought under the law's protective umbrella. "I may not like it much myself. But philosophers argue moral rights; judges decide legal rights. And so I present a legal, and not a philosophical, argument for the dignity-rights of nonhuman animals."[5] If this sounds as if Wise hopes to impose animal rights on society via judicial fiat, that is precisely because he does.

Wise knows that animal rights—as distinct from laws against cruelty—are unlikely to be enacted through democratic processes anytime soon. But *the courts* might be willing to force the door open to animal rights if proponents are not too ambitious at this early stage and can liken the treatment of the most intelligent mammals to that of people with disabilities. Thus, like any good lawyer, Wise tailors his claims to seem sufficiently narrow to gain judicial rulings that establish the broader legal principle he seeks: "Advocating for too many rights for too many nonhuman animals," he warns, "will lead to no nonhuman animal's attaining rights."[6]

Obtaining a court order ruling that an animal was entitled to protection as a "person" would be, Wise contends, "the first and most crucial step toward unlocking the cage,"[7] because once a court accepted practical autonomy as equaling personhood, the movement would be well on the road to total victory. Wise licks his lips in anticipation of the argument that would come to the fore once being human ceased to be the sole basis for recognizing formal individual personhood:

> On what nonaribitrary ground could a judge find the [profoundly disabled] girl has a common law right to bodily integrity that forbids her use in terminal biomedical research, but that Koko [a gorilla] shouldn't have that right, without violating basic notions of equality? Only a radical speciesist could accept a baby girl who lacks consciousness, sentience, even a brain, as having legal rights just because she is human, yet the thinkingest, talkingest, feelingest apes have no rights at all, just because they're not human.[8]

Thus, opening the door to rights for what are often called higher mammals—chimps and dolphins, for example—would not be the ceiling of animal rights advances, but a launching pad for a cascade of legally enforceable rights and privileges for most animals, and not just mammals, but also perhaps birds and sophisticated insects such as bees, the "tiny brains" of which, Wise claims, produce "sentience" if not full practical autonomy.[9]

Seeking Legal Standing for Animals in Courts

Animals don't have the right to sue in human courts because they are not legal persons, and hence they lack "standing" to seek redress for grievances. This legal principle constrains animal rights activists from attacking animal industries "from the inside" by having, say, a steer sue a feedlot alleging abuse. This limitation requires animal rights groups to find other legal pretexts on which to bring litigation against animal-using industries.

For example, in 2006 the Humane Society of the United States filed a federal lawsuit against Hudson Valley Foie Gras, described in the HSUS publicity release about the case as a "notorious factory farm."[10] *Foie gras* is considered by some to be an especially delicious delicacy, but animal rights/liberationists detest the manufacturing of *foie gras* because it is made from the livers of ducks and geese that have been fattened through forced overfeeding so that their livers swell to three times the normal size.[11] HSUS's lawsuit, however, technically had nothing to do with the treatment of Hudson Valley's birds. Rather, HSUS—which is *not* an environmental protection organization—charged the company with violating the federal Clean Water Act, contending that the farm permitted bird feces to pollute the Hudson River.

The pollution case was not the first time HSUS had filed suit against Hudson Valley Foie Gras. In another case, the animal rights group claimed that the company was delivering tainted food to the marketplace. And just months before filing the pollution suit against the farm, HSUS had lost a suit that sought to prevent New York's Empire State Development Corporation from awarding the farm a $400,000 grant intended to help it *upgrade and expand its water treatment facilities*. In other words, HSUS first tried to prevent Hudson Valley Foie Gras from receiving state money that would help it run a cleaner operation with regard to water pollution, and then turned right around and charged the company with polluting water.[12]

Clearly, pollution isn't the real issue driving HSUS's legal war against Hudson Valley; it is a pretext. HSUS's actual gripe against Hudson Valley is over the company's raising, force-feeding, and slaughter of geese. So, why sue over a public policy matter with which HSUS is not primarily concerned? Because these were the only legal avenues open to it. As a private nonprofit juridical entity, *it would not have legal standing* to bring a private case against Hudson Valley for alleged animal abuse or to have the *foie gras* manufacturing process declared a form of illegal animal abuse. Thus, wanting to impede Hudson Valley's business operations, HSUS was forced to instead avail itself of the private right to sue its enemy as permitted under the Clean Water Act. Animal rights organizations often hit animal industries with lawsuits that have little to do with protecting animals or directly improving their welfare. They pursue this tactic because the law rarely permits private litigation to enforce animal welfare standards.

But what if animal rights organizations such as PETA and HSUS could sue cattle ranches, leather merchants, pet food manufacturers, fishing fleets, hunters, meat processors, dog breeders, any and all animal-using enterprises directly for alleged animal abuse? Or, better yet from the animal liberationist's perspective, what if instead of HSUS suing Hudson Valley for pollution violations, *the company's geese could sue the company directly for abuse?* What if animal liberationists could provide lawyers so that animals could bring legal cases? They could easily use their considerable budgets to pay lawyers to flood the courts with lawsuits fair and foul—and thereby tie animal industries into hopeless knots, raising their cost of doing business, and perhaps making insurance companies unwilling to provide coverage for fear of financial losses.

Animals bringing lawsuits? Don't laugh. Granting animals the right to sue—known as "legal standing"—is a major long-term goal of the animal rights movement. (Of course, it would be the liberationists who would bring the cases on behalf of the oblivious animals as their "guardians.") Moreover, there is a dedicated cadre of lawyers and law students eagerly working toward achieving this and other legal goals of animal rights through the courts. (At last count there were nearly a hundred law schools offering animal law classes or programs, often at the behest of animal rights groups such as the Animal Legal Defense Fund.)

Imagine the consequences if a court declared or a legislature created legal standing for animals to bring lawsuits. The issue of personhood for animals would receive a huge boost as the shift in law handed animal rights activists a sizeable club with which to pound animal industries into submission. No wonder many animal rights legal activists are so eager for animals to be granted the right to sue! And the first steps toward obtaining legal standing for animals have already been taken. As you read these words, activists are crafting the intellectual hooks—articles in professional journals and sample legal briefs complete with bounteous citations—upon which future judges or legislatures could hang their policy hats in granting legal standing to animals.

Unfortunately, animal standing has friends in surprisingly high places. The law professor Cass Sunstein—a close friend of President Obama who has been appointed to be "regulations czar" and is rumored, as of this writing, to be on the fast track for the United States Supreme Court—explicitly advocates that animals be granted legal standing to sue. For example, writing in the *UCLA Law Review*, Sunstein argued for amending federal and state animal welfare laws so as to permit private "individuals"—by which he meant both human and animal—to bring suit against abusers "to supplement currently weak agency enforcement efforts."[13] The article, moreover, notes that there is already legal precedent that could open the door wide to such private standing against putative abusers: a case in which the courts permitted an offended individual to sue a zoo based on "injury to his aesthetic interest in observing animals living under inhumane conditions."[14] Similarly, in *Animal Rights: Current Debates and New Directions*, a book for which he was an editor as well as a contributor, Sunstein wrote:

> It seems possible . . . that before long, Congress will grant standing to animals to protect their own rights and interests. . . . Congress might grant standing to animals in their own right, partly to increase the number of private monitors of illegality, and partly to bypass complex inquiries into whether prospective human plaintiffs have injuries in fact [required to attain standing]. Indeed, I believe that in some circumstances, Congress should do exactly that, to provide a supplement to limited public enforcement efforts.[15]

Where Sunstein focused primarily on legislative action, David Favre, a professor at the Detroit College of Law and chairman of the Animal Legal

Defense Fund, wants the courts simply to impose legal standing for animals via judicial decree. Writing in the journal *Animal Law*, Favre argued that a new tort (a right to bring a civil action) be created as a "next step" toward legal recognition of full animal rights. While Favre ultimately hopes to prevent all use of animals by humans, an intermediate goal is to permit animals to sue if their "fundamental interests" are being infringed for reasons that are not of compelling benefit to humans. Under the cause of action envisioned by Favre, the plaintiff animal would have to demonstrate the following:

1. An interest of fundamental importance to the animal plaintiff, and
2. interference with that fundamental interest or harm by the actions or inactions of the human defendant, and
3. that the weight and nature of the animal plaintiff's interests substantially outweigh the weight and nature of the human defendant's interests.

Knowing that legislatures are unlikely to enact such radical measures, Favre urges that courts impose this scheme upon society:

> Fundamental to the concept of a tort is the creation and existence of a duty obligating one being to take into account the interests of another. It is the role of the common law courts to determine whether a particular moral claim or interest asserted by a plaintiff will be accepted by a court, resulting in the imposition of a legal duty upon others to accommodate the newly affirmed interest. As moral perspectives change and society evolves, courts may find the existence of a duty where none existed before.[16]

Adding heft to the worry that animal standing is not just a fringe agenda item, none other than Lawrence H. Tribe, the famous Harvard Law School constitutional scholar, has spoken in support of enabling animals to bring lawsuits.*

On February 8, 2000, Tribe delivered a speech praising the crusading animal rights lawyer Steven Wise—whose ideas we have already discussed— at

---

*Tribe has been mentioned often as a potential Supreme Court nominee. Among his many famous cases, Tribe represented Vice President Al Gore in one of the hearings before the United States Supreme Court in the federal litigation that eventually culminated in George W. Bush winning the 2000 presidential election.

Boston's historic Faneuil Hall; a transcript of his remarks was later published in the journal *Animal Law*. Claiming a "deep intuition that chimps and dolphins and dogs and cats are infinitely precious—like ourselves,"[17] Tribe argued for granting animals the right to sue:

> Recognizing the animals themselves by statute as holders of rights would mean that they could sue in their own name and in their own right.... Such animals would have what is termed legal standing. Guardians would ultimately have to be appointed to speak for these voiceless rights-holders, just as guardians are appointed today for infants, or for the profoundly retarded.... But giving animals this sort of "virtual voice" would go a long way toward strengthening the protection they will receive under existing laws and hopefully improved laws, and our constitutional history is replete with instances of such legislatively conferred standing.[18]

Meanwhile, as legal thinkers argue the intellectual case for granting animals standing, animal rights lawyers aren't waiting until the law is changed before listing animals as litigants in lawsuits against animal-using industries or lawsuits to prevent endeavors that may threaten animal welfare. Unsurprisingly, these efforts so far have all been turned back, but occasionally they have received a respectful hearing in courts of appeal.

For example, an environmental lawyer sued in the name of the "Cetacean Community," allegedly consisting of all the world's whales, porpoises, and dolphins; the "Cetaceans" sought an injunction preventing the federal government from conducting underwater sonar tests. When a trial court found that the "Community," being animals, had no standing, the attorney Lanny Sinkin—the actual litigant—appealed. The Ninth Circuit Court of Appeals addressed the standing issue in a published opinion "as a matter of first impression." In language that must have warmed every liberationist's heart, the court ruled that in theory, animals *could* be granted standing to sue:

> It is obvious that an animal cannot function as a plaintiff in the same manner as a juridically competent human being. But we see no reason why Article III [of the U.S. Constitution] prevents Congress from authorizing suit in the name of an animal any more than it prevents suits brought in the name of

artificial persons such as corporations, partnerships or trusts, and even ships, or of juridically incompetent persons such as infants, juveniles and mental incompetents.

The court then looked into the statute under which the case had been brought, the Endangered Species Act, and ruled that only "a 'person,' as defined [in the law], may sue in federal district court to enforce the duties the statute describes." The court further noted:

> Animals are not authorized to sue in their own names to protect themselves. There is no hint in the definition of "person" . . . that the "person" authorized to bring suit to protect an endangered or threatened species can be an animal that is itself endangered or threatened.[19]

To which it would be prudent to add the word "yet." Remember, another major agenda item for animal liberationists is to have animals declared to be legal persons. If that effort ever succeeds, the court's analysis denying standing might no longer apply.

Another animal standing case was litigated in the Texas Court of Appeals in early 2008. Sponsored by PETA, the case involved a dispute over the proper sanctuary in which to care for some chimpanzees and monkeys. The appeals court agreed with the trial court, ruling that primates had no standing to sue in their own names.[20]

Of all the ubiquitous advocacy thrusts by animal rights advocates, successfully obtaining legal standing for animals could prove the most impactful. First, it would accomplish a major animal rights goal of undermining the status of animals as property, moving them forcefully toward legal personhood. Second, imagine the chaos that would result once animals—that is, liberationists—could bring cases directly. Hundreds if not thousands of lawsuits "filed by animals" would immediately clog the courts: cattle against ranchers, elephants against zoos, horses seeking injunctions against stables, monkeys demanding habeas corpus against research labs, perhaps even dogs and cats suing their owners.[21] Animal industries would be thrown into crisis. And on an existential level, the perceived exceptional nature of human life would suffer a significant blow from the blurring of one of the clear definitional lines that distinguish people from animals. But of course, this is the future for which animal rights/liberationists devoutly yearn.

And for those who take comfort in the exceedingly dangerous notion that "it will never happen," a warning note: It already has. In 2005 a Brazilian court allowed a chimpanzee to bring a lawsuit in his own name—and awarded the chimp a writ of habeas corpus against his keeper.[22]

Of even greater concern, when animal rights activists in Austria sought to have a court grant personhood to a chimpanzee so they could be named its legal guardians, they got nowhere, but the European Court of *Human* Rights saw matters differently. In 2008, the court agreed to hear the case and determine whether a chimpanzee should be considered a legal person—a foreboding event given that rejecting the right would have been most easily accomplished by rejecting the appeal.[23]

The Silver Spring Monkey Case

Misguided ideas and beliefs aside for the moment, there are actually some things to admire about the animal rights/liberation movement. While its activist core are relatively few in number, in twenty or so short years they have elevated their movement from being the butt of jokes to a disproportionately influential social force that refuses to be ignored.

And they—along with animal welfarists—have unquestionably pricked our consciences. Animal protection advocacy has encouraged people to care far more about animal pain, suffering, and intrinsic value than we would have otherwise. Tens of millions of people have changed their individual lifestyles solely out of concern for animal well-being, for example by becoming vegan or vegetarian, or restricting their meat intake to animals that have been "compassionately" raised. Dubious areas of research using animals have been curtailed or terminated, and concerted efforts are well under way to find alternatives to animal research whenever feasible. Meanwhile, zoos have been redesigned to make animals more comfortable, while trophy hunting is, thankfully, on the wane.

There are reasons for such remarkable successes: Perhaps more than any other contemporary social/political advocacy community, animal rights activists are utterly devoted to pursuing their ideas and achieving their goals. They are indefatigable, imaginative, edgy, zestful, energetic, often funny, yet filled with righteous rage and indifferent to being unliked—a key to bringing any minority view into the mainstream. To its most committed adherents, animal rights activism is a quasi-religious call-ing, an all-encompassing way of life.

Unfortunately, our greatest strengths can lead to our worst failings. Too often, activists' commitment devolves into fanaticism. Liberationists are prone to propagandizing more than educating, personally attacking rather than legitimately protesting, and intentionally mischaracterizing and distorting instead of steadfastly sticking to the truth. Moreover—and this is where things can get dangerous—some turn into "true believers" (in the Hofferian sense), whose hopelessly utopian and romantic zeal for the cause leads all too frequently to treating those with whom they disagree not just as misguided but as cruelly sadistic and evil—as enemies to be stopped by any means necessary, rather than adversaries to be either per-suaded or defeated in the marketplace of ideas.[1] Such an absolutist mind-set can make it all too easy to think: What difference does it make if "animal abusers" get hurt?

We will explore the propensity to engage in lawlessness, violence, and terrorism that has infected the animal rights/liberation movement a little later. But for the next few chapters, let's focus on some of the more notable animal rights advocacy actions and policy proposals that reveal the move-ment's radical core.

Pictures That Lie

In their zeal to protect animals, liberationists often engage in coercive and fundamentally dishonest tactics that can leave broken careers and even ruined lives in their wake. And this has been true almost from the begin-ning of the modern movement. In 1981, a newly hatched PETA soared from obscurity into a major political and social force as a consequence of pulling off a nasty and cruel subterfuge against Edward Taub, a medical researcher then working in a lab in Silver Spring, Maryland.[2] To this day, PETA's promotional material brags about its part in the case of the Silver Spring monkeys:

> PETA first uncovered the abuse of animals in experiments in 1981 and
> launched the precedent-setting "Silver Spring monkeys" case. This resulted in

the first arrest and criminal conviction of an animal experimenter in the United States on charges of cruelty to animals, the first confiscation of abused laboratory animals, and the first U.S. Supreme Court victory for animals in laboratories.[3]

But the real story of the Silver Spring monkeys bears little resemblance to the myth spun by PETA propaganda. It is a tale in which the dirty hands belonged to the PETA cofounder Alex Pacheco, not the medical researcher he targeted.

Pacheco, like his PETA colleague Ingrid Newkirk, is an animal rights fanatic who, as we have already seen, believes that killing an animal is as bad as killing a human being. "The time will come," he once said, "when we will look upon the murder of animals as we now look on the murder of men."[4] He has also justified criminality for the cause, telling the Associated Press in 1989, "Arson, property destruction, burglary, and theft are 'acceptable crimes' when used for the animal cause."[5] It is thus hardly surprising that Pacheco resorted to misrepresentation and personal betrayal to thwart an animal experiment and disgrace a promising medical researcher.

Here's the story: In 1981, shortly after PETA's founding, Pacheco decided to target Dr. Edward Taub, who was then engaged in basic research aimed at learning whether paralyzed people could be taught to use limbs that had no feeling. Pacheco infiltrated the lab and gained Taub's trust by pretending to be a "student volunteer." Taub recalls: "Pacheco came to me and told me he was a part-time student at Georgetown University, and that he had done fieldwork with animals and was now considering a career in animal research. He said he wanted to find out if laboratory work was as interesting as being in the field."[6] Little did Taub know that Pacheco lied: His true purpose was to discredit Taub's scientific research and destroy his life.

Taub was not experimenting on monkeys to gain a sadistic thrill. He hoped to find out if the primate brain and nervous system could exhibit "plasticity" after traumatic injury, that is, whether the biology of the brain and nervous system could actually be altered and trained to function even in the absence of feeling. If so, he hypothesized, perhaps stroke patients could be rehabilitated and taught to use arms numbed by their brain injury. This was a new field of study at the time as the dominant belief in neuroscience was that the mechanism of movement depended absolutely on spinal cord reflex capacity.

"Our experiment sought to determine whether by using behavioral techniques we could induce monkeys to make use of an arm that had no reflexes,"[7] told me. As part of his study, the nerves in the monkeys' forelimbs were severed surgically (deafferented). To measure their loss of sensation, research animals were placed in a chairlike device in which their arms, legs, and head were held motionless to facilitate precise measurements. "This was not a major part of the experiment," Taub recalled. "It was done to an animal maybe once or twice for an hour at a time. It was not painful. The only distress caused in the animals came from their being held immobile."[8]

This aspect of the study would later become an important element of the story. So would the fact that some of the animals injured themselves because they could not feel their forelimbs. This did not cause them pain but it was unsightly and disturbing.

More importantly, by the time Pacheco began "volunteering" in the lab, Taub's work with the monkeys had substantiated his hypothesis. Based on the results of his work with monkeys, Taub believed his hope to find an effective therapy for some paralyzed stroke patients could be realized. As he wrote in 1980, just before the events that caused him so much difficulty, "It is not anticipated that all patients with long enduring motor deficits will be amenable to training methods based on our work with deafferented monkeys. However those individuals for whom these methods do work will have had extremities that would have remained useless for the remainder of their lives converted into limbs that can be employed for a variety of purposes."[9]

Not that Pacheco cared. The animal rights activists had one goal: Stop Taub from researching on monkeys.

Unaware that his student volunteer was actually waiting for a chance to subvert his research, Taub left on vacation, fully expecting that the lab would be maintained properly during his absence: two animal caregivers were supposed to tend to the animals daily and Pacheco was also available as a failsafe to alert administration if anything went wrong. As it happened, Taub's leaving coincided with the sudden failure of the previously reliable caregivers to do their jobs. "Both of my animal room cleaners were absent on all but two of the days in the week before the raid on my laboratory," Taub remembers, absences he still finds "inexplicable" because "for the previous one and one-half years in which they had worked in my laboratory they had a documented near-perfect record of showing up for work."[10] To say the least, the "timing" of the workers' unprecedented unreliability is odd. I asked Taub of the maintenance workers ever explained themselves. "They said they were sick," Taub recalled skeptically.[11] Whatever the cause, the dereliction of the maintenance workers played right into Pacheco's hands.

Sanitation in the lab fell well below approved standards. Moreover, the caretakers' many absences left Pacheco with unfettered access to the monkeys. He took the opportunity to bring fellow animal rights activists into the lab at all hours of the day and night to witness the "poor" conditions that now existed in the lab. The group, which included animal use professionals, took photographs to present to the media and legislators as proof of abuse and cruelty allegedly occurring routinely in Taub's lab.

"The pictures that were brought forward publicly were fabricated," Taub told me. "They were not those taken during actual research."[12] Pacheco used the force of visual media to create a powerful but false impression about Taub's work—a tactic that, as we shall see later, remains a staple of animal rights advocacy.

At some point in Pacheco's work in the lab, a monkey was placed in the chair device incorrectly so that it could struggle and looked as if it were suffering. *Flash/Click:* Pacheco took one of the most famous photographs in animal rights advocacy, depicting the monkey tied with its limbs spread-eagled almost in crucifixion style, struggling against its bonds.

The photo was deceptive. Had it been taken during an actual experiment, it would have shown the animal seated quietly, not struggling. But the falseness of the image never mattered; what counted was the emotional jolt experienced when viewers of the photo believed they were watching a monkey being tortured. This "visual aid" is still often used to turn people against animal research in animal rights propaganda.

Taub remains justifiably bitter. He told me, "The monkey was put improperly in the device so that it was partially free to struggle, a situation that he [Pacheco] had been specifically instructed never to allow to occur. He knew that if a monkey was in distress and he couldn't handle the situation, he was to call the head of the monkey lab for help."[13] But Pacheco wasn't really there to participate in important medical research or ensure that the monkeys were cared for properly. He was intent on discrediting animal research in the promotion of animal rights.

When he thought he had enough material to bring Taub down, Pacheco reported him to the authorities for cruelty to animals. The lab was shut down and the monkeys were confiscated.

When Taub returned from vacation he was stunned to be charged with 119 counts of cruelty to animals. The researcher's life and professional career went into a tailspin. He was accused of being a "Dr. Frankenstein" in the *Washington Post*. He had to suspend his professional activities to defend himself. The whole ordeal extracted a terrible toll: "I was working sixteen hours a day to clear my name," Taub told me. "My wife had to work three jobs to support the family. We received death threats by telephone and in the mail."[14]

Eventually, the truth fully vindicated Taub. When it became clear that the monkeys were not being mistreated in his lab, that their injuries were not due to cruel neglect, and moreover, that the experiment was fully sanctioned and funded by the National Institutes of Health, all but six of the criminal counts were dropped. The remaining charges involved failing to provide adequate veterinary care for six monkeys, one charge per monkey. There were three trials, exonerations, and in the end no convictions—six initial guilty verdicts having been overturned on appeal.

Not only was Taub criminally nonculpable, but he was eventually cleared of any wrongdoing. Indeed, *five* subsequent independent investigations of the incident by five separate scientific groups, including an ethics committee of the Society for Neuroscience and a committee from the American Psychological Society, exonerated Taub of abusing the animals or engaging in any inhumane practices whatsoever.

For Pacheco, the ultimate outcome of Taub's criminal trials and his eventual complete exoneration by his peers were completely beside the point. His true goals were to end the experiments, boost PETA's profile, and garner publicity to influence congressional subcommittee hearings about pending revisions of the Animal Welfare Act. The guerilla theater worked brilliantly. Pacheco's congressional testimony was a media sensation providing a cornucopia of free publicity for PETA, helping it to become the international animal rights powerhouse that it is today.

Oh, and the vaunted victory in the United States Supreme Court about which PETA brags in its self-promotion? That too was much less than meets the eye, having had nothing whatsoever to do with Taub's experiments on the monkeys. Rather, the case involved a civil lawsuit contesting their custody. The owners of the animals wanted the federal court to hear the case, but the animal rights activists wanted the case heard in the state courts of Louisiana. The U.S. Supreme Court ruled on limited jurisdictional grounds that under the pertinent federal statutes the case was a matter for Louisiana, not the federal courts. In other words, the decision had nothing whatsoever to do with animal rights.

There is no question that animal rights activists won a huge propaganda victory in the Silver Spring monkey case, but it was not one founded on justice or integrity. Rather, it was a vicious and slanderous crusade to destroy the reputation of a respected medical researcher, whose career was almost ruined because of the factual distortions and character assassination to which he was subjected. Worse, it established a pattern of disingenuous activism that continues as an animal rights staple to this day.

A Medical Breakthrough

It took Dr. Taub eight years after his arrest to get back to his research. To the great benefit of humankind, he developed a promising new therapy, called "constraint-induced movement therapy" (CIMT), that can restore mobility to people whose arms have been paralyzed by stroke or other neurological causes.

Taub's groundbreaking research has reaped tremendous benefits for people suffering from paralysis caused by stroke, traumatic brain injury, cerebral palsy, and multiple sclerosis. In 2006, the American Stroke Association reported that CIMT patients showed "large to very large" improvements in the functional use of their affected arm in daily life, adding that a growing number of clinics are beginning to offer the therapy: "In 2004, few rehab facilities offered CIMT; today, CIMT is increasingly common because it has proven effective at improving survivors' lives."[15]

A 2006 study published in the *Journal of the American Medical Association* similarly concluded, "Among patients who had a stroke within the

previous 3 to 9 months, CIMT produced statistically significant and clinically relevant improvements in arm motor function that persisted for at
least 1 year."[16] And it now appears that children with cerebral palsy will
benefit from research that began with the use of monkeys at a lab in Silver
Spring. A 2007 report in the medical journal *Clinical Rehabilitation*
reported that a "clinically controlled trial demonstrated a significant treatment effect favoring modified CIMT using the Assisting Hand Assessment at two and six months," and another study "showed a significant
treatment effect at six weeks on the self-care component" of the therapy.[17]

Taub's monkey research was a crucial early step in achieving this magnificent medical breakthrough. "Before we began the experiments," Taub
told me, "we didn't have the information we needed to know whether the
theory of brain and nerve plasticity was even true. To learn the answer, we
needed to conduct experiments that might fail or could harm the subjects.
The only choice we had was to use animals or not find the answers we
believed might be there. Without the work carried out on the Silver
Spring monkeys, I could never have developed CIMT."[18]

It is infuriating to think that if Pacheco had succeeded in ruining Taub
and preventing his research from progressing, CIMT might have been lost
to humanity. Tens of thousands of people who have already had some
motor function restored in limbs they cannot feel—improving their quality of life and empowering them to achieve levels of independence once
thought impossible—would still be unable to use their arms. "People can
now comb their hair, turn a doorknob, bring a fork to their mouths, pour
a cup of coffee," even though their limbs have no feeling.[19] None of this
would have happened but for the monkey experiments.

And here's more good news: CIMT is no longer considered "experimental," meaning that it will increasingly be covered by health insurance.
This means that millions of people may benefit—even if they lost the use
of their arms decades ago. "In the United States alone there are four million stroke survivors, three-quarters of which could be helped by CIMT,"
Taub told me. What's more, the improvement in function can be achieved
years, even decades after the loss of mobility: "We had one case in which a
person who was fifty years post-stroke benefited from therapy."[20]

CIMT is now being taught to therapists from around the world.
Taub and his colleagues have trained therapists from Germany, the

United Kingdom, China, Sweden, the Netherlands, Brazil, Portugal, and Japan.[21]

Still, much has been lost: The sudden termination of his research with the monkeys and the years Taub took to clear his name kept him from gaining more information that may have had medical or scientific value. Taub was not only researching the plasticity of the brain's role in the nervous system—which has now been proved—but also whether the spinal cord and nerves would show a similar capacity. But PETA and Pacheco's attack prevented further investigation of the question. "I never was able to get back to that area of inquiry," Taub says.[22]

The development of CIMT proves the importance of animal work in developing medical therapies and treatments. (We will explore this topic in more detail later.) This point was explicitly made by the American Psychological Association in granting Taub its Distinguished Scientific Award for the Applications of Psychology in 2004:

> For undaunted brilliant research bridging from the primate laboratory to the bedside, Edward Taub's work has benefited thousands of patients suffering from what are otherwise irremediable long-term motor impairments from brain damage, including stroke and, in children, cerebral palsy. To counter a hitherto undetected phenomenon of learned nonuse obscuring recovery potential, he devised a highly successful therapy using basic behavioral principles. Related research with others has yielded surprising discoveries that the adult cerebral cortex is capable of substantial plastic reorganization that is use-dependent on and supportive of motor performance and recovery. His contributions against odds testify to his persistent scientific rigor.[23]

Unfortunately, most animal rights activists disingenuously refuse to admit that animal research leads to beneficial human applications. And those liberationists with the intellectual integrity to acknowledge the benefit we receive from animal research believe that people have no moral right to obtain it at the "expense" of the animals. Taub disagrees. "We have two sides of the scale to ponder," he told me. "On one side is the real and potential hope that animal research offers to countless suffering human beings. On the other is the difficult knowledge that obtaining many of these benefits means that some animals will be harmed."[24]

Taub has it exactly right. Animal rights/liberationists believe that monkeys matter as much as stroke victims and children with disabilities. People like Taub and this author believe that the suffering of animals is a serious matter and that it should never be countenanced for frivolous reasons. But alleviating the suffering of human beings and promoting human thriving matter most. That, in a nutshell, is the nub of the entire animal rights debate.

The Death of a Thousand Cuts

Fully achieving the ultimate goal of the animal rights/liberation movement will require the utter eradication of all animal-using industries. The resulting shock waves would not only affect businesses that deal directly with animals, but given the ubiquitous use of animal products throughout the economy and society, it would have deleterious consequences up and down the line.

Being obsessed with animals, liberationists know this better than anyone else. None other than Steven Wise, a lawyer who (as we saw earlier) advocates granting "practical personhood" status to some animals, recognizes that our society today is "enmeshed in the use of nonhuman animals":

> Today, the use of nonhuman animal products is so diverse and widespread that it is impossible to live in modern society and not support the nonhuman animal industry directly. For example, the blood of a slaughtered cow is used to manufacture plywood adhesives, fertilizer, fire extinguisher foam, and dyes. Her fat helps make plastic, tires, crayons, cosmetics, lubricants, soaps, detergents, cough syrup, contraceptive jellies and creams, ink, shaving cream, fabric softeners, synthetic rubber, jet engine lubricants, textiles, corrosion inhibitors, and metal-machining lubricants. Her collagen is found in pie crusts, yogurts, matches, bank notes, paper, and cardboard glue; her intestines are used in strings for musical instruments and racquets; her bones in charcoal ash for refining sugar, in ceramics, and cleaning and polishing compounds. Medical and scientific uses abound. And there is much, much more.[1]

Rather than being impressed by the nothing-goes-to-waste efficiency of animal use, Wise is, of course, utterly appalled, equating such practices to human slavery and other assorted actual evils. And he understands—as do all the movement's leaders—that ending all human use of animals would require a wrenching economic and cultural revolution. Because such a revolution would be "impeded by physical, economic, political, religious, historical, and legal obstacles," the goal of total animal liberation is the work of generations.[2]

Understanding this reality, animal liberationists such as the leaders of PETA, the Humane Society of the United States (HSUS), and Farm Sanctuary have adopted a "one-step-at-a-time" strategy intended to undermine the economic and cultural foundations for the domestication and humane use of animals—in essence destroying their perceived enemies slowly but implacably, in a death of a thousand cuts.

This goal is pursued ubiquitously by means both fair and foul. For example, activists sometimes engage in mendacious PR campaigns. They harness the vitality of democratic processes, sponsoring legislation and voter initiatives intended to make animal husbandry increasingly difficult and meat products consequently more expensive. As we have already seen, they file lawsuits, some of which are righteous and others frivolous. They publish video or photographic exposés claiming abuse by animal industries—some true and others, like those of the Silver Spring monkeys, distorted or false—that serve as the bases for official investigations and PR campaigns. They mount public protests and boycotts, sometimes based on inaccurate or incomplete information.

The purpose of all this frenetic activity is not primarily to improve animal welfare—remember, liberationists disdain animal welfarism, although some do engage in welfare-type campaigns—but rather to impede the functioning of animal-using industries, damage their profitability, and, like termites in the basement, undermine their legitimacy in the public eye, with the ultimate goal of eradicating all domestication and other uses of animals by humans. Here are a few of the most notable campaigns against animal use in recent years.

"Kentucky Fried Cruelty"

On May 7, 2003, Cheryl Bachelder, the president of KFC (formerly Kentucky Fried Chicken), went crawling (figuratively) to the offices of PETA to petition Ingrid Newkirk for an end to the organization's "Kentucky Fried Cruelty" campaign. It hadn't taken much to break the corporate will. PETA's threat to disrupt a Los Angeles appearance in *The Producers* by KFC's television pitchman at the time, Jason Alexander, had the *Seinfeld* star pulling a real-life George Costanza, begging KFC to get PETA off his back. (Alexander and KFC parted company soon thereafter.) Then, when PETA announced plans to picket Bachelder's home, it was Munich time.[3]

Bachelder "jumped on the corporate jet and flew to PETA's hometown of Norfolk," PETA's website triumphantly crowed afterward, acquiescing to five of PETA's eight demands. According to PETA's victory report, Bachelder pledged, among other things, to install cameras in all of KFC's twenty-nine contract slaughterhouses by the end of 2004 (the chain does not raise or slaughter the chickens it uses), with a plan to audit the tapes monthly. KFC also agreed to ensure that its suppliers add stimulation devices to the perches in the chicken sheds; quickly move to kill chickens in electric stun baths rather than merely stunning them before manual slaughter; implement humane mechanized chicken-gathering systems; and provide increased space for chicken housing. KFC promised to report back to PETA on a regular basis to verify its compliance.

In return, PETA didn't have to agree to do much of anything. PETA would not picket KFC's annual shareholder meeting for 2003. It agreed to modify its website assertions about KFC and suspend "all planned billboards." And it promised not to undertake further "step-ups" in the anti-KFC campaign for sixty days—which only meant that it would be at least sixty-one days before Bachelder's home was picketed by animal rights protestors.

The promised reforms might all have been humane and appropriate changes in the raising and slaughter of chickens by KFC's suppliers—although it must be pointed out that the American Veterinary Medical Association approves of stunning chickens and then manually killing them as a humane method of ending their lives.[4] Indeed, it shouldn't take pressure from animal liberationists for corporate executives to do the right thing. And from a purely strategic standpoint, acting under such pressure—as Bachelder did—merely adds to the power of animal rights activists, making them an ever-greater threat to the legitimate use of animals.

Be that as it may, if KFC thought that it had bought peace and security from PETA by so clearly and publicly caving in to the organization's threats and intimidation, it didn't know its enemy. As we have already seen, PETA's goal is not to reform food industry practices. The organization is not ultimately seeking a more enlightened universal standard for humane treatment of chickens by food producers. Accomplishing these goals would be mere tactical moves toward the strategic end of, quite literally, driving KFC—and all other meat-serving fast food restaurants—completely out of business.

Predictably, appeasing PETA did not work. In a six-page follow-up "Dear Cheryl" letter dated May 8, 2003 (and subsequently made public by PETA, including Bachelder's home address), Ingrid Newkirk warned darkly that the Kentucky Fried Cruelty campaign would continue more energetically than ever unless KFC agreed to the rest of PETA's demands. Not only that, but Newkirk more than hinted that the agreed-upon actions were "bare minimums" of what PETA would ultimately seek from the fast food behemoth.

In a preview of coming attractions, Newkirk served notice that PETA would one day require that KFC's chickens be "given sunlight, fresh air, the ability to dust bathe or raise their families—in other words to *be the animals nature intended them to be.*" This would mean nothing less than the end of the chicken restaurant business. After all, from PETA's perspective, nature intended chickens to be allowed to run wild without *any* interference from people, particularly those who might want to eat them. Not coincidentally, it would be virtually impossible to raise the hundreds of millions of chickens KFC sells as food each year in what would essentially be free-range conditions, and still charge low prices. But of course, that would suit Newkirk just fine.

Another of PETA's demands in the Dear Cheryl letter was highly ironic:

KFC must pledge to implement gas killing, using the latest technology, of all KFC chickens.... You said that you "can't do this overnight," and we don't expect you to. We do, however, expect you to do it, as the present method of slaughter is terrifying for the animals and abusive, as we have spelled out in detail in our report on this issue.[5]

As we saw in our earlier discussion of the Holocaust on Your Plate campaign, PETA explicitly compared eating meat to the Holocaust, created a moral equivalence between the raising of chickens in cages and the imprisonment of Jews in concentration camps, and stated that "the leather sofa and handbag are the modern equivalent of the lampshades made from the skins of the people killed in the death camps." And now PETA was demanding that KFC's inmates (from the liberationist point of view) be killed in the same way as the death-camp victims. It was enough to make one's head explode.

Not only that, but PETA had previously *decried killing fur animals by carbon monoxide*, even though this method of slaughter is condoned for chinchillas and minks by the American Veterinary Medical Association's *Guidelines on Euthanasia* because it causes "loss of consciousness without pain and with minimal discernible discomfort" within two minutes and cessation of heartbeat in five to seven minutes.[6] (More on this later.) Not that PETA's (non) fact sheet about the fur industry admitted this. Rather, it spread the false charge that fur animals are "poisoned with hot, unfiltered engine exhaust from a truck. Engine exhaust is not always lethal, and some animals wake up while they are being skinned."[7]

The truth is rather different, according to Theresa Platt, executive director of the Fur Commission USA, an industry-financed nonprofit educational organization. As she explains,

One could accomplish the task with engine exhaust but no one does and if they did, they could be charged with cruelty under state cruelty statutes. The gas must be cool, not hot, as per the AVMA report on euthanasia. For this reason, and because the chambers are mobile, farmers use canisters of gas. The animals are killed in the small barns (sheds) where they are raised, just a few feet from their pens. Transport, of course, is stressful to the animals so it is preferable to do the process on the farm.[8]

But truth and consistency are not important to PETA. What matters is impeding animal-using industries in pursuing their businesses. So, to make it harder to process fur animals, PETA decried gassing the animals and falsely depicted how that is done. At the same time, PETA spoke from the other side of its mouth in condemning chicken processors for *not* gassing their birds, even though the stunning by electricity and then manually killing the chickens is also approved by the AVMA's 2007 report. (The chickens cannot be killed by chemical agents because they are intended for human consumption.)[9]

To anyone with any knowledge of PETA's tactics and ideology, it was clear that KFC would find no lasting peace from PETA even if it agreed to gas chickens instead of using other means of slaughter. Not surprisingly, the detente between PETA and KFC was short-lived. Before the moratorium was up, a PETA animal rights activist poured fake blood over David Novak, the CEO of Yum! Brands, the parent company of KFC, while he was visiting Germany.

PETA and KFC have since gone to their respective corners. PETA continues its Kentucky Fried Cruelty campaign, attempting to deprive KFC of profits and, not coincidentally, raise money for its own operations. KFC understands that it is up against a relentless adversary that seeks to harm its business as much as alleviate the suffering of fryers sent to market.

This is the bottom line: KFC and other businesses that use animals must understand that they can never treat animals humanely enough to satisfy the animal rights/liberation absolutists. Their only hope is to treat their animals humanely *before* PETA pounds on the door and then to stand firmly against activists' intimidation whenever and however it occurs—even if it means their presidents' homes are picketed, their stockholder meetings disrupted, and their executives' business suits stained by fake blood. Pursuing a less courageous course will bring KFC and other animal industries peace all right—the permanent peace of the corporate grave.

Putting Pregnant Pigs into the Florida Constitution

In November 2002, Florida voters passed an amendment to their state's constitution that granted pregnant pigs a constitutional right not to be kept in gestation crates.[10]

On the surface, the issue in Amendment 10 was merely a controversial method of animal husbandry. To prevent mother pigs from accidentally rolling on and crushing their offspring and to increase productivity, some pig farmers confine sows in crates during pregnancy and for a time after birthing. Supporters of this practice claim that the crates, which are seven feet long and two feet wide, ensure the safety and health of pregnant pigs and new piglets, and promote successful breeding. Indeed, peer-reviewed studies published in professional journals do show that crates improve breeding efficiency and prevent pigs from harming each other in fights. Moreover, the use of gestation crates was explicitly approved in a resolution passed in 2002 by the American Veterinary Medical Association:

> The American Veterinary Medical Association supports the use of sow housing configurations that: (1) minimize aggression and competition between sows; (2) protect sows from detrimental effects associated with environmental extremes, particularly temperature extremes; (3) reduce exposure to hazards that result in injuries; (4) provide every animal with daily access to appropriate food and water; and (5) facilitate observation of individual sow appetite, respiratory rate, urination and defecation, and reproductive status by caretakers.[11]

(Subsequent efforts within the AVMA to reverse this position have repeatedly failed.)

But animal rights activists see it differently. They claim that immobilizing the sows in crates causes a wide range of physical and psychological problems. Farm Sanctuary (FS), an animal rights organization based in Watkins Glen, New York, wants to see not just an end to the use of gestation crates, but the total eradication of pig farming. "In an ideal world, there would be no need for Farm Sanctuary," the organization asserts on its website. "There would be no factory farms or stockyards and cows, pigs, chickens, and other farm animals would not be abused. They would be free to laze in the breeze, bathe in the sun, scratch at the earth, and enjoy life."[12] Farm Sanctuary is not an animal welfare organization devoted to reforming animal husbandry practices. Rather, its goal is to eliminate all meat industries—no matter how humanely the food animals are raised: "Farm Sanctuary opposes the slaughter, consumption and commodification of farm animals. . . . Farm Sanctuary has never and will never support so-called 'humane' meat. We maintain that the words 'humane' and 'slaughter' are mutually exclusive."[13]

The Humane Society of the United States also seeks to ban gestation crates. HSUS is an intriguing organization: While its advocacy activities top even those of PETA in scope (and budget), it does not claim to be in favor of (or against) animal rights/liberation and it wisely avoids the wackier aspects of animal rights polemics. HSUS does not, for example, refer to cattle as "slaves," nor does it explicitly call for the abolition of all domesticated animals. Rather, HSUS defines itself as promoting "animal protection," and in fact it is the richest and most powerful organization in the field, with assets in excess of $200 million and an annual expense budget of about $108 million in 2006.[14] (HSUS is not to be confused with local humane societies that run animal shelters and the like. HSUS does not operate shelters, although it does give a small percentage of its budget to groups that do.)

Still, there is abundant cause to believe that, as least in the hearts of its leaders, animal rights rather than protection or welfare is the real name of the game for HSUS. Its president, the always professional Wayne Pacelle, has said—quite aptly—that HSUS is "the NRA of the animal rights movement," meaning that its public advocacy on behalf of animals is on a par with the National Rifle Association's support of gun rights.[15] Sounding very much like the abolitionist Gary Francione, Pacelle, who like Francione is a vegan, once told a publication called *Animal People*, "We have no ethical obligation to preserve different breeds of livestock produced through selective breeding.... One generation and out. We have no problem with the extinction of domestic animals. They are creations of human selective breeding."[16] J. P. Goodwin, once the executive director of the Coalition to Abolish the Fur Trade and a self-described (as reported by the *Dallas Morning News*) former member of the terrorist Animal Liberation Front, is now HSUS's grassroots coordinator.[17] He has stated, "My goal is to abolish all animal agriculture."[18] Adding fire to this plume of smoke, in the published proceeds of a 1980 conference at which HSUS apparently resolved to pursue a more radical course, the organization asserted, "There is no rational basis for maintaining the moral distinction between the treatment of humans and other animals."[19]

Be that as it may, Farm Sanctuary and HSUS (among others) despise gestation crates because they allegedly lead to such disorders as joint damage, leg weakness, urinary tract infections, and emotional stress, supposedly because the pigs are prevented from living in natural "communal nests."[20] Toward this end, the two organizations—neither of them based in Florida—took advantage of Florida's easy qualification process for voter initiatives and, working with animal rights activists in the state, qualified a proposed state constitutional amendment that would make it *unconstitutional* to confine a pregnant pig "in a cage, crate, or other enclosure, or tether a pregnant pig on a farm so that the pig is prevented from turning around freely."[21]

Here we can't settle the gestation crate controversy, which is unquestionably a legitimate subject of public debate and government regulation, with respectable arguments on both sides. (In this regard, it is worth noting that the country's largest pork processor has required its suppliers to phase out gestation crates, not because they are inhumane, but because of "questions from customers.")[22] Our primary concern is whether it was appropriate to make gestation crates a matter of *constitutional rights* for pigs.

According to its preamble, the Constitution of the State of Florida was ordained and established by the people to "secure the benefits" of "Constitutional Liberty," "perfect our government, insure domestic tranquility, maintain public order, and guarantee equal civil and political rights." In other words, the Florida Constitution is about the rights and responsibilities of people, not pigs.

This point is not a mere intellectual abstraction to be discussed over a morning *latte* or debated at some arcane academic symposium. The content of constitutions is crucial to our own self-perception. Constitutions are about maintaining and protecting *human* liberty and dignity. Through constitutions we establish our forms of government and mutually guarantee that none of us will be denied certain fundamental human rights. The articles of constitutions are far more important than simple statutes, and far more profound. They provide the philosophical and structural bases from which flow our freedom and our sacred honor.

Granting constitutional rights to animals cheapens these charters. Worse, making humans and animals common beneficiaries of constitutional liberties undermines the principle that humans enjoy a unique status, elevated above the natural world of flora and fauna. And that is precisely why animal rights activists used the Florida initiative process to challenge the idea of constitutions as guarding *human* rights exclusively: their purpose was not so much to protect pigs as to blur the moral distinctions between animals and humans.

There is plenty of circumstantial evidence supporting this assertion. Florida was not exactly known as the Pig Farm State when Amendment 10 was placed on the ballot: At the time, there were only *ten* pork suppliers in the entire state—and of these, only *two* pig farms even used gestation crates, involving only three to six hundred animals.[23] Yet proponents spent $1.2 million to promote Amendment 10.[24] Farm Sanctuary even violated Florida election law in soliciting money to pass the measure—resulting in a $50,000 fine—and raised suspicion that Florida was selected precisely because there would be little organized opposition in a state with so few pig farms.[25]

If that was the plan, it worked like a charm. With more than a million dollars spent on the campaign and no effective opposition, Amendment 10 passed by about 55 to 45 percent.

As if to demonstrate that helping pigs wasn't the real point of the initiative, the two pork growers in Florida that used gestation crates immediately sent the sows affected by the amendment to slaughter, along with the rest of their stock. But that was fine with the animal liberationists who had supported the measure. As a story in the *St. Petersburg Times* noted about the slaughter:

> [D]on't look for sympathy from the animal rights groups that pushed for the ban. Running hog farms out of business and keeping new ones from coming to Florida is exactly what they were after. "We think that's an excellent thing," said Mike Winikoff, spokesman for the Animal Rights Foundation of Florida. "And the fact that some of the pigs might get slaughtered earlier, in the big picture, we see that as a good thing. It's going to lessen their suffering and hasten the end of their miserable lives."[26]

Some stories reported that the two pig farms were going out of business even before the initiative.[27] But whichever version is true, the paucity of pig farms in the state surely indicates that other political agendas were at work beneath the surface in the Florida initiative, which could have only a minimal impact on pig welfare.

This is a continuing pattern: Liberationists and animal protection activists claim to be acting on behalf of animals—even if it results in mass slaughter of the very animals for which they purport to advocate. Thus, several years ago, when an African animal park agreed to ship elephants to the San Diego Zoo and the Lowry Park Zoo rather than kill them in a cull, a coalition of animal rights groups including PETA and In Defense of Animals, along with animal protection organizations such as Born Free USA, filed suit seeking an injunction against the importation. According to the district court's opinion denying the injunction, when the judge pointed out to the plaintiffs' lawyers that granting the injunction would result in elephants' deaths, "counsel for plaintiffs explained that, from plaintiffs' perspective, the elephants will be better off—and thus plaintiffs' interests will be more fully advanced—if the elephants are killed rather than imported and placed in zoos."[28]

Of course, granting limited state constitutional rights to pregnant pigs is a long way from expanding coverage of the Bill of Rights to include all animals. But considering the clearly stated goals of the animal rights movement and the explicit agendas of advocacy organizations such as the Great Ape Project, the successful effort to grant constitutional rights to pigs can reasonably be seen as merely one small step on the proverbial thousand-mile journey that leads to the eradication of any moral distinction between animals and people.

Making False or Misleading Charges

On November 13, 2007, PETA filed serious charges with the United States Department of Agriculture against the Primate Research Center at the Oregon Health and Science University (OHSU). Based on the assertions of an "undercover" plant that had obtained employment with OHSU under false pretenses, PETA alleged at a press conference that the lab failed to provide timely veterinary care to monkeys suffering from chronic vomiting and kidney stones, as well as failing to prevent monkeys from being physically harmed, experiencing behavioral stress, and suffering trauma.

As we saw in the Silver Spring monkey case, a favored tactic of liberationists is to infiltrate animal labs and industries, gather "secret evidence,"
and then emerge to tell vivid and bloody tales of horror and supposedly
rampant abuse generally accompanied by lurid photographs or videotapes.
Sometimes, the claims made are true, as when HSUS exposed the abuse
of cattle by employees of the Hallmark/Westland Meat Packing Company, in which "downer" animals—those too sick to walk, and hence unfit
for the food supply—were cruelly prodded into standing up and walking
so they could pass pre-slaughter inspection. The exposé of this inexcusably abusive and unhealthy lawbreaking resulted in the biggest beef recall
in history: 143 million pounds.[29]

Unfortunately, liberationists often make bogus or broadly overstated
charges against their enemies in the animal industry. And indeed, in the
matter of the Primate Research Center, federal inspectors quickly cleared
the OHSU lab—one of the most prestigious in the world—of all charges.
In response to its vindication, the acting head of the center aptly stated:
"Our business involves offering hope to people with disease. My colleagues
and I will not be deterred by extremist organizations or those who choose
to campaign based on false information and harassment."[30]

This was not the first time that animal liberationists leveled false or
misleading allegations against animal researchers, nor will it be the last.
Sometimes these allegations are based on manipulated evidence. A classic
example of this occurred back in 2000 when twelve animal rights organizations accused IBP, Inc., a beef-processing plant of cruelty to animals. On
May 31, 2000, the Humane Farming Association, PETA, the Physicians
Committee for Responsible Medicine, and HSUS (among others) filed a
"Petition for Enforcement of the Humane Slaughter and Animal Cruelty
Laws" with the State of Washington. The groups accused IBP of inhu-
manely slaughtering cattle, of allowing meat to become contaminated, and
of creating unsafe work practices that resulted in injuries to employees.

The charges were based on videotapes taken by an infiltrator, which,
true to the standard liberationist playbook, were released to an ever-eager
media and aired by Seattle's KING-TV. The allegations and the video
seemed serious enough to spark the Washington State Department
of Agriculture to lead a multiagency investigation, which included the Washington State Department of Labor and Industries, the

state's attorney general, the USDA, and other government and law enforcement agencies.

After nearly a year of checking, the WSDA issued a detailed report finding that the charges were almost entirely without merit across the board. Concerning the charge of inhumane slaughter, the summary report of the investigation concluded:

> Investigators did not discover any evidence that IBP had a written or unwritten policy of either encouraging or permitting employees to mistreat livestock. Persons who had signed affidavits alleging mistreatment of animals, when making statements to the WSP detective, were unable to provide dates, times, or names of individuals involved in particular incidents of animal abuse; nor did such statements indicate that supervisors had sanctioned or encouraged the mistreatment of animals. The investigation did not reveal any benefit to the corporation from systematic or sanctioned abuse of animals. To the contrary, animal experts told investigators that animals that are mistreated or arrive at the stunning area in an excited condition produce lactic acid and depleted glycogen stores in their tissues. This depletion ... produces "dark cutters" with dark, discolored meat.... An animal in this condition produces meat of undesirable quality and its value is significantly reduced.[31]

In fact, investigators found only one incident of mistreatment, when two animals were "excessively prodded"—and this had been corrected at the time by on-site USDA inspectors.

Evidence of food safety violations were also determined to be substantially without merit. After conducting interviews with employees about such alleged violations, the WSDA "found no evidence to support the allegations." And while on-site inspectors had found some deficiencies to have occurred between 1999 and 2000, IBP "had demonstrated effective implementation of corrective actions that preclude ... system plan failures."[32] Similarly, worker safety violations also proved to be a dry hole, with health and safety problems on the line being primarily "ergonomic issues" rather than unsafe methods of animal processing, and in any event these were "not related to the allegations in the petition."[33]

Most interestingly, the investigation concluded that the five-minute videotape of alleged abuses—the public release of which had sparked the controversy—*had been taken from three and a half hours of actual footage.*

Moreover, when investigators compared the edited scenes with the unedited footage, they found that the edited version created a materially false impression. In describing a video of its own correcting the record, investigators noted that either the activities were legal, albeit "disturbing"—after all, the activity depicted is the slaughter of cattle—or, "In several instances, what appears to be a 'bad act' on the edited version is corrected by IBP employees during the next few seconds of the unedited video."[34] In other words, the video clip produced by the animal rights activists was mere propaganda, not an accurate exposé of systemic abuse.

And this brings up an important point: We should be careful to reserve judgment when considering videos released by animal rights groups purporting to document abuse or other illegal practices. Likely as not, the depictions will have been taken out of context or cherry-picked to heighten the emotional impact. After all, the unbending goal of animal rights ideologues is to turn the public against all animal-using industries and impede their operations. Thus, while a photograph may be worth a thousand words, when distributed by animal rights propagandists it may well be a thousand lies.

Attacking Australian Sheepherders

Animal rights propagandists often tell only part of the story—leaving out crucial information and context—when attacking supposed animal abuses. A classic example came out of the PETA shop in 2005 when the group attempted to launch an international boycott against the Australian wool industry.

The protest began in 2004 with a large PETA-sponsored billboard near Times Square depicting a lamb with red flesh showing around its anus because skin had been removed. The text of the sign read: "Did your sweater cause a bloody butt? Boycott Australian wool."[35] PETA's press release explained why it was mounting the protest:

> PETA launched the boycott in October after the Australian government ignored repeated pleas to ban live sheep exports, in which thousands of sheep die each year, and to end "mulesing," a little-known crude mutilation in which farmers use gardening shears to cut large chunks of flesh from lambs'

hindquarters without any painkillers. Australia is the largest producer and exporter of wool, accounting for 28 percent worldwide. Prestigious retailer Abercrombie & Fitch has joined the boycott, and J. Crew, an $800 million company, and New Look, a $1 billion company based in London, have also announced that they have examined their inventory and sources and do not sell cruelly produced Australian wool.[36]

Sounds awful and gratuitously cruel, doesn't it? But wait: There is far more—and less—to this story than some apparent sadism by Aussie sheepherders.

Here is what PETA didn't highlight as it attempted to destroy Australia's sheepherders: Australia is home to a nasty species of fly called the blowfly, which reproduces by laying eggs in wet wool, particularly around wounds or in healthy but damp areas soiled by feces and urine. When the eggs hatch, the maggots literally eat into the flesh of the sheep and feed for several days—a condition known as "flystrike"—before falling off onto the ground to pupate and become mature insects, starting the cycle anew. This parasitic maggot infestation, *which partially eats the infected animal alive,* not only is agonizing to the sheep, but releases toxins often causing afflicted animals to die lingering and terrible deaths.[37]

Mulesing protects tens of millions of Australian sheep for their entire lives from suffering flystrike. During the procedure, small patches of wool-bearing *skin* (not "large chunks of flesh") are snipped and removed from young lambs around the rump. When the wound heals, no wool grows in the area and thus wet waste is far less likely to stick to the animals and attract blowflies. Moreover, the skin around the anus tightens and becomes smooth so that even if flies do land, they do not lay eggs.

No eggs means no maggots. No maggots means no flystrike. No flystrike means that sheep will not suffer a torturous parasitic affliction and potentially agonizing death. Thus, rather than being cruel, mulesing is actually a necessary preventive measure *that protects sheep against much worse suffering* than the transitory pain the procedure causes. Indeed, without mulesing, up to three million sheep would die terrible deaths during a bad flystrike year.

PETA mentions flystrike without dwelling on the awfulness of the affliction, and claims that mulesing isn't necessary to prevent it anyway.

Instead, PETA suggests, sheep ranchers could continually shear the wool off the rumps of each of the hundred million or so sheep in Australia. But that wouldn't work as well as mulesing does, since the flies lay eggs in healthy sheep in the wrinkly skin around a sheep's anus. It takes *both* the tightening of the skin and the removal of wool to prevent flystrike in healthy, uninjured sheep. And PETA's suggestion is ironic considering its belief that the shearing of sheep itself is abusive, as evidenced in the organization's "Inside the Wool Industry" documents, where readers are told that premature shearing causes sheep to die of exposure,[38] and that "the shearing shed must be one of the worst places in the world for cruelty to animals."[39]

Insecticides and flytraps could also reduce the flies, we are told. In fact, such methods are already in use. Sheep are also dipped to prevent the disease. But there is currently nothing as effective as mulesing in preventing flystrike over the long term.

PETA also suggests that ranchers change breeds to those without so many wrinkles. But according to Sarah Llewellyn-Evans, a spokeswoman for the Australian wool industry, wrinkled merino sheep "produce the finest and of the highest quality wool in the world. Changing to a different breed of sheep would not allow us to produce the wool that the market demands."[40] Thus, changing breeds would destroy the Australian wool industry and severely damage the livelihoods of Aussies who work directly or indirectly in the wool industry—which, of course, would be PETA's dream come true.

Any objective and informed view must thus conclude that mulesing is an unfortunate but necessary and appropriate animal management practice until a better method can be developed. Since the 1930s, the Australian wool industry has in fact tried to find a better alternative, although there is little doubt that PETA's campaign has spurred more action in this area. The Australian Veterinary Association, which also advocates finding alternatives to mulesing, has stated:

> Fly strike is particularly painful for the sheep as maggots eat the live flesh of the animal. Mulesing is an animal husbandry practice currently used to prevent fly strike in sheep, which the AVA considers to be necessary in terms of the overall welfare of the sheep likely to be affected by fly strike.[41]

Even the Royal Society for the Prevention of Cruelty to Animals (RSPCA), which deeply dislikes the practice, "considers mulesing a necessary means of eliminating or minimizing the pain and suffering caused by flystrike" in those areas where "there is a high risk" and "no acceptable alternative."[42]

None of this matters to PETA. In its zest to destroy Australian wool producers, it announced an international boycott using vividly colored— and, it should be mentioned, out-of-date—photographs of restrained lambs that had just undergone mulesing, intended to convince people (who have never heard of flystrike) that Aussie sheep are routinely being abused. Of course, PETA never disseminated any pictures of flystruck sheep dripping blood and maggots on its website or billboards. Doing so would have demonstrated that the Australian wool producers are actually protecting their sheep. Indeed, the singer Pink initially supported PETA's call for a boycott, but reversed her position when she learned the full story and apologized for acting before discovering all the facts. The Academy Award–winning actress Toni Collette also rescinded her initial support for the boycott after getting more information.[43] (Demonstrating PETA's lack of intellectual integrity, as of January 8, 2008, its website still had the Pink video available for playing without alerting viewers that she had withdrawn her support of the wool boycott.)[44]

Would that retailers possessed the same wisdom. Companies such as Abercrombie & Fitch and J. Crew supported the boycott soon after PETA threatened public pressure against them. After the Abercrombie & Fitch announcement, the Australian wool producers vowed to phase out mulesing by 2010, thus appearing to cave in to PETA's demands.

But long before PETA entered the picture, the wool industry had invested millions of dollars in searching for effective alternatives. It had paid university researchers, for example, to study the genome of the blowfly to learn whether genetic science can be applied to eradicate the threat. In another promising approach, which appears close to becoming usable, researchers developed a protein that would be applied noninvasively to lambs' rumps, preventing all growth of wool and constricting the skin to smooth out posterior wrinkles. If the protein experiments pan out, mulesing can be phased out.

Not surprisingly, Australian Wool Innovation sued PETA as a result of the boycott. Also, not surprisingly, the case settled in what appears to have been a victory for the wool growers. PETA called off its boycott, agreeing to "maintain a Moratorium on their Australian Wool industry campaign until 31 December 2010." For its part, the industry agreed to continue to seek an alternative to mulesing—which it was already doing in any event. It also agreed to establish a training program to help teach sheep farmers "who mules their sheep about animal husbandry and farm management practices that may . . . reduce the incidence of fly-strike to reduce mulesing." A method was to be created that would identify "unmulesed Australian wool throughout the Australian wool supply chain." And the wool industry would "encourage the development . . . of products to provide relief from pain associated with mulesing." Finally—and this seems a very big concession on PETA's part, demonstrating clearly that at the time of the settlement there simply was no viable alternative to mulesing to prevent flystrike—the wool industry agreed to "fast track the development of Genetic-Based Mulesing Alternatives and . . . encourage the adoption of such alternatives *when developed.*" (My emphasis.)[45]

The problem for the woolgrowers is that PETA often has a loose definition of what it means to keep its word. Despite the legal agreement to call off the boycott, in early 2008 the Swedish clothing company H&M stated its intent to boycott Australian wool over mulesing, apparently based on PETA's advocacy. Rather than noting that PETA had agreed to a boycott moratorium until 2010, Ingrid Newkirk applauded the decision, claiming it "would hasten the day when the Australian wool industry is seen as nothing more than lamb mutilators and sheep abusers."[46] Of course, the story does not mention that in Newkirk's view, raising any sheep for wool is, by definition, abuse.

PETA apparently broke its word again in March 2008 when Matalan, a British discount chain, announced it would comply with the boycott after meeting with PETA representatives. Amusingly, according to Norman Blackman, a spokesman for the Australian Sheep and Wool Industry Task Force, "This retailer has not been using Australian wool and, given the nature of their product range, they are unlikely to do so in the future."[47] In other words, PETA convinced a company to desist from an activity in which it had never engaged. No matter. The point for PETA was the publicity—another notch on its boycott gun, even though it had agreed to put the gun back in its holster.

Nobody relishes mulesing, including sheep ranchers, but it sure beats flystrike. Until the practice can be phased out and replaced with an equally effective and less painful prophylactic, the one-time procedure is necessary to prevent sheep from falling prey to an awful and very painful maggot infestation. And shame on PETA for slandering Australian sheepherders as so many sadists who gratuitously harm their sheep, and for misleading the public as they try to ruin the ranchers' livelihoods.

8

Proselytizing Children

Several years ago, I spoke to an honors class for seniors at a high school in Canada. I was asked by the organizers to defend the intrinsic value of human life as a predicate for guaranteeing universal human rights. During the presentation, I warned against following the Siren song of Peter Singer–style personhood theory, in part because it could lead to the killing and exploitation of vulnerable human life. As part of my thesis, I noted how Singer is well known not only for jump-starting the animal liberation movement but also for promoting infanticide as appropriate in some circumstances on the ground that babies, in his view, lack personhood and hence are not yet full members of the "moral community."[1]

Even though I only mentioned the animal liberation aspect of Singer's utilitarian theories in passing, a very bright-eyed young woman approached me after the speech and, in a voice brimming with the righteous earnestness of youth, said in an accusatory tone, "You are saying that the life of a human has greater value than the life of a bunny."

Surprised that she seemed put off by that idea, I said, "Ye-e-e-s."

"No!" she emotionally interjected. "A bunny feels pain just like a human. That means we are equal."

I was disturbed by this exchange and the conversation that followed, in which the girl refused to consider that humans have greater value than animals. Her adamancy so struck me that it helped plant the seed for this book.

A year or two later I appeared on the *Lee Rodgers and Melanie Morgan Show*, a morning talk show on KSFO radio in San Francisco, to discuss an article I had written about the ideology of the animal rights movement. As I recounted the story of my exchange with the Canadian high school student, Morgan's eyes widened and she gasped, "Oh my gosh: My thirteen-year-old son came home from school yesterday and insisted that our dog is equal to humans."

In preparing to write this chapter, I called Morgan and asked if she remembered the interview and her son's statement. She did and agreed to ask her son, now sixteen years old, if he still believed that dogs and people are equal and, regardless of his current belief on the matter, how he got this idea. She e-mailed me the following response (and granted permission to quote it here): "I spoke with my son C.J. and asked if he remembered our conversation [about humans and dogs]: Answer: 'I said dogs were equal to humans because it is true. They can *think*.' Question: 'Where did you learn that?' Answer: 'From school because it is *true*. Dogs think, and so they are the same as humans.'" Morgan told me that her son was apparently taught that dogs and humans are moral equals at a public school in Marin County.[2]

Clearly, C.J. and the Canadian girl—and other children and teenagers who accept animal rights ideology that I have spoken with, received e-mails from, and heard about from their concerned parents in the last few years—did not come to believe in human/animal equality by accident. There is no question that animal rights organizations emphasize proselytizing the young into accepting their "a rat is a pig is a dog is a boy" dogma, and that these views are sometimes foisted on children by teachers in school. As Dan Matthews, PETA's vice president, once put it, "Our campaigns are always geared towards children and they always will be."[3]

Converting the young to animal rights dogma makes abundant sense from the liberationists' perspective, and it is among the youth that they find their most receptive audience. The primary arguments made by liberationists are hyperemotive and highly anthropomorphic, an approach that seems particularly suited to an era in which feelings are often deemed more important than thinking. Moreover, as we will discuss in more detail in the last chapter, our youth have been exposed all their lives to explicitly antihuman attitudes, to accusations that humans are an "invasive virus" afflicting nature and destroying the planet.[4] Besides, people of a certain age, for whom the word Metamucil has taken on a whole new meaning, remember all too vividly the era when KKK racists compared African Americans to animals and the unprecedented horrors of Auschwitz, and are markedly less likely to be sympathetic to explicit comparisons between animal husbandry and the unequivocal evils of the Holocaust and human slavery. Besides, the more mature generally find it hard to take an ideology seriously when its adherents accuse beekeepers of abusing hive queens on "rape racks"[5] and contend that wood cockroaches "are monogamous [and] raise one group of children" as if insect broods were akin to human families.[6]

Not surprisingly, PETA is the most aggressive organization seeking to lasso the young to the animal rights cause with hyperemotional appeals and romanticizing of the animal world and special pleading to youthful innocence. PETA even seeks to interfere with the relationship between children and their parents in tracts called the "PETA Comics," aimed at convincing children to stop their mothers from wearing fur and their fathers from fishing.

The cover of *Your Mommy KILLS Animals!* depicts an evil-looking "mother" in an apron and pearls, stabbing an innocent rabbit to death with a huge Bowie knife, splattering blood and gore all over the page. The cover says, "*Ask your mommy: How many animals she killed to make her fur coat? The sooner she stops wearing fur, the sooner animals will be safe!*" On the inside page, the "comic book" then claims that "*nasty men in boots catch animals with traps that have metal claws that snap shut on animals' legs.... Trapped animals that don't get away from the traps are stomped to death by the nasty men.*" (Remember, this is distributed to young children.)

Then, the PETA propagandists shamefully plant the seed in children's minds that a woman who wears fur might kill the family's pets. "*Tell her that you know she paid men to hurt and kill animals. Everyone knows. And the sooner she stops wearing fur, the sooner the animals will be safe. Until then, keep your doggie or kitty friends away from mommy—she's an animal killer!*"[7] Whatever one might think of wearing fur or trapping animals for their pelts, to present such disturbing images *to children* and plant seeds of worry that their mothers might kill a beloved pet is utterly inappropriate and wrong.

PETA unrepentantly repeated the same approach in its second "PETA Comic," *Your Daddy KILLS Animals!*, an anti-fishing diatribe with a cover that vividly depicts an "evil daddy" wearing a hat affixed with lures and fish hooks (and a skull and crossbones) eviscerating a fish. In lurid large red letters, the cover says: *"Ask your daddy why he's hooked on killing!"* On the inside, the children are told: *"Imagine that a man dangles a piece of candy in front of you. So you reach for it. But, as you grab the candy, a huge metal hook stabs through your hand and you are ripped off the ground. . . . You'd feel really scared, wouldn't you? That would be an awful trick to play on somebody, wouldn't it?"* Then comes the anthropomorphism so thick it can be cut with a knife. *"Fish may not be cuddly or cute like kitties and puppies, but fish are really smart. They learn from each other and can remember things for a long time. Just like people, fish eavesdrop to get info and they can even use tools!"* And it wouldn't be a PETA Comic without warnings against parents killing pets. *"Until your daddy learns that it's not 'fun' to kill, keep your doggies and kitties away from him. He's so hooked on killing defenseless animals that they could be next!"*

After the release of *Your Daddy KILLS Animals*, PETA pushed the theme that kittens are the same as tuna and trout even further on its PETA Kids website, which is devoted to proselytizing children.[8] Here, fish are called "sea kittens" and depicted with cute feline faces. Another section of PETA Kids offers free merchandise in return for engaging in advocacy "missions":

> Who wants free stuff? Right—everyone does, and this is the place to get it . . . but there's a catch: You have to *earn* it. Don't worry, we're not going to ask you to build an animal shelter from scratch over the weekend with three of your best friends or jet to Washington, D.C., to convince Congress to pass stricter laws to protect animals. The stuff that we'll be asking you to do is all easy-squeezy and, of course, fun.
>
> Missions will change monthly, so be sure to check back for new ways to score swag. This month's mission is here [linking to a PETA URL] and we're sure that you can handle it.[9]

In January 2008, the site listed fifteen different missions. One was to download animal rights "stencils" such as a chick saying "I am not a nugget," cut them out, and then "get spraying." Another was to download a petition against KFC and send it to the company's CEO, whose address was listed. Yet another was to get more children into PETA's clutches:

> OK. Ready? Your first mission is to convince 10 of your friends to sign up for PETA Kids E-News. Once you've done that, send their e-mail addresses to us at PETAKids@peta.org. Put "PETA Kids E-News Mission" in the subject line, and don't forget to include your name and mailing address. **If you don't give us all the info, you won't get your stickers!** Now that wasn't so bad, was it?[10]

PETA propagandists are unquestionably thorough, playing every thinkable angle. Pandering to kids' interest in popular culture and movie stars, the "Celebs and Music" link brings readers to a section that dishes the gossip:

> Love is definitely in the air for PETA pals this summer. Wedding bells were ringing for two of our favorite peeps in June when the lovely "World's Sexiest Vegetarian 2004" Alicia Silverstone married her longtime boyfriend, the equally sexy S.T.U.N. frontman, Christiane J. Congrats to the happy vegan couple, who were married in a beautiful seaside ceremony in Lake Tahoe, followed by what else? . . . A *totally* vegan reception, of course.[11]

Not coincidentally, Silverstone also appears in a video for PETA extolling vegetarianism in which she sensually emerges nude from a swimming pool—a presentation clearly designed to attract teenage boys![12]

The PETA Kids site also offers children the opportunity to play video games. In a section titled "Milk Sucks," kids can access a game called "Make Fred Spew" in which the player uses the computer mouse to scroll ice cream, yogurt, cheese, and other milk products to "Fred's" mouth. (Fred is depicted as a bumpkin who lives in a small trailer and cooks on a barbeque.) Fred then "spews" green vomit and makes a gross noise guaranteed to make kids giggle with glee.

Ingrid Newkirk, PETA's alpha wolf, even targets children through her MySpace site. One photo of Newkirk on the site depicts her making a funny face with flowers in her mouth. Another has her hugging a dog. Declaring, "Meat is murder," the entire site is brilliantly constructed to appeal to children and teenagers, particularly girls. For example, Newkirk identifies herself as a Pisces. And true to PETA's unrelenting approach, she never stops pushing the agenda, with the celebrity gossip, the books aimed at kids, and the cutesy comments of appreciation complete with images of dogs wagging their tails.[13] It is both brilliantly targeted and worrying.

The Center for Consumer Freedom, a nonprofit organization funded by the food industry to combat the animal rights agenda, published a large pamphlet titled *Your Kids, PETA's Pawns*, highlighting the many areas in which PETA seeks to proselytize children for the animal rights cause.[14] According to the center, at the elementary school level, in addition to distributing its "comics" about Mommy and Daddy being animal killers:

+ PETA sends its interns and employees to visit schools dressed in colorful mascot costumes designed to attract inquisitive kids.
+ In-school curriculum materials from PETA emphasize the alleged animal "exploitation" contained in *The Three Little Pigs* and *Cinderella*.
+ Activists distribute colorful anti-milk and anti-meat trading cards (and tofu "ice cream") to children as they walk home from school.
+ A newsletter called *Grrr! Kids Bite Back* introduces young children to the vocabulary and history of the animal liberation movement.[15]

At the middle school level:

+ PETA distributes free curriculum materials to teachers featuring anti-meat messages and discouraging kids from "chowing down on one of your friends."[16]
+ PETA "Humane Education Lecturers" preach strict vegetarianism to teen audiences. (One of PETA's humane education lecturers was a convicted animal rights felon named Gary Yourofsky, whom PETA hired in 2002 despite his being "sentenced in 1999 to six months in a Canadian maximum security prison for a felony raid on a fur farm.")[17]
+ The PETA Kids website instructs children on what to eat and tells them how to avoid field trips to the zoo or circus.[18]

PETA also targets high school students:

+ Curriculum material encourages students to ponder whether it's "acceptable to break a law" to promote animal rights.

+ Pre-written "homework" packets on animal rights topics are offered for students to use in essays, class presentations, and persuasive speeches.
+ PETA distributes literature encouraging students to refuse dissection assignments in biology class and offers legal assistance to those whose requests for a waiver are denied.[19]

PETA is not alone in this focus on children and youth in support of animal liberation. The animal rights organization called Farm Sanctuary, which "opposes the slaughter, consumption and commodification of farm animals," also targets children for "education" about animal rights.[20] The goal clearly is to have teachers inculcate animal rights belief in their students in the classroom. Thus, in its "Humane Education Project," Farm Sanctuary distributes a series of age-specific booklets titled *Cultivating Compassion: Teachers' Guide and Student Activities*, for use by teachers to promote the cause.

A pamphlet accompanying the *Cultivating Compassion* series describes the explicitly ideological and political purposes undergirding the Farm Sanctuary curricula, which appear to extend beyond animal rights:

> Good news for teachers! Farm Sanctuary's *Cultivating Compassion* program makes it even easier for caring teachers to bring compassion to their classrooms. In an increasingly violent world in which making profits often takes precedence over seeking peace, *Cultivating Compassion* offers materials designed to encourage respect and kindness toward all living things and the environment. . . . If, as Margaret Mead said, a small group of concerned individuals can change the world, just imagine what a lot of caring children could do![21]

In a "Dear Teacher" letter that comes with the booklets, a Farm Sanctuary "humane educator" named Carol Moon writes:

> Cultivating Compassion Teachers' Guides offer lesson plans, hand-outs, and activities for teaching that farm animals have feelings too. The material offers a gentle, thought-provoking, sometimes humorous, but always realistic, approach to a difficult subject often ignored in the classroom: The welfare of farm animals. The packets include ten $8^{1}/_{2}$ x 11 inch color photos of rescued animals who live at our sanctuaries and four photos of animals in factory farms.[22]

Since these materials are sent directly to teachers, there would appear to be no official oversight by school boards for quality and accuracy, nor any requirement that the sensitive subject of the care and treatment of animals receive balanced handling in the classrooms.

This much is sure: The booklets are anthropomorphically aimed at directing the children to reach specific pro-animal-rights conclusions. The three lesson plans (for grades 3–5, 6–8, and 9–12) urge children to oppose the meat industry and even to become vegans. Thus *Cultivating Compassion*, Elementary Level,[23] teaches children ages 8–10:

+ Cow Fact: Mother cows separated from their calves by a fence will moo loudly and seem very upset. They'll wait through hunger, cold, and bad weather to be with their calves.[24]
+ Cow Fact: Cows share babysitting duties. If there are several calves in a herd, one or two cows (or bulls!) stay with the calves while the others go look for food and water.[25]
+ Chicken Fact: Mother chickens teach their children to eat, drink, roost and avoid enemies.[26]
+ Chicken Fact: Hens sitting on nests often cluck and chirp to their chicks while they are still inside the egg.[27]
+ Pig Fact: Pigs are nearly house-broken when they are born. They will use one corner of the nest as a toilet and keep the nest clean.[28]
+ Pig Fact: Happy pigs rest for over 82% of the day.[29]
+ Pig Fact: Pigs are great swimmers. In the wild, they sometimes swim for miles.[30]

There are also animal "stories" that appeal to the emotions of children, such as this one steeped in anthropomorphism about a supposedly heroic pig:

Spammy was born on a small farm in California. She was named Spammy so the farmer's children wouldn't forget that she would someday become food. Spammy shared a shed with a young calf, named Spot. The two of them were friends who liked to cuddle and rub noses.

One day a fire broke out in the shed. Spammy was then just a 40-pound piglet, but she saved herself and her friend. People later figured out from looking at the scratch marks, burn blisters, and soot marks on her behind, that she had pushed a hole in the shed wall with her rump, and led Spot out after her. Perhaps her bravery saved her from becoming bacon. What do you think?[31]

Teachers are also told to have their young students experience "Life on the Factory Farm," an exercise intended to illustrate the purported cruelty of food production. The lesson instructs teachers to have "two volunteers take off their shoes and stand on [two] plastic milk crates. They are to remain their quietly while the class continues." Other children are "to get on their hands and knees between desks or chairs placed in such a way that they cannot turn around without standing up." Another volunteer "should have a paper collar around his/her neck with a dangling chain." Then, "Group the rest of the class into a space so small that no one can spread their arms. Ask for complete silence and shut off the lights for 1 minute."[32]

The next step is to have the students "process information":

Ask the students: Now that we have looked at the way chickens, calves, pigs, and turkeys live on factory farms, do they need sanctuaries? Why or why not? What things could they get at a sanctuary that they could not get at a factory farm? (Write answers on a chalkboard.)[33]

Not surprisingly, the last step in this lesson plan makes the vegan pitch, complete with an appeal to our celebrity-crazed popular culture:

When they're not making movies, TV shows, or recordings, many celebrities take time to help animals. Some, like Alicia Silverstone, Joaquin Phoenix, Drew Barrymore and Jonathan Taylor Thomas have even become vegans because they don't want to cause animal suffering. Imagine that one of them is coming to your house for the weekend. If you went to the store to help your mother buy groceries for their visit, what things do you suggest she serve them?[34]

This isn't education. It is propaganda.

Some organizations go even further. In Defense of Animals strives to convince students to refuse to dissect dead frogs or other animals in science class. The group's website encourages children to exercise their "right to choose" not to participate in dissection.

CHALLENGING DISSECTION: **Your Right to Choose**
Objecting to dissection may be as simple as talking to your science teacher or bringing a note to class from your parents. But when a teacher is unwilling or unable to meet your request for a humane alternative, refusing to dissect can become a test of your persistence, patience and convictions.

The site provides strategies, such as speaking to the teacher early, finding "safety in numbers" by organizing group protests, and suggesting alternatives such as using models or viewing videos. But if all else fails, the site offers access to legal assistance with a phone number to call to obtain redress.[35]

The site also provides a sample letter to the editor for interested students to send to newspapers objecting to dissection in science classes. It states in part:[36]

> As a student dedicated to respecting all life, I will not slice into, cut apart or kill, in short, dissect any animal, for any reason. These procedures amount to nothing more than classroom curiosity....
>
> [D]issection desensitizes. It is impossible to condone killing an animal for the sake of a science class and at the same time still believe that life is sacred.
>
> Dissection teaches superiority: I will cut apart an animal because I can.
>
> It teaches selfishness: I will repeat another unnecessary and useless dissection, already performed for decades by millions of students before me.
>
> It teaches poor ethics and condones cruelty: I accept that this animal may be a stolen companion animal, and that he or she most likely suffered severe trauma before dying.
>
> The very act of dissection and the companies that support it are defined by carelessness, deception and cruelty. How can anything scientific come from such an unscientific foundation?
>
> For the animals who die in silence and the students who suffer in silence, I ask that our school district ban dissection as a science curriculum requirement.
>
> Sincerely,[36]

We have barely touched the surface of the many and varied ways in which the animal rights movement seeks to persuade children—including the very young—to convert to the vegan cause. How deeply animal rights activists have penetrated into the education of our children isn't known. But their influence seems to be growing. In 2003, for example, the Sacramento School Board approved a K-6 charter school called the "Humane Education Learning Community," the math curriculum of which would help students "explore economic costs as they relate to environmental degradation, the loss of wildlife and companion animal overpopulation."[37]

At least we know how a Canadian honors student might have come to think that a bunny is equal to a human and how Melanie Morgan's son learned that the family's dog was equal to the human members of the family. The question now is: What are *your* kids learning about animals in school?

PART TWO

By Any Means Necessary

9

Advocating Terror

W
hile in London in early December 1998 doing research for a
previous book, I was stunned that a group of liberationist
extremists, who called themselves the Animal Rights Mili-
tia, announced "a list of ten vivisectors who will be assassinated if animal
liberation hunger striker Barry Horne dies through Labour's broken
promises."[1] The brouhaha began when animal rights campaigners accused
Prime Minister Tony Blair of breaking a campaign promise to create a
Royal Commission on Animal Vivisection to find ways to limit the use of
animals in research. When Blair failed to create the commission, a convicted terrorist named Barry Horne—imprisoned for torching a department store because it sold fur coats—undertook a hunger strike. When it
appeared that he might die, the ARM issued its assassination threat as a
pledge of retaliation.

The story filled the front pages of the London newspapers and led the
television news throughout my stay. Much to my surprise, a troubling
wave of public sympathy developed for Horne—if not agreement with the
death threats. Not only did people write letters to the editor praising his
courage, but a sizeable group of supporters gathered in a round-the-clock
vigil at the hospital to which Horne had been transferred from prison. A
national debate soon mushroomed over whether Horne was a martyr or a
terrorist.

The misanthropy that permeates the "animal rights" movement came
clearly into focus as the controversy continued. As reported by the *Times*

of London, Ronnie Lee, the founder of Britain's Animal Liberation Front, denigrated farms and ranches as "the concentration camps of the human Reich," opining, "True animal liberation will not come merely through the destruction of the Dachaus and Buchenwalds, but demands nothing less than the driving back of the human species to pre-invasion boundaries," by limiting the world's human population to fifty million. Bigotry toward people with disabilities also came to the fore as ALF members railed against research on animals intended to find ways to alleviate or cure spinal injuries and other disabilities. One ALF activist was reported to have informed a disabled medical researcher, "I am so glad you're in a wheelchair. You don't deserve to live on this earth."[2]

Horne ended his hunger strike just as he reached the point of real danger. With his life no longer at risk, the violent threats ceased and the crisis passed. But it wasn't the end of the war. One ALF member stated, "I would be overjoyed when the first scientist is killed by a liberationist activist."[3] As we shall see, he is not alone in expressing such murderous sentiments. (Horne eventually died of liver failure. Seven hundred people attended his funeral, with his coffin bearing the banner, "Labour Lied and Barry died." One of Horne's co-activists told the *Guardian*, "Animal rights is a war. We are at war for the animals.")[4]

That trip to London was my first real exposure to the dangerous extremes to which some animal rights/liberationists are willing to go. And while violence in the name of animal liberation began in the United Kingdom—where the children of one researcher were actually sent an *HIV-infected hypodermic needle in the mail*[5]—it has since been imported to the United States, with arson, threats, and intimidation against those denigrated as animal abusers becoming commonplace. Indeed, as I have focused on the movement in the last several years, read its literature, listened to its speakers, followed the news reports of what seems an alarming crescendo of intimidation and violence directed against animal researchers, fur farmers, and other animal industries, and noted an appalling refusal by most "mainstream" activists to condemn these practices unequivocally, I have concluded that the impetus toward violent and coercive tactics within the movement is growing stronger.

Terrorism in the Name of Animal Rights

When Morris Dees, co-founder of the Southern Poverty Law Center (SPLC), sued a white supremacist organization to collect damages on behalf of the mother of a lynching victim, Michael Donald, he came to the depositions wearing a bulletproof vest and packing heat. Dees had reason to worry about his safety: the suit was against the Ku Klux Klan. The case ended as a triumph against racism, and not coincidentally bankrupted the odious United Klans of America.[6]

Over the years, Dees and the SPLC have broken the financial back of other hate groups as well. Tom Metzger, founder of the White Aryan Resistance, saw his organization destroyed when Dees and the SPLC convinced a jury to find Metzger liable for the beating death of an Ethiopian student named Mulugeta Seraw, a despicable racist crime.[7] Similarly, Dees and the SPLC obtained a huge verdict against the KKK in North Carolina and South Carolina for the part these terrorists played in the burning down of a black church.[8]

Why do I bring this up in a book about animal rights? The SPLC is such an implacable enemy of hate and ideologically inspired violence in all its guises and political persuasions that, to paraphrase a famous commercial, when the SPLC speaks about terrorism, the country listens. And the SPLC's quarterly magazine, *Intelligence Report*, has repeatedly and energetically warned about the dangers posed to public safety, life, and property by animal rights and environmental extremists—a topic that has received far too little attention from the mainstream media. Militant groups have to be especially odious to appear alongside the KKK and the American Nazi Party in the pages of the *Intelligence Report*.

In the fall 2002 issue, a ten-page exposé titled "From Push to Shove" reported on the terrorism of Stop Huntingdon Animal Cruelty (SHAC) in its effort to drive Huntingdon Life Sciences, an animal testing laboratory, out of business by terrorizing its employees as well as the workers of its banks, insurance companies, and customers—a pernicious tactic known as "tertiary targeting":

> Since 1999 ... members of both groups [ALF and the Earth Liberation Front, or ELF] have been involved with SHAC's campaign to harass employees of Huntingdon—and even distantly related business associates like Marsh [USA,

an insurance firm]—with frankly terrorist tactics similar to those of anti-abortion extremists. Employees have had their homes vandalized with spray-painted "Puppy killer" and "We'll be back" notices. They have faced a mounting number of death threats, fire bombings and violent assaults. They've had their names, addresses and personal information posed on Web sites and posters, declaring them, "wanted for collaboration with animal torture."[9]

"From Push to Shove" describes a crescendo of criminality in the name of animal rights and environmental advocacy, with 137 "direct actions" committed in 2001 alone. Kevin Jonas (a.k.a. Kevin Kjonaas), a former ALF spokesman and onetime leader of SHAC, told the *Intelligence Report*, "When push comes to shove, we're ready to push, kick, shove, bite, do whatever to win."[10]

"Whatever" is precisely what ALF, ELF, SHAC, and others of their ilk have in mind. When Huntingdon Life Sciences moved from the UK to the USA to escape the terrorism being mounted against its employees and those of its service providers, it found no respite. As described by the *Intelligence Report*, "SHAC-USA's Web site boasted that a company vice president here 'was visited several times, had several car windows broken, tires slashed, house spray painted with slogans. His wife is reportedly on the brink of a nervous breakdown and divorce."[11] And in July 2002, Dr. Michael Podell, a veterinarian at Ohio State University, was driven away from AIDS studies using cats when he "received nearly a dozen death threats after PETA put the experiment on its 'actions alert' list. Podell was sent a photograph of a British scientist whose car had been bombed. 'You're next' was scrawled across the top of the photo."[12]

The increase in animal rights and ecoterrorist threats has also alarmed the Federal Bureau of Investigation, which along with the Bureau of Alcohol, Tobacco, Firearms, and Explosives (ATF) branded animal rights and eco-extremists as being among the nation's leading domestic terrorist threats.[13] According to congressional testimony delivered by John E. Lewis, deputy assistant director of the FBI's Counterterrorism Division:

> One of today's most serious domestic terrorism threats comes from special interest extremist movements such as the Animal Liberation Front, the Earth Liberation Front, and [the] Stop Huntingdon Animal Cruelty campaign.

Adherents to these movements aim to resolve specific issues by using criminal "direct action" against individuals or companies believed to be abusing or
exploiting animals or the environment.

"Direct action" is often criminal activity that destroys property or causes
economic loss to a targeted company. Traditional targets have ranged from,
but have not been limited to, research laboratories to restaurants, fur farmers
to forestry services. Extremists have used arson, bombings, theft, animal
releases, vandalism, and office takeovers to achieve their goals. ...

While most animal rights and eco-extremists have refrained from violence
targeting human life, the FBI has observed troubling signs that this is changing.
We have seen an escalation in violent rhetoric and tactics. ... Attacks are ...
growing in frequency and size. Harassing phone calls and vandalism now co-
exist with improvised explosive devices and personal threats to employees.[14]

Lewis testified that there had been 1,200 criminal incidents involving this
cadre of terrorists between 1990 and 2005. In the FBI report *Terrorism
2002–2005*, fifty-one out of fifty-eight domestic terrorist acts listed—including bombings, arson, and burglary/vandalism—were suspected to have been
perpetrated by ALF, ELF, or individual animal rights extremists. What stands
out in the summary is how dramatically the primary sources of domestic terroristic criminality shifted after 1999, from mostly right-wing racism or sur-
vivalist extremism to radical animal rights and environmentalist ideology.[15]

Unfortunately, as we have seen, such terroristic tactics are often successful. Adrian Morrison, a professor of veterinary medicine at the University of Pennsylvania and an outspoken supporter of animal research,
explained to me why this is so:

It is important to be free in our lives if we are to be creative in our work. To
have to comply with government regulations [for the use of animals in
research] is one thing. But to have these added fears of being harassed or
threatened, or having one's work stolen or destroyed, definitely burdens
research activities. And because most scientists won't engage in public education, at least in part for fear of attracting the attention of animal rights
activists, the public is often unaware of the tremendous benefits it receives
from using animals in research. That creates a doubly harmful effect because
it makes people more apt to support laws that would unduly restrict research

because they don't understand how crucial it is to medical and scientific advancement. It becomes a vicious cycle.[16]

Morrison's point is echoed by P. Michael Conn and James V. Parker, the associate director and a former public information officer respectively at the prestigious Oregon National Primate Research Center. In their book *The Animal Research War*, Conn and Parker trace the cumulative harm caused to science by animal rights intimidation and criminality:

> We do know from the National Academies' Research Council Report, *Critical Needs for Research in Veterinary Science*, that the nation faces a critical shortage of research veterinarians, especially those trained in veterinary pathology, lab animal science, and veterinary research.... The inability of the nation's twenty-eight veterinary colleges to graduate enough trained veterinary researchers will result in a shortfall of hundreds of such critical professionals as early as this year [2008].[17]

The authors blame the threat of terrorism as a major cause of this shortfall and the consequent impediment to America's scientific progress—to which the believers in animal rights, no doubt, will issue a loud cheer.

Terrorism School

Animal rights terrorists hijack the Internet and modern communications technologies to brag about their exploits; communicate the names, addresses, and phone numbers of targeted individuals; teach fellow travelers how to commit crimes without being caught; and develop tactics designed to prevent their infiltration by law enforcement. Toward this end, activists have published several terrorism primers on the Internet or had them released through anarchist bookstores. Each, in its own way, promotes violence in the name of animal rights and constitutes a how-to-be-a-terrorist instruction book. One of the more alarming of these is *A Declaration of War: Killing People to Save the Animals and the Environment*, written under the *nom de guerre* Screaming Wolf, and on its cover exhorting: "Strike a match, light a fuse, we've only got the earth to lose."

To read *A Declaration of War* is to enter a world of misanthropic and anarchic surrealism. In a mad screed bordering on psychopathology, Screaming Wolf writes (with emphasis):

> Liberators have come to one unavoidable conclusion: HUMANS WILL NEVER MAKE PEACE WITH ANIMALS! **It is not in their natures or in the natures of the societies they have created. In fact, liberators believe that if people really want to save the animals, they must stop wasting their time trying to improve the human race and its societies. They must declare war against humans. They must join in this revolution!**
>
> Liberators believe this is the only logical, consistent and morally correct conclusion stemming from a true belief that animals should be free to live their lives unshackled from human exploitation. **They believe that the nature of human society and its laws are implicitly and irrevocably immoral. Liberators are people of conscience who feel morally obligated to break those laws and revolt against this oppressive regime.**[18]

Claiming that "all beings are equal," Screaming Wolf understands that there "is no way that people will stop eating flesh, driving cars, wearing leather, hunting, and doing all other overt and covert abuses of animals simply because a handful of 'lunatics' feel compassion for the beasts." But Screaming Wolf knows what must be done:

> The liberator solution is the use of physical force. They believe force is a necessary method for defending animals against their human being oppressors. The fact that we are human need not stop us. But it does demand, they say, that each person reassess his or her loyalties. **If you are of the family of all creatures, brother or sister to other animals, then you must stop cooperation with society and participating in the slaughter, and fight for your family.** If you are of the family of man, then don't call yourself an agent or defender of the animals. You have a conflict of interest, and not admitting it is doing animals more harm than good. It can mislead people who are of the family of creatures, and who may be willing to fight for their family.[19]

A Declaration of War urges "defenders of animals" to stop criticizing liberators such as the Animal Liberation Front, which seek to secure the ultimate goal:

> Liberators hope that those who do not join them can at least admit to
> themselves that such a life, with its strategies of withdrawal and militant
> interventionism, is the *most consistent position* to take if one wishes to live
> as a true animal defender, and the *most effective method* for liberating our
> family of creatures from human oppression. If they admit this to them-
> selves, and consider the liberation ethic and ideal, liberators hope they can
> also admit it to others. **At the very least, they can stop condemning libera-
> tion activities, such as Animal Liberation Front raids, as unacceptable
> acts of "terrorism."**[20]

Alas, Screaming Wolf can rest easy: As we shall see, there is scant condemnation of ALF-style tactics from within the "mainstream" animal
rights movement.

A Declaration of War is an antihuman ideological rant, which does not
discuss the actual techniques that can make for a successful campaign of
animal rights terrorism. But other pro-ALF publications fill that gap. One
of the most pernicious of these is *Arson-Around with Auntie ALF: Your
Guide to Putting the Heat on Animal Abusers Everywhere*, written by "Auntie ALF, Uncle ELF, and the Anti-Copyright Gang." The line drawing on
the cover depicts an ALF member dressed in wolf costume with a lit
match, standing in front of a fire-gutted building.

Arson-Around is a far more dangerous publication than *A Declaration
of War*. Assuming that readers are already such fervent zealots that they
will readily commit serious crimes "for the animals," the online publication
eschews polemics and gets right down to the business of instructing readers how to burn down buildings. Why set fires? Readers are told that it is
an especially effective tool of animal liberation:

> Arson is not always used by the A.L.F in the course of an action, but when it
> is, it can be devastatingly effective. Millions of dollars in damage has been
> caused against fur-feed companies, slaughterhouses, department stores and
> fur shops, fast food restaurants and transport trucks belonging to animal
> abuse industries.[21]

Activists are advised to "tell no one" of their plans and to make sure to
"leave no evidence behind at the scene."[22] Readers are given the plusses and

minuses of different destructive devises as calmly as a cookbook might explain recipes for pie crust:

> Good incendiaries can be improvised more easily than explosives and the materials are more easily obtained. On a pound for pound basis, incendiaries can do more damage than explosives against many types of targets if properly used. There is a time lag, however, between the start of a fire and the destruction of the target. During this period the fire may be discovered and controlled or put out. An explosive once detonated has done its work.

Under the "Tools and Techniques" section, Auntie ALF teaches her students that good incendiaries can be made from common items such as jars, pots, and bottles. Extended treatment is given to "igniters" such as "potassium chlorate and sugar," "flake aluminum-sulfur," and "homemade black powder."[23] In the section "incendiary materials," recipes for "homemade napalm" and something called an "incendiary brick" are provided—complete with specific step-by-step instructions for their manufacture. The proper application of these explosives and incendiaries is also covered, to ensure the successful commission of a felony.

Finally, ALF trainees are told how to burn and run so they will be free to continue their terrorist campaign indefinitely:

> LEAVE NO EVIDENCE—always wear gloves and protect your workspace and materials from hair, fiber, fingerprints and DNA traces that might lead back to you or your active cell. Good luck![24]

Defenders of *Arson-Around* will no doubt remark that "Auntie" tells readers not to harm humans or animals in the fires they will be setting. But that is a veneer to rationalize committing inherently dangerous and life-threatening felonies while pretending to be peace-loving protestors.

The ALF Primer: When Darkness Falls provides broader instructions on the commission of various criminal acts and terroristic activities. Knowing that novice ALF criminals might be nervous before their first direct action, the book remarks that "the first time is the hardest" and advises them to start small, for example by gluing locks or spray-painting a building such as "a fur shop, a butcher shop, a factory farm or slaughterhouse, maybe a fast food restaurant."[25] New ALF members are instructed how to maintain internal security by starting their own cell, "since if you know of an existing one, their security obviously isn't too good."[26]

The primer offers guidance on various forms of vandalism, including how to make stink bombs, destroy toilets, and cut phone lines. Methods for committing more serious felonies such as arson, and even how to wreak future havoc in buildings under construction, are also provided for the especially intrepid animal rights terrorist:

> Salt greatly weakens concrete. If a large amount can be introduced into cement bags or sand piles for making concrete, foundations and the like would be weakened. After the foundation is poured, connections for plumbing, especially sewage, are exposed. They are often covered in duct tape to avoid objects being dropped inside. If the duct tape were to be carefully removed and clogging elements such as concrete, epoxy, or plaster dropped down the pipes and the tape carefully put back in place it could cause major problems not realized until after the building is completed. After drywall is put up electric wiring is put in. Once sheet-rock or other wallboard is hung this wiring is very hard to get to. After drywall is erected, wiring can be cut in inconspicuous places like behind studs, and then taped or glued into positions.[27]

The fact that weakened concrete or fires caused by short circuits could kill people is of no obvious concern.

Making sure that ALF gets credit for the carnage is deemed especially important. Note the reasonable assumption that other animal rights activists will collaborate in the crucial public relations phase of the terrorist strike:

> If you choose to report your actions to a support group, send news clippings or your own report, including the date, place, and what was done. Write the reports on plain paper using block capital letters, or a publicly accessible typewriter or computer, like the ones available at a library. Photocopy the report a couple of times at a public copier to obscure details making it harder to trace. If handwriting it, you may want to have more than one person write each letter.... Obviously don't sign the report or include your address in the report or put a return address. Spell everything correctly, since certain spelling errors

are often common to certain individuals. Wet the envelope glue and stamp with a sponge, don't lick them as saliva is traceable. Always drop in a public mailbox, and avoid using the same one frequently.... Dropping it off anonymously at a supportive groups' office, or the house of a supportive above ground activist is safer than mailing it.[28]

That last point is telling: As we shall see below, ALF, SHAC and other such criminals are often supported by animal rights believers, who may not commit such acts themselves, but respect and even applaud those who do.

10

Tertiary Targeting

C riminal attacks and threats against research facilities and businesses that use animals have infected animal rights advocacy like a low-grade fever over the last twenty years. Much of the terrorism has been directed against medical researchers. According to research published by *USA Today* at the end of 1999, "more than 80 scientists have received letters booby-trapped with razors. Others have received death threats and been intimidated in their homes." Moreover, vandalism has been a constant threat against researchers since 1981. Extremists have "attacked university labs and federal research centers nationwide, inflicting millions in damage and destroying years' worth of data." *USA Today* rightly labeled participants in such actions as "brown shirts."[1]

An entire book could be written describing the chaos caused by the Animal Liberation Front and kindred groups in recent years. For example, according to an FBI report:

> In the early morning of July 7, 2005, fire officials responded to a vehicle fire in the driveway of a private residence in Los Angeles, California. In extinguishing the fire, authorities recovered a partially melted, plastic gasoline container from behind the vehicle's left front wheel. The car belonged to a representative for the Animal Care Technicians Union, which represents employees for the Los Angeles Animal Services (LAAS). LAAS and its affiliates have been targeted by local animal rights extremists, and the LAAS union representative had been placed on a "targets" list of individuals profiled by extremists for "direct actions." The incident remains under investigation.[2]

Activists apparently attempted arson against Los Angeles Animal Services, where the issue involved euthanasia of dogs and cats at the city's animal shelters:

> On September 16, 2005, fire officials responded to a fire at the high-rise condominium home of the director of Los Angeles Animal Services, after residents observed smoke coming from a recyclables/janitorial closet. First responders recovered an improvised incendiary device consisting of a four-inch-long tube labeled "TOXIC" and using a cigarette as a fuse. The device, which had been placed next to a stack of newspapers in the recycling/janitorial closet, had malfunctioned and only scorched the concrete floor of the closet. The Animal Liberation Front claimed responsibility for this incident.[3]

Note that the fire was set in a high-rise condominium building, where it was first reported by other "residents." So much for ALF's blithe assurances that its affiliated terrorists ignite only unoccupied buildings.

Also in 2005, criminals claiming the mantle of ALF followed the wife of a pharmaceutical executive to her job, broke into her car, and stole a credit card. They used the card to buy $20,000 in traveler's checks, which they "donated" to four charities. Then came the terrorist death threat posted on an animal rights website: "If we find out a dime of that money granted to those charities was taken back we will strip you bear [sic] and burn your [expletive]. This is OUR insurance policy."[4]

In December 2007, the mayor of Los Angeles, Antonio Villaraigosa, received a thinly veiled death threat from the North American Animal Liberation Press Office, an attempt to force him to change the practices of city animal shelters. As reported by the LA Weekly, the NAALPO posted a "communiqué" on its website reading: "Villaraigosa deserves to be bumped off like the dogs and cats we witnessed with their eyes wide, terrified before they were bumped off. He got off way to [sic] easy." The same terrorist bragged about vandalizing the car of the mayor's sister, a tactic celebrated by a Press Office spokeswoman named Lindy Greene: "It's a brilliant concept. Even though Deborah [the mayor's sister] is not entirely involved, the idea is that she would be very upset and she'll call Antonio and say, 'Why do I have to suffer for something you're not doing?' There's a hope that she'll apply pressure on him, or he would feel guilty for what's happening to his sister."[5]

Such actions, which have happened throughout the United States and all over the world, are simply too numerous to recount. In the Netherlands, a developer rescinded plans for a science park after executives' houses were vandalized with paint and the ALF threatened that its next action would not be so "friendly."[6] Oxford University academics have had letter bombs mailed to their homes in an attempt to coerce them into ceasing all animal research.[7] Cambridge University canceled plans to build a primate laboratory that would have researched for cures to diseases such as Parkinson's and Alzheimer's, due to the "financial risks" of threatened violence at the proposed facility and the costs of security.[8] An ALF extremist named Donald Currie was sentenced to twelve years in prison for conducting a fire-bomb campaign in England against animal researchers, including bombs placed under cars and a fire that caused £140,000 damage.[9]

In December 2007, one of America's more dangerous animal rights fanatics, Rodney Coronado—previously imprisoned for four years after burning down an animal testing laboratory in Michigan—pleaded guilty to a felony for showing people how to make a destructive device with the goal of having someone commit a violent crime.[10] In October 2007, the ALF terrorist Jonathan Paul was sentenced to fifty-one months in prison after pleading guilty to burning down a horsemeat slaughterhouse—certainly not the only direct action in which Paul had engaged. With regard to ALF, Paul warned in an interview on the progressive NPR program *Democracy Now!* that "a lot of these people"—his co-believers—are "just on a rampant rage."[11]

One of the most insidious innovations developed by animal rights terrorists has been the strategy known as "tertiary targeting," the primary tactic employed by SHAC in a nearly decade-long campaign to drive Huntingdon Life Sciences out of business. Huntingdon became enemy number one of the entire animal rights movement after a PETA infiltrator videotaped several HLS employees in the UK badly abusing animals, including punching a beagle in the face, in 1997. When the video was shown on television, British authorities justifiably revoked the company's license. Three employees were suspended from the company and later held to criminal account for their terrible actions, as was appropriate.[12]

Huntingdon took the necessary remedial action to bring their animal care and supervision up to proper standards, and the company reopened six months later under new management. In this regard, it is worth noting that despite heightened scrutiny from authorities and never-ending attempts by the animal rights movement to find further wrongdoing, Huntingdon has not been found since to have engaged in any more illegal animal abuse.

But correcting such wrongdoing wasn't the point of the PETA infiltration, nor is promoting good animal care protocols within laboratories and slaughterhouses the goal of the animal rights movement. Rather, activists want to drive *all* testing labs and all animal industries completely out of business. And they saw a golden opportunity in the circumstances of Huntingdon's derelictions, involving the mistreatment of *dogs*—which even among animal rights believers evoke a unique, one might say speciesist, emotional response—and its business of doing nonmedical testing (which is often required by law) as well as medical testing. Branding Huntingdon "puppy killers," movement activists hatched a plan to drive the company completely out of business. In 1999, activists created Stop Huntingdon Animal Cruelty and declared war on HLS. Ever since, SHAC and ALF thugs have subjected Huntingdon's employees and executives to an unremitting campaign of harsh and often illegal harassment and intimidation.

Knowing that direct actions taken solely against the company and its employees would not destroy its quarry, militants asked the question: How does one go about obliterating a thriving international business? Their answer was to expand their focus to the complex interrelated commercial relationships that any modern enterprise requires to function: Buildings need to be insured; auditors are required to verify financial integrity; banks are needed for the many financial transactions in which any business engages; customers are needed to generate income; and so forth.

Tertiary targeting strikes at HLS's service and product providers. The tactic is as cruel as it is effective: By terrorizing employees of banks, insurance companies, and other enterprises that have contractual relations with Huntingdon—even stationery suppliers[13]—SHAC and ALF intend to destroy Huntingdon by withering it on the vine. If the company can find no banks in which to deposit funds, insurance companies from which to purchase protection, independent auditors to check the books, or customers from which to generate an income, the company will not survive.

Toward this pernicious end, SHAC, ALF and others launched a vicious international campaign of terroristic harassment against industries that use no animals but do business with Huntingdon, a campaign that continues to this day. In testimony before the Judiciary Committee of the House of Representatives in 2005, William Trundley, vice president of corporate security and investigations for GlaxoSmithKline, a leading pharmaceutical company that has used Huntingdon to conduct animal research, said that SHAC members distribute a "SHAC Terror Card" to potential victims with the warning:

> Do you do business with Huntingdon Life Sciences? ... If you do, there's something you should know.... Radical animal rights activists have been targeting executives and employees of companies that work with HLS, with criminal activity including: smashed windows; spray painted houses; glued locks; vandalized cars; stolen credit card numbers; ID theft; fraud; and continuous acts of harassment and intimidation against employees, their children and spouses.

The card gives notice that "the only way to end or prevent such attacks ... is to stop doing business with Huntingdon."

If the tertiary targeted company does not immediately yield, the intimidation begins. Imagine the pressure on a bank or insurance company's executives, for which HLS is just one of a multitude of customers, to appease SHAC in the face of terrorizing behavior of the kind that Trundley described as targeting GSK's employees:

- Theft of mail from a GSK employee, which revealed divorce proceedings and an alcohol treatment program recently completed by his spouse. Animal Rights Extremists left a bottle of beer at her front door and a note stating "Have a drink Bitch." The same day AREs [animal rights extremists] visited the school of her son placing slanderous flyers throughout the campus depicting one parent as an animal killer and the other an alcoholic. Similar defamatory statements were e-mailed to the school's staff. On a previous visit to the spouse's residence an anonymous message was left on her answering machine stating "We have been watching you and we know you are alone."
- A GSK senior executive had his home attacked twice in the middle of

the night resulting in spray painting of the exterior of the house with the words "Puppy Killer Dave" and a rock thrown through a large front window. He has also been subjected to anonymous late night threatening calls and numerous daytime intimidating demonstrations, where defamatory flyers and the SHAC "terror card" were distributed to neighbors.

+ During a Hugs for Puppies (a NJ/PA based animal extremist group) protest at GSK's Philadelphia parking facility, a female GSK employee was threatened by a Hugs for Puppies protestor, when he yelled at her, "I have your license plate, we will track you down and kill your family."

+ A GSK physician was contacted in the middle of the night by someone posing as an employee of the Baltimore City Morgue, requesting her to come to the morgue to identify a relative who had died. Upon arrival at the morgue she learned that the call was a hoax, and was then fearful that someone was lying in wait for her upon returning to her home in the middle of the night.

+ Another GSK employee was subjected to several ARE demonstrations at his home, including leafleting the neighborhood with the SHAC Terror Card. The employee's eight year son was traumatized by the incident, waking up in the middle of the night staring out the window for fear that the terrorists would return.[14]

It is important to reemphasize at this point that tertiary targeting is not about peaceful picketing or even good old-fashioned civil disobedience. The SHAC website identifies targets to be harassed and provides information for use by anonymous terrorists, including victims' home addresses, phone numbers, and the names and ages of their children and even where they attend school. They also publish Social Security numbers and other information about a target's neighbors, inviting identity theft. Targeted people may receive videotapes of their family members taken by SHAC activists, or anonymous death threats, or hundreds of harassing phone calls. A Canadian stockbroker who buys and sells Huntingdon securities on behalf of his clients once received 450 calls in a single day accusing him of being a "puppy killer."[15]

Companies have been bombed.[16] Homes have been invaded and vandalized. In one case, animal rights activists broke into a lawyer's house and flooded it with the garden hose because his company once did business with Huntingdon Life Sciences and refused to vow never to do so again.[17] In the UK, a nursery school rescinded vouchers to Life Sciences employees due to threats of violence.[18]

Imagine the terror experienced by a Japanese executive and his family whose home was attacked by SHAC activists because his company does business with HLS:

> They came in the early hours of the morning, four hooded thugs trying to smash down the door. Besieged in his Home Counties house, the company executive desperately phoned the police and prayed they would arrive in time. His wife and terrified young daughter were hiding upstairs. They feared for their lives. The attackers had activated rape alarms and thrown them around the house. The noise was unbelievable. Then came the crack of broken windows. Thankfully, the police made it and the masked men fled.[19]

London, North England, and Northern Ireland residents were victims of a poisoning hoax when a nebulous terrorist cadre called the Animal Rights Militia claimed to have contaminated bottles of an energy drink because the manufacturer did business with Huntingdon:

> In a series of coordinated actions on the 10th December by the ARM 49 bottles of Lucozade Energy have been contaminated with sodium hydroxide and replaced onto shop shelves in the North of England, London, and Northern Ireland. The affected flavours are Original, Orange, Apple, and Lemon of the sizes 500ml and 1l.
>
> Jean-Pierre Garnier the choice is yours, either you cut your companies ties with Huntingdon Life Sciences or these actions will continue. We've been watching GlaxoSmithKline closely and we know what you're up to, Novartis paid the price when we hit its products a couple of months ago the question is how higher a price are you willing to pay? As you can rest assured we will be back.
>
> This action is dedicated to the 500 animals who die at the hands of HLS workers every day.[20]

In Britain, SHAC terrorists caused Barclay's Bank to withdraw financing from Huntingdon when their executives came under assault. Similarly, after it was subjected to terrible threats and intimidation, the Stephens

Group of Arkansas withdrew a promised $33 million loan. After Marsh USA and its executives were warned by SHAC to revoke the insurance of a Huntingdon facility and SHAC published executives' home addresses, phone numbers, and Social Security numbers, the company stopped insuring Huntingdon. Meanwhile, attacks against HSL employees continued. According to the Southern Poverty Law Center's *Intelligence Report*, a U.S.-based Huntingdon vice president has been so badly and repeatedly harassed that the man's "wife is reportedly on the brink of a nervous breakdown and divorce."[21] In the face of this fury, the company's value plummeted at one point from £360 million to £5 million, and in 2000, HLS was delisted from the New York Stock Exchange "for failure to remain in compliance with the Exchange's financial continued listing requirements."[22]

In 2005, the NYSE engaged in an act of such abased appeasement in the face of a SHAC attack that Neville Chamberlain would have blushed. After Huntingdon announced that its parent company (Life Sciences Research) would be listed on the Big Board,[23] SHAC and another extremist group called Win Animal Rights (WAR) pounced. True to the tertiary targeting playbook, their minions posted the names, phone numbers, and e-mail addresses of a hundred Exchange leaders and staffers. Thousands of e-mails went out to animal liberationists pointedly declaring that the NYSE was the "primary focal point" of the anti-Huntingdon campaign. When an executive's yacht was damaged by animal liberationists, the Exchange blinked. The Huntingdon Life Sciences counsel told a congressional committee what happened:

> On the morning of September 7 our senior management team went to the NYSE's Wall Street headquarters for the original listing celebration. But only minutes before we were to go down to the trading floor to watch the first trade in LSR stock, the President of the NYSE told us that they would not be listing LSR stock that day, and that our listing was postponed. One of my LSR colleagues and I spent the next hour or so meeting with senior NYSE officials. We spoke only about the animal rights campaign against the Company. It was patently clear to me that the only reason the NYSE postponed our listing was because of concerns about the SHAC campaign. All Americans took pride when the New York Stock Exchange reopened for business only four business days after the 9/11 terrorist attacks. Yet, apparently purely

on the basis of a perceived threat from SHAC, the NYSE postponed plans to list LSR. A handful of animal extremists had succeeded where Osama bin Laden had failed.[24]

Adding to the certainty that the NYSE executives folded out of fear of SHAC, Catherine Kinney, the Exchange's president, refused an invitation to appear before the committee and explain the decision, and the lawyer sent in her place provided no details as to why, precisely, LSR's listing was suddenly rescinded.[25] This much is sure: Animal liberationists thought they knew the cause, and they celebrated the delisting decision as "a score of biblical proportions" for animal rights.[26] (In December 2006, in settlement of a lawsuit filed by LSR against the New York Stock Exchange, LSR was finally listed on an electronic stock trading platform owned by the NYSE called ARCA, which permits anonymous trading. The company's stock value immediately soared 40 percent.)[27]

Tertiary targeting is terrorism most foul—and unfortunately, it is working. At present, SHAC's website lists more than one hundred companies that have complied with its demands to cease doing business with HLS, including Johnson & Johnson, Washington Mutual, UBS Global Capital, Nucryst Pharmaceutical, and Chubb.

SHAC is so brazen that it requires targeted companies to capitulate to its demands publicly. The SHAC website instructs:

> TO ALL SUPPLIERS: If you have severed your links with Huntingdon Life Sciences, please let the campaign know. You can send a simple email to info@shac.net stating the following: "... (name of your company) have severed their links with HLS and terminated their contract, and will not be dealing with them now or in the future, directly or indirectly." This will enable supporters to be kept up to date with which companies are still involved with Huntingdon Life Sciences.[28]

Failing to comply exposes company employees and their families to continued and relentless assault. Fear of being targeted explains the abject appeasement by many in the medical research community: they realize that if Huntingdon can be taken down by tertiary targeting, so can any medical company, including their own. For example, here is a promise posted on the SHAC website from Brian Brockway, president, CEO, and chairman of Transoma Medical, an implantable diagnostic company:"We at Transoma Medical and DSI do not deal with Huntingdon Life Sciences (HLS) or Life Sciences Research (LSR) and would not conduct business with them in the future or via any third parties."[29]

My call to Mr. Brockway for an interview to explain his posting was not returned.[30]

11

Praising with Faint Condemnation

When I began research for this book, I believed that the "mainstream" of the movement—if that term is appropriate for such a radical notion as animal rights—should be considered distinct and apart from the violent extremists, such as ALF and SHAC liberationists. No more. My immersion in the field has convinced me that most animal rights activists actually support the direct-action approach. Thus, the terrorist wing is not disconnected from peaceful protestors; they all belong to a single, mutually supportive social movement. To be sure, different groups pursue the common goal using different tactics, and it is certainly true that most activists do not engage in active criminality. But all work in support of the same goal. And while there isn't a central command structure coordinating the movement's many protest approaches, terrorism in the name of animal rights can be thought of as one arm of an octopus, with PETA, HSUS, philosophers, financiers, and the like being other tentacles. They may appear separate, but they are parts of the same organism.

Here is how I drew this conclusion. First, despite the discredit that ALF and SHAC types bring to the overall reputation of the movement, there is little active opposition to their overt criminality among its leadership. The most notable exception to this general rule has been Gary Francione, whose "abolitionist" approach to animal rights is explicitly nonviolent and noncoercive. I asked Francione why he believes animal rights activists should eschew all violence. He told me:

As a theoretical matter, the animal rights movement should represent the ideals of nonviolence because the movement should represent the ultimate affirmation of life. I see the animal rights movement as a logical progression of the peace movement, which seeks to end conflict between humans. The animal rights movement ideally seeks to take a step further and to end conflict between humans and nonhumans.

As a practical matter, violence makes no sense. Anyone who has ever used violence claims to regret having to resort to it, but that some goal justifies its use. It is precisely that sort of consequentialist thinking that leads to more violence. It is important that the animal rights movement stand clearly and unequivocally for an end to the cycle. Moreover, it is not clear to me what those who support violence hope to achieve. They certainly are not causing the public to become more sympathetic to the plight of nonhuman animals. If anything, the contrary is true.

Noting that most violent and coercive actions are, at present, aimed against medical researchers, Francione said:

The problem is that we live in a world where virtually anyone who can afford to eat animal products does so. That is, most people engage in a form of animal use that is transparently frivolous and wholly unnecessary. In such a world, there is no context in which violence against vivisectors can be interpreted in any way other than as irrational and extreme. If we have not gotten a significant number of people to the point where they reject the completely unnecessary suffering of nonhumans used for flesh, dairy, or eggs, what hope is there that violence in the cause of ending an activity [vivisection] that is perceived by most of the public to be necessary and to provide benefits for humans is going to resonate?

I am constantly criticized by the so-called "animal rights community" for being rigid in my promotion of veganism. But the reality is that the many animal advocates who are not vegans are participating in the direct exploitation of nonhumans in the same way that vivisectors are. I do not see the pro-violence people urging violence against their ovo-lacto-vegetarian colleagues. So why against the vivisectors?[1]

Peter Singer has opposed violence, as has Wayne Pacelle, the head of HSUS. For example, when a medical researcher's house was bombed in

Santa Cruz, HSUS offered a token reward, a mere $2,500 from an organization with more than $200 million in assets, for the capture and conviction of the culprits—which infuriated other animal rights activists. Steven Best blew his stack for this "treachery," castigating Pacelle and HSUS both for publicly opposing animal rights terrorism and for the small reward it offered in the Santa Cruz bombing case.[2]

Unfortunately, Francione, Singer, and Pacelle are the proverbial exceptions that prove the rule. Most other prominent animal rights leaders and organizations either are silent about ALF and SHAC-type direct actions, or praise it with faint damnation, or sometimes openly support it. Perhaps most notably, PETA explicitly refuses to condemn ALF on its website, where the "Ask Carla" feature says:

QUESTION: What's PETA's position on the Animal Liberation Front?

ANSWER: Throughout history, some people have felt the need to break the law in order to fight injustice. The Underground Railroad and the French Resistance are both examples of people breaking the law in order to combat injustice. PETA is a legal activist organization, but we realize that other groups have different methods and we try not to condemn any efforts in behalf of animals in which no one is harmed. "The ALF," which is simply the name adopted by people acting illegally in behalf of animal rights, breaks inanimate objects such as stereotaxic devices and decapitators in order to save lives. It burns empty buildings in which animals are tortured and killed. ALF "aids" have provided proof of horrific cruelty that would not have been discovered or believed otherwise.

They have resulted in officials' filing of criminal charges against laboratories, the citing of experimenters for violations of the Animal Welfare Act, and, in some cases, the shutting down of abusive labs for good. Often ALF raids have been followed by widespread scientific condemnation of the practices occurring in the targeted labs. Anyone can be an activist. It does not take any special skills or superhuman abilities. You just need to care enough about animals to want to help them.[3]

Forget for the moment that comparing lab rats to freed slaves is profoundly insulting and that the French Resistance summarily executed collaborators. Consider the kinds of activities that PETA expressly approves as acceptable forms of advocacy: arson, threats of death and physical harm, attempted and actual bombings, theft, vandalism, harassment of the most vile sort. Moreover, PETA maintains a deafening silence about tertiary targeting and other such tactics of SHAC.

PETA has gone even further than refusing to condemn animal rights terrorism: It has also financially supported those engaged in such felonious conduct. And this has been true from the time PETA first became a potent political force. When the ALF activist and PETA member Roger Troen was convicted in 1986 of theft, burglary, and conspiracy for breaking into a lab and stealing 156 rabbits, PETA "quietly paid the ALF member's $27,000 legal tab and also picked up the hefty $34,900 fine levied against him."[4]

As determined by its Form 990 federal income tax return from 1988, PETA gave $7,500 to a fund created to defend Fran Stephanie Trutt.[5] This is significant because Trutt didn't "just" burn an empty building but *plotted the murder* of the head of a research laboratory. As reported by *Time*:

> Acting on a tip from an informant, police in Norwalk, Conn., arrested Trutt seconds after she placed a powerful pipe bomb studded with roofing nails outside the headquarters of the U.S. Surgical Corp., a firm that animal-rights activists have accused of cruelty to the dogs it uses for medical research and training. On the seat of Trutt's rented Chevy pickup was a remote-controlled detonator from which a battery had been removed to prevent an accidental explosion. A subsequent search of her apartment turned up three more bombs and a shotgun. Trutt was charged with possession of explosives, manufacturing a bomb and attempted murder.[6]

Trutt eventually pleaded guilty in a plea bargain and went to prison.

Rodney Coronado is one of the most notorious animal rights criminals, who as we saw earlier was imprisoned in 2007 for showing people how to make a destructive device with the goal of having someone commit a violent crime. He also has an explosive personality. David Martosko, who works with the Center for Consumer Freedom, a food industry-financed nonprofit organization that opposes animal rights activism, recalls a close call he had when Coronado saw him observing a group of demonstrators that had picketed Huntingdon Life Sciences:

After the protests were over, most of the activists retreated to a public park to eat and (it was rumored) break into smaller groups to hold evening protests at the homes of Huntingdon researchers. Most of them had masks on during the protests, and even at the speaker event the night before. But I thought they'd have to take their masks off to eat, and I figured that might be my only opportunity to see who the rank-and-file troublemakers were.

I drove my rental car to the park, walked a safe distance from the activists' picnic site, and started taking pictures. About five minutes later, a handful of activists noticed me. I imagine now that they thought I was an undercover police officer, which makes what happened next even more bizarre. Three of them, including Rodney Coronado, Lauren Gazzola, and a third man, suddenly started running toward me at sprint speed.

The third activist tripped and fell, but Gazzola and Coronado headed straight for me. By the time I ran back to the rental car and started the engine, they were about twenty yards behind me. Coronado was brandishing a tire iron menacingly. Gazzola was holding a large rock, which she threw at the car (missing by a mile) as I peeled out of the gravel lot.

In retrospect, getting that close to the animal rights movement's violent vanguard is something I would never do again. The experience was something like encountering a bear in the forest without being armed. If I had known how dangerous these two were, I would never have gotten out of the car.[7]

In 1995, PETA donated a whopping $45,200 to a defense fund established for Coronado when he was charged with arson. Here's the story: After breaking and entering into a Michigan State University lab—and stealing records and documents—he set it on fire. This was apparently only one of many crimes committed as a key ALF activist for which he was not caught. In the government's sentencing memorandum, the assistant U.S. attorney Timothy P. Verhey laid out Coronado's violent history:[8]

- He had, as a member of the Sea Shepherd Society, "sabotaged a whaling station and sunk two whaling ships in Reykjavik, Iceland."[9]
- In 1987, Coronado became associated with ALF and vandalized nine fur salons in Vancouver, Canada.
- He fled Canada after an arrest warrant was issued.

+ He came to the United States government's attention for advocating arson.
+ Credit cards and phone records proved Coronado's presence in the area either before or immediately after most ALF attacks and intentionally set fires.[10]
+ After he torched a lab at Michigan State University, Coronado went on the lam and was finally found living under an assumed name on an Indian reservation, after which he pleaded guilty to committing arson.

The sentencing memorandum is also very pertinent to PETA's winking at violence in the name of animal rights. Apparently after the break-in and fire, Coronado sent two Federal Express packages to animal rights activists. One package, intercepted before delivery, contained stolen MSU documents. The second went to PETA co-founder Ingrid Newkirk, who, the report pointedly noted, "had arranged to have the package delivered *before* the MSU arson occurred." (Emphasis in the original.)[11]

Search warrants disclosed a further nexus between Newkirk and PETA's co-founder Alex Pacheco (of Silver Spring Monkey infamy) and Coronado's criminality, which would appear to have included the commission of other crimes such as obtaining of false identification:

> The first warrant ... was executed at the home of Maria Blanton, a longtime PETA member who had agreed to accept the first [intercepted] Federal Express package from Coronado after being asked to do so by Ingrid Newkirk.[12] Records found during the search of Blanton's home demonstrated that Coronado and others planned a raid at Tulane University. These records showed that Coronado, Alex Pacheco and others had planned a burglary at Tulane University's Primate Research Center in 1990. (In 1990, Tulane housed the "Silver Spring Monkeys," a group of lab monkeys that had been the focus of furious criticism by PETA.) The records seized included surveillance logs; code names for Coronado, Pacheco and others; burglary tools; two-way radios; night vision goggles; phone identification for Coronado and Pacheco; and animal euthanasia drugs.[13]

It is important to emphasize that neither Pacheco nor Newkirk was charged in the case. But their seemingly close working relationship with

Coronado demonstrates, at the very least, that such direct actions have their moral support.

PETA's federal income tax return for 2001 shows further channeling of financial resources toward the defense of animal rights activists accused of crimes. For example, PETA paid $5,000 to the "Josh Harper Support Fund"[14] when Harper, who had previously been jailed for assaulting a police officer and also the crew of a whaling ship, was held in contempt of court for refusing to testify before a grand jury about the activities of ALF and ELF.[15] PETA also paid $1,500 to the North American Earth Liberation Front to "support their activities," which, as we have seen, include arson and other forms of terrorism.[16]

According to the Southern Poverty Law Center's *Intelligence Report*, PETA and HSUS were sponsors of an animal rights conference where perpetrators of violence from ALF and ELF were asked to speak—which clearly indicated an acceptance of their tactics. One speaker was ELF's Craig Rosebraugh, who had stated before a congressional committee that he wasn't worried about ELF killing anyone because he was "more concerned with massive numbers of people dying at the hands of greedy capitalists if such actions are not taken."[17] The conference also had an authorized table where ALF and SHAC representatives handed out pamphlets and T-shirts.[18]

At the conference, Bruce Friedrich, PETA's vice president of International Grassroots Campaigns, stated that he didn't personally use violent tactics, but he explicitly cheered those who did:

> If we really believe that animals have the same right to be free from pain and suffering at our hands, then, of course we're going to be, as a movement, blowing things up and smashing windows.... I think it's a great way to bring about animal liberation.... I think it would be great if all of the fast-food outlets, slaughterhouses, these laboratories, and the banks that fund them exploded tomorrow. I think it's perfectly appropriate for people to take bricks and toss them through the windows.... Hallelujah to the people who are willing to do it.[19]

Mainstream support for ALF among the leaders of the animal rights movement is even more clearly seen in the book *Terrorists or Freedom*

Fighters?, edited by Steven Best, a philosophy professor at the University of Texas, El Paso, who is one of the intellectual luminaries of animal rights, together with the self-described "peace activist" Anthony J. Nocella.[20] Among the other contributors to the book supporting ALF are the arsonist Rodney Coronado; PETA's head, Ingrid Newkirk; PETA's former "humane educator" Gary Yourofsky, a convicted felon; and the SHAC activist Kevin Jonas, also a convicted felon.[21] Even the animal rights theorist Tom Regan, while not supporting ALF at this time, offers a theoretical defense of acting violently in behalf of animal rights under certain circumstances.

The book's ideological thrust is made clear in its dedication to the late British arsonist Barry Horne, whose hunger strike, readers will recall, led animal rights terrorists to threaten the assassination of British scientists. Demonstrating the close link between animal rights and the hard edge of anarchist and far-left politics, the preface is by Ward Churchill, who became infamous after the attacks of September 11 for referring to the victims at the World Trade Center as "little Eichmanns."[22]

The overarching theme of most of the essays in *Terrorists or Freedom Fighters?* is that ALF belongs within the broad spectrum of animal rights advocacy. Justifying terror in the name of animal rights is both implicit and explicit in the book's pages. In "Direct Actions Speak Louder Than Words," Rodney Coronado justifies ALF's many felonies—which he calls "uncivil disobedience"—and endorses its terrorism as a necessary adjunct to legal means of protest:

> Those in industry and government can rest assured that in the coming years, the ALF will continue to exist to provide an avenue of freedom for those innocent victims the animal rights movement is unable to rescue legally. The ALF brings hope when others feel hopeless. For the peaceful warriors of the ALF, nonviolent action to save lives remains not a choice, but the obligation of every enlightened human being.[23]

Gary Yourofsky offers further praise for ALF direct actions, asserting that the way to end terrorism is to give in to the coercion:

> If people truly want to end terrorism, then they should discard animal flesh from refrigerators, toss bows and bullets into the trash, insist that universities close down their vivisection laboratories, demand that department stores

close their fur salons, drop animal acts from circuses, abolish the rodeo once and for all, and support the courageous ALF activists who liberate animals from places of terror. People who yearn for a compassionate world should have nothing but praise for these amazing altruists.[24]

The support of ALF as a legitimate arm of the overall animal rights movement is also explicit in *Terrorists or Freedom Fighters?* Comparing the animal rights movement to the feminist struggle, Pattrice Jones—who once said that "animals are people and people are animals"[25]—argues that ALF should be seen as an essential partner in the effort to gain rights for animals:

> Feminism also offers challenges to all animal activists—ALF and non-ALF alike—concerning cooperation, coordination, coalition, and communication. Because social change struggles have always been most effective when diverse tactics have been deployed within the context of a coordinated strategy, these principles of feminist practice can help us build a more effective animal liberation movement.
>
> Cooperation means, at minimum, not impeding the actions of one's allies and at best, facilitating their work. The rest of the animal liberation movement must recognize ALF activists as allies and vice versa. Mainstream animal advocates need not jump to distance themselves from the ALF and certainly should not find reasons to criticize the ALF in public. Similarly, ALF activists ought not harshly condemn liberationists who include within their work efforts to improve the lives of animals until such a time as freedom is achieved.[26]

Ingrid Newkirk likewise describes the ALF as an indispensable arm of the broader animal rights movement, saying that without its threat of destruction, change will not happen:

> I would hazard to say that no movement for social change has ever succeeded without "the militarism component." Not until black demonstrators resorted to violence did the national government work seriously for civil rights legislation.* In the 1930s labor struggles had to turn violent before any significant

---

*Not true. For example, the Civil Rights Act of 1964 preceded the race riots of the 1960s.

gains were made. In 1850 white abolitionists, having given up on peaceful means, began to encourage and engage in actions that disrupted plantation operations and liberated slaves. Was all that wrong?[27]

Asserting that "the ALF wouldn't hurt a mouse" and calling it "the animals' greatest hope" because it gives "a prod in the ribs of both conservative animal protectors and animal exploiters alike,"[28] Newkirk makes her endorsement of ALF-style terrorism abundantly clear:

> Isn't the chicken house today's concentration camp?—or do we not believe that it is wrong to make victims and to deride and persecute those we do not relate to? Will we condemn its destruction or condemn its existence? Which is the more violent wish? If a property stands as a mechanism, a platform, or a vehicle for violence, shouldn't it be destroyed?[29]

PETA's Bruce Friedrich again gives direct action his explicit seal of approval in his essay, calling ALF attacks "a reasonable response to the level of violence inflicted against animals."[30] And he places ALF (and by implication its ideological twin, SHAC), within the mainstream of the animal rights movement:

> If we believe that animals have as much right to be free from pain and suffering as human beings do, and if we understand the degree of the animals' suffering, how can we disdain actions that liberate them, actions that treat their suffering as important? ... In addition to totally disagreeing with the argument that ALF activities alienate people (certainly, they shake people up, and some people will claim to be alienated), I can't imagine arguing, even if that were true: "Well, yes, animals were saved, but you know, some people are now alienated from our message." Imagine applying similar logic to some movement for human liberation.

Friedrich concludes with a clarion call to let ALF be ALF:

> I am convinced that it is our innate speciesism, deeply ingrained in most of us, that allows this discussion [about whether ALF tactics are justified] to even occur.... In the end, it seems to me that the most important thing is that those of us who take the animals' side simply stop the internecine fighting and name calling, which does not help animals at all, and get back to the essential work of animal liberation.[31]

Even one of the movement's most notable philosophers, Tom Regan—
who believes that animals have rights as "moral patients"—refuses to issue
a clear condemnation of ALF violence. In a chapter titled "How to Justify
Violence," Regan writes that he admires the terrorists' "sincerity" and "commitment" as well as "the courage these activists embody."[32] Regan's criticism
of ALF is mild, based mostly on the view that it's a tactical error. He also
believes that before violence is warranted, activists must first "exhaust nonviolent alternatives," something he regards as not yet done.[33] On the other
hand, Regan sees animal husbandry as far worse than the kind of terrorism employed by SHAC and ALF.

> The violence done to things by some ARAs [animal rights activists] (by
> which I mean the destruction of insensate property) is nothing compared to
> the violence done to feeling creatures by the major animal use industries. A
> raindrop compared to an ocean. On a day-to-day basis, by far the greatest
> amount of violence done in the "civilized" world occurs because of what
> humans do to other animals. That the violence is legally protected, that in
> some cases (for example vivisection) it is socially esteemed, only serves to
> make matters worse.

Given this view of what humans do to animals, it isn't surprising that
Regan does not argue persuasively for ALF activists to cut out the violence. Instead, he shrugs:

> Finally, and lamentably, one thing seems certain. Unless the massive amount
> of violence done to animals is acknowledged by those who do it, and until
> meaningful steps are taken to end it, as certain as night follows day, some
> ARAs somewhere, somehow, will use violence against animal abusers them-
> selves to defend the rights of animals.[34]

When one of the most influential leaders of the animal rights/libera-
tion movement cannot do more than mildly criticize ALF because peaceful approaches have not been exhausted, the movement is clearly not as
peaceable as its boosters suppose. This acceptance of the criminality and
terrorism committed by activists such as ALF and SHAC bodes ill for the
future. Will the next step taken by the most extreme fanatics "for the animals" be murder?

Murder They Wrote?

When confronted with the violence of the ALF wing of the animal rights movement, their apologists invariably fall back on the claim that felonious acts such as arson and threats of violence against entire families are not really terroristic since no one has been murdered. Rodney Coronado actually claims that his arson crimes and those of other ALF militants are *nonviolent* actions!

> The ALF has never endorsed or participated in physical violence and never will. Our 19-year record of no injuries or deaths is no coincidence. It is the product of a determined nonviolent underground movement sincerely committed to alleviating physical violence—not rationalizing it as our opponents regularly do.[1]

"Nonviolent arson" is an oxymoron. If the KKK burned a cross in front of the home of an African American but hurt nobody, would anyone say it wasn't terrorism? Not a chance.

When ALF or SHAC or other animal liberationists send death threats, burn buildings, invade houses, it isn't civil disobedience or peaceful protest. When a British animal researcher "received two letter bombs, one of them wrapped in HIV-infected needles and addressed to his daughters," it was terrorism in the truest sense of the term even though nobody was physically injured.[2]

We need only look at the legal definition of terrorism in the United States to see clearly that ALF and SHAC are terrorist groups. Terrorism is defined by the Code of Federal Regulations as "the unlawful use of force or violence committed against persons or property to intimidate or coerce a government, the civilian population, or any segment thereof in further-ance of political or social objectives."[3] ALF, SHAC, and their apologists readily acknowledge that their intent is to intimidate their enemies into ceasing legal activities by means of property crime and threats of violence.

Besides, given the flow of events, murder in the cause of animal rights may only be a matter of time. As we have seen, attacks on animal researchers and companies that use animals have been growing steadily in seriousness, including the exploding of incendiary devices. In February 2008, masked terrorists invaded the home of a UC Santa Cruz professor who had been the subject of threats from animal rights extremists because he used animals to research the causes of breast cancer and neurological diseases. From the story:

> Santa Cruz police reported that six people wearing bandanas tried to break into a Westside home just before 1 P.M. and that one of the family members, not the faculty member, was attacked before the intruders fled. The male vic-tim made sure his wife and children were safe in the back of the house before he confronted the attackers. He suffered minor injuries after being hit with an unknown object. None of the other four people in the house were injured.[4]

Home invasions are among the most serious of crimes, not only because of the utter terror they cause to the residents, but also because the situa-tion can easily escalate until attackers or defenders engage in deadly force.

A few months later, the names, addresses, and photos of UC scientists were published in a pamphlet that read like a wanted poster. According to a newspaper report on the incident, "The crudely-constructed pamphlet titled 'Murders and Torturers Alive and Well in Santa Cruz' warns, 'We know where you live. We know where you work. We will never back down.'"[5] It was about a week after this that the home of a scientist identi-fied in the pamphlet was firebombed in the early morning hours. The large incendiary device caused the front porch to catch fire and filled the house with smoke. The scientist and his family, including two small children, "were forced to escape a smoke-filled house using a second-story lad-der.... One family member sustained injuries requiring brief hospitalization, and police are calling the firebombing, which occurred shortly before 6 A.M., a case of attempted homicide." At about the same time, another animal researcher's car was firebombed.[6]

Bombings are unquestionably terrorist actions. Two San Francisco Bay Area companies, Chiron and Shaklee, were bombed in 2003 because of their relationship with Huntingdon Life Sciences. The *San Francisco Chronicle*'s report made clear that the attacks were designed to injure people:

> The bombs were made out of materials readily available off the shelf. "The device left at Shaklee was covered with nails to create shrapnel," said Andy Traver, assistant special agent in charge of the Bureau of Alcohol, Tobacco, Firearms and Explosives. "The only purpose of adding this shrapnel is to cause damage or bodily harm to people," Traver said.

The FBI offered a $50,000 reward for the arrest of an animal rights extremist named Daniel Andreas San Diego for the bombings, but he disappeared, probably with the assistance of other animal rights extremists.[7] In 2006 the reward for San Diego's arrest was raised to $250,000 and he was added to the FBI Most Wanted list.[8] As this book went to press, San Diego had not been apprehended.

Smash the State—Crush the Cage

Advocacy usually precedes action, which is why we should be so concerned about the nexus tying the extremist flank of the animal rights movement with nihilistic anarchists and earth-worshipping environmentalists. "Smash the State, Crush the Cage," an animal rights conference held in 2007 at Hampshire College in Amherst, Massachusetts, typified the radical core that has been driving the animal rights movement into increasingly dark and dangerous territory. One description of the conference put it this way:

> Looking back in time, it becomes clear that the struggle for animal liberation is no different than other struggles against oppression. In 1860, human slavery was every bit as legal as enslaving animals in laboratories and circuses,

factory farms and zoos is today. Back then there were people like Old John Brown willing to put their actions where their words were, and today is no different. Brave warriors with the ALF, the Animal Rights Militia, the Revolutionary Cells and the Justice Department are putting their lives and freedom at risk to liberate the enslaved and to continue to push our movement forward just as in other, more "human liberation" struggles.[9]

It isn't a coincidence that "Old John Brown" (who my family tradition holds is a distant relative) would be extolled in such a radical gathering: To his credit, Brown adamantly opposed slavery; but unlike the generally pacifistic abolitionists, he committed five coldblooded murders in "Bloody Kansas," where he infamously kidnapped and executed five pro-slavers at Pottawatomie. His raid on Harper's Ferry, intended to ignite a slave rebellion, instead resulted in the murder of the town's mayor, who was known for being kind to slaves, and it helped ignite the Civil War.[10]

With similar intensity of fervor, Rodney Coronado tied the cause of animal liberation to lethal insurgencies:

> We are warriors. Like Geronimo, we must fight and never lose hope if we are to remain true to the principles of animal liberation. This struggle will not end in our lifetime. We are at the threshold where the same forces that sought to contain the spirit of Geronimo and his people on reservations, are now directing their pursuit towards the Animal Liberation Front and the Earth Liberation Front in an attempt to preserve the invader's worldview that demands that animals and the Earth remain property to be exploited.... If Geronimo and thirty-seven renegade Apaches could hold back the tide of Western Expansion, there's reason to believe our small movements can do the same towards preserving the natural world and preventing animal exploitation.[11]

Perhaps somebody should remind Coronado that Geronimo hunted animals and rode horses into battle, making him an oppressor of animals.

The former PETA "humane educator" Gary Yourofsky, who is a big draw on the college lecture circuit,* displays the lava-hot rage that

---

*In early 2008, Yourofsky claimed to have "given 1,403 lectures in 27 states at 134 institutions to more than 35,000 students."

motivates many of the most radical animal liberationists. Writing in a college newspaper, he expressed a desire to see violence done to people who use animals or animal products:

> Deep down, I truly hope that oppression, torture and murder return to each uncaring human tenfold! I hope that fathers accidentally shoot their sons on hunting excursions, while carnivores suffer heart attacks that kill them slowly. Every woman ensconced in fur should endure a rape so vicious that it scars them forever. While every man entrenched in fur should suffer an anal raping so horrific that they become disemboweled. Every rodeo cowboy and matador should be gored to death, while circus abusers are trampled by elephants and mauled by tigers. And, lastly, may irony shine its esoteric head in the form of animal researchers catching debilitating diseases and painfully withering away because research dollars that could have been used to treat them were wasted on the barbaric, unscientific practice of vivisection.[12]

The increasingly radical thrust of the animal rights movement goes far beyond the sentimental embrace of a murderer like John Brown, identification with a violent insurgent such as Geronimo, and wishes for women to be raped. Some liberationists seem to be literally preparing for violent armed conflict. In 2004, animal rights extremists "set up a combat skills training camp" and declared "an escalation in what participants call 'the animal liberation war.'"[13] Liberationists expanded on this alarming approach two years later, when a conference was convened in 2006 to train attendees in "lethal" techniques of personal combat. The explicit point of the conference, as reported by the *Telegraph*, was to export animal rights violence into Eastern Europe:

> The SHAC spokesman said that the group would pay to fly people from Russia and Eastern Europe to Britain to learn defence techniques that could be used against security guards at pharmaceutical companies and huntsmen. At previous camps, activists were taught how to deliver punches to key areas of the body and to damage optic nerves by sticking their fingers into adversaries' eyes.[14]

Murder is the Rubicon toward which the animal liberation army seems to be marching with its violent imagery, training in lethal techniques, and hysterical Holocaust analogies. And the marchers include some of the movement's most prominent leaders. In a disturbing chapter of *Terrorism or Freedom Fighters?* titled "It's War! The Escalating Battle between Activists and the Corporate-State Complex," Steven Best warned of pending bloodshed:

> More and more activists grow tired of adhering to a nonviolent code of ethics while violence from the enemy [presumably, he means against animals] increases. Realizing that nonviolence against animal exploiters in fact is a pro-violence stance that tolerates their blood-spilling without taking adequate measures to stop it, a new breed of freedom fighters has ditched Gandhi for Machiavelli and switched principled nonviolence with the amoral (not to be confused with immoral) pragmatism that embraces animal liberation "by any means necessary."
>
> A new civil war is unfolding—one between forces hell-bent on exploiting animals and the earth for profit whatever the toll, and activists steeled to resist this omnicide tooth and nail. We are witnessing not only the long-standing corporate war against nature, but also a new social war *about* nature.[15]

In Best's paranoid imagination, animal rights is no longer merely about stopping the abuse of animals but about thwarting a looming totalitarian state that threatens to spread tyranny throughout the earth. Against this American monster, Best seems to be urging his readers in effect to take up arms:

> The animal rights community can no longer afford to be a single-issue movement, for *now in order to fight for animal rights we have to fight for democracy*.... Attacks on foreigners are preludes to attacks on U.S. citizens, which are overtures to assaults on the animal rights and environmental activist communities, which augur the fate of all groups and citizens in the nation. In the world of Bush, Cheney, Rumsfeld, Ashcroft, the FBI, the CIA, and the corporate conglomerates, *we are all becoming aliens*, foreigners to their pre-modern barbarity by virtue of our very wish to uphold modern liberal values and constitutional rights. Like "the war on drugs," the "war on terrorism" is phony, a front for the war on privacy, liberty, and democracy. Only counter-terrorists can defeat terrorists. May the armies of the animal, earth, and human liberationists rise and multiply in a perfect war against the oppressors of the earth.[16]

Not surprisingly, Best was banned from entering the United Kingdom under the country's antiterror laws in 2005, his presence being deemed "non conducive to the public good."[17]

The animal rights fanatic Jerry Vlasak was similarly banned from Britain in 2004 due to his violent advocacy.[18] An emergency room physician, Vlasak is an energetic apologist for SHAC and has been associated with many other radical animal rights and environmental groups; he has served as a spokesperson for the Physicians Committee for Responsible Medicine, treasurer of the Sea Shepherd Conservation Society, and science adviser for In Defense of Animals.[19] He is also the primary spokesperson for the North American Animal Liberation Press Office, a conduit for the public release of ALF post-terrorism "communiqués" and future terrorist threats.[20]

Vlasak is a showman and has made many intentionally incendiary comments over the years, but he is most infamous for hoping that scientists who do research with animals will one day be assassinated. He told the *Observer*:

> I think violence is part of the struggle against oppression. If something bad happens to these people [animal researchers], it will discourage others. It is inevitable that violence will be used in the struggle and that it will be effective. I don't think you'd have to kill too many [researchers]. I think for 5 lives, 10 lives, 15 human lives, we could save a million, 2 million, 10 million nonhuman lives.[21]

Not surprisingly, Vlasak's encouragement of assassination outraged the scientific community and government representatives, resulting in the ban from the UK. After being declared *persona non grata*, he dug the hole he was digging for himself even deeper as he sought to "respond to media lies," writing on a radical website:

> People have been killed over absolutely ridiculous things like oil, power, and money. It would be "speciesist" of me to say that in a battle for the moral and ethical high ground, in the fight on behalf of the most oppressed, abused, and tortured beings the world has ever known, that there will never be casualties. I'm not encouraging or calling for this, I am simply stating that the animal rights movement is and has been the most peaceful and restrained movement

the world has ever known considering the amount of terror, abuse, and murder done to innocent animals for greed and profit. If by chance violence is used by those who fight for non human sentient beings, or even if there are casualties, it must be looked at in perspective and in a historical context.[22]

Vlasak pledged to file a libel suit against the *Observer* for claiming that he encouraged violence. Truth being an absolute defense to libel, needless to say, the lawsuit was never filed.

Despite denying feebly that he advocated the murder of animal researchers, Vlasak validated the *Observer*'s journalism in testimony before a United States Senate subcommittee. Here is a partial transcript of an exchange he had with Senator James Inhofe (R-ID):

> SENATOR INHOFE. One of the statements you made at the animal rights convention when you were defending assassinating people, murdering people, you said, let me put it up here to make sure I'm not misquoting you, "I don't think you'd have to kill, assassinate too many. I think for five lives, ten lives, fifteen human lives, we could save a million, two million, or ten million non-human lives."
>
> You're advocating the murder of individuals, isn't that correct?
>
> DR. VLASAK. I made that statement, and I stand by that statement. That statement is made in the context that the struggle for animal liberation is no different than struggles for liberation elsewhere, whether the struggle for liberation in South Africa against the apartheid regime, whether the liberation against the communists, whether it was the liberation struggles in Algeria, Viet Nam or Iraq today, liberation struggles occasionally or usually, I should say, usually end up in violence.
>
> There is plenty of violence being used on the other side of the equation. These animals are being terrorized, murdered and killed by the millions every day. The animal rights movement has been notoriously non-violent up to this point....
>
> SENATOR INHOFE. And so you call for the murders of researchers and human life?
>
> DR. VLASAK. I said in that statement and I meant in that statement that people who are hurting animals and who will not stop when told to stop, one

option would be to stop them using any means necessary and that was the context in which that statement was made.

SENATOR INHOFE. Including murdering them, is that correct?

DR. VLASAK. I said that would be a morally justifiable solution to the problem.[23]

As the statements of Jerry Vlasak and Steven Best (among others) illustrate, there is little inclination within the animal rights movement to squelch the growing pressure for physical violence against "animal abusers," which is building like a boiler ready to explode. It may be only a matter of time before an unhinged fanatic, steeped in the twisted ideology that equates animal husbandry with the Holocaust, makes the jump across the Rubicon. Then it will be Katie bar the door.

It May Have Already Started

In actuality, there have already been a few serious physical assaults—perhaps even murders—committed by animal rights extremists against people they regard as animal abusers. According to the Southern Poverty Law Center's *Intelligence Report*, a Huntingdon Life Sciences executive was viciously attacked because of his work for the company.

In February 2001, Huntingdon's managing director in Great Britain, Brian Cass, was badly beaten outside his home by three masked assailants swinging baseball bats. Shortly after the attack, a British animal rights activist named David Blenkinsop, a friend of SHAC-USA's Kevin Jonas, was arrested and sentenced to three years in prison for the assault.[24] Blenkinsop was later sentenced to a further four and a half years in prison for a bombing spree.[25]

Another Huntingdon executive was nearly blinded by animal rights terrorists. As he was emerging from his car, two attackers suddenly sprayed a caustic substance in his face and punched him when he tried to protect his face. He fully recovered but spent hours not knowing whether his sight would be permanently impaired.[26]

In 2002 a rising Dutch politician named Pym Fortuyn was assassinated by an animal rights extremist and vegan named Volkert van der Graaf. While the killer has never explained why he murdered Fortuyn except in general terms, many suspect that Van der Graaf's zeal for animal rights was a contributing factor. For example, Fortuyn was something of a libertarian who in his last campaign decried what he called untruths spread by the environmental lobby and who had announced he would work to lift the legal ban on fur farming in the Netherlands if his party came to control the government.[27] Moreover, Van der Graaf was also implicated—albeit not charged—in the murder of an environmental officer named Chris van de Werken. "The picture that has emerged from interviews with those who know Van der Graaf," reported the *Sunday Times*, "... is of a gifted but obsessive man so fanatical about the rights of animals that he was prepared to take human life."[28]

According to the *Sunday Times* report, Van der Graaf began his activist career by spray-painting the walls of restaurants that served frog legs. He founded the Zeeland Animal Liberation Front and became a vegan and formed a group opposed to all animal farming, which frequently clashed with local farmers, politically impeding their attempts to improve their property or enlarge their herds. When farmers were granted a license to increase the size of their herds, Van der Graaf came to believe that Van de Werken was siding with the farmers. One day, Van de Werken went for a walk in the woods and never returned; he had been shot to death. While that crime was never solved, the *Sunday Times* noted some disturbing similarities between the two killings:

> Like Fortuyn, Van de Werken was killed with 9mm silver-tip hollow-point bullets, a rare form of ammunition similar to dumdum bullets. Both men were shot in cold blood at extremely close range. Police confirm that Van der Graaf was among those questioned at the time. Documents found on the hard disk of a computer seized from his home also point to a possible link with arson attacks in November 1999 on a plant in Milheeze, a few miles to the south, that produces feed for minks, and a series of incidents at a local poultry farm that started in 1995.... Fortuyn was dismissive of the green movement ... [and] was also known to favor easing restrictions on farming, especially the rearing of mink. There could be no stronger symbol of everything Van der Graaf so passionately opposed.[29]

At his sentencing for Fortuyn's murder, Van der Graaf claimed he had "no choice" but to kill his victim, telling the court:

> I got the impression he was looking for a scapegoat he could use to increase his popularity. That was a great concern to me. In my eyes, this was a highly vindictive man who used feelings in society to boost his personal stature. The ideas he had about refugees, asylum-seekers, the environment, about animals . . . He was always using or abusing the weak side of society to get ahead.[30]

Thus Van der Graaf echoed the sentiments of animal rights activists throughout the world who create a false analogy between what is done to animals and what is done to people.

Will there be more Pym Fortuyns and Chris van de Werkens in the future? The Southern Poverty Law Center is justifiably concerned, worrying that "further violence is almost inevitable."[31]

The Animal Enterprise Terrorism Act

Clearly, something must be done by authorities to temper the flames of violent animal rights activism and to keep innocent people from being terrorized by the brownshirts of animal rights. A good step forward toward this goal was made on November 27, 2006, when President George W. Bush signed an updated law to combat animal rights thuggery, known as the Animal Enterprise Terrorism Act.

The AETA significantly strengthened existing legal sanctions against animal rights terrorism by including tertiary targeting within its scope. The new law provides important protections not only for enterprises such as research centers, fast food restaurants, and zoos, but also for customers, employees of ancillary service businesses, and others who might be the tertiary targets of animal rights terrorism. Under this law, it is now a federal crime to assault the vice president of a bank that handles the accounts of Huntingdon Life Sciences (or any other animal enterprise) or to threaten her children, as just two examples.[32]

Predictably, the "peaceable" animal rights movement howled in outrage, claiming that their First Amendment rights were being infringed. The

Humane Society of the United States came out forcefully against the bill, stating:

> The Humane Society of the United States has no tolerance for individuals and groups who resort to intimidation, vandalism, or violence supposedly in the name of animal advocacy, and we have spoken out repeatedly against violence in any form. . . .

Then came the expected "however":

> However, the Animal Enterprise Terrorism Act (AETA) threatens to sweep up—criminalizing as "terrorism" or otherwise chilling—a broad range of lawful, constitutionally protected, and valuable activity undertaken by citizens and organizations seeking change.

How could a bill that punishes acts of terrorism and threats intended to terrify people be said to interfere with constitutionally protected activities? According to HSUS:

> The legislation uses vague, overbroad terms such as "interfering with" which could be interpreted to include legitimate, peaceful conduct. For example, someone who uses the Internet to encourage people not to buy eggs from a company producing eggs with battery cages could be charged with terrorism for causing the company a loss of profits. Likewise, someone who videotapes the cruel treatment of horses at a slaughter plant, potentially causing loss of profits if that footage is used in legislative or media efforts, could be labeled a terrorist.[33]

Meanwhile, the fanatical Steven Best—who declared that "it's war" on the "corporate-state complex"—made a similar argument in more hysterical language. "Welcome to the post-constitutional America," he wrote, "where defense of animal rights and the Earth is a terrorist crime."[34]

Time for a little sanity: Rather than targeting the legitimate rights of protest and assembly, as the law's critics contend, the authors of the AETA went out of their way to protect free speech and other legal activities taken against the use of animals. For example, under the "definitions" section of the law, the term "economic damage" is defined to explicitly protect the right to organize boycotts, a favored tactic of PETA:

(d) 3) the term "economic damage"—

(B) does not include any lawful economic disruption (including a lawful boycott) that results from lawful public, governmental, or business reaction to the disclosure of information about an animal enterprise.

Moreover, the very worries expressed by HSUS, Best, and others are revealed as baseless by the section that specifies how the law is to be enforced (emphasis added):

(e) Rules of Construction—*Nothing* in this section shall be construed—

(1) *to prohibit any expressive conduct (including peaceful picketing or other peaceful demonstration)* protected from legal prohibition by the First Amendment to the Constitution;

(2) *to create new remedies for interference with activities protected by the free speech or free exercise clauses of the First Amendment to the Constitution, regardless of the point of view expressed,* or to limit any existing legal remedies for such interference; . . .[35]

Given that the law explicitly protects legitimate means of protest and advocacy, one has to wonder why HSUS, which as we have seen has mildly opposed violence, would also oppose a law that brings to justice the terrorists who so discredit the movement.

The good news is that the law is working. The convictions of six of the so-called SHAC-7 in New Jersey, after a six-year investigation by the FBI, involved the very kind of terroristic and felonious actions that the law was designed to punish. One of those convicted, the notorious Kevin Jonas, had asserted that "innocents are not being targeted, only those 'combatants' who are involved in the suffering of animals."[36] But this claim was bogus; in fact, the victims of Jonas and his SHAC co-conspirators included children, as the U.S. Justice Department's press release indicates (emphasis added):

Testimony from victims revealed that SHAC and its organizers routinely posted personal information on their websites, including the names, addresses and phone numbers of employees of HLS and other targeted companies and their employees. Other information published on the Internet included names of employees' spouses; *the names and ages of their children and where the children attended school,* even in some instances teachers' names; license plate numbers and churches attended by employees and their families and more.

Victims of the SHAC campaign, several of whom testified at trial, often endured vandalism of their homes in the dark of night, including rocks being thrown through windows, cars being overturned, messages in red paint plastered on their homes and property, unrelenting bullhorn protests in front of their homes and harassment of neighbors.

In compelling testimony from one victim in Texas, an executive with an insurance broker doing business with HLS, she described vandalism to her suburban home, disruptive protests outside her home by SHAC members and other threatening activity. *One day, the doorbell rang and, she testified, she went to the door and found her 7-year-old son inside the door crouched down with a kitchen knife, telling her that he would protect her from "the animal people."*[37]

This wasn't free speech cruelly repressed. It wasn't civil disobedience. It wasn't peaceful protest. It was terrorism pure and simple.

The sentences imposed on the convicted criminals ranged from three to six years, plus an order to pay a million dollars in restitution—an order that was properly rendered and richly deserved.[38] And let us hope that there are more prosecutions until animal rights extremists come to realize that the adrenalin thrill they get from engaging in acts of terrorism is not worth the price to be paid for their criminal conspiracies.

Given what we have seen in the last three chapters—which is not a complete recounting of such activities—I think it is fair to say that the animal rights/liberation movement is not peaceable. Nor is it democratic, since these tactics are meant to coerce rather than persuade. Indeed, the "war" declared by animal rights terrorists against animal enterprises is a serious threat to the rule of law and to peaceful means of reforming society.

In this regard, more is at stake in thwarting violence in the cause of animal liberation than saving companies such as HLS, university research centers, or fast food restaurant chains from ruin—as important as those goals might be. If animal rights terrorists succeed in eradicating animal husbandry and other uses of animals through the means of violent and terroristic criminality, if terrorism proves to be a potent tool for a protest movement, then no controversial human activity will be immune from being similarly victimized.

Success always breeds imitation. If animal rights terrorism prevails, why wouldn't antiwar radicals apply tertiary targeting to businesses that contract with the Defense Department? Or antiglobalists use the method to take down an international bank? Or anti-abortion radicals target the insurers of Planned Parenthood clinics? Or gay rights extremists harass the landlord of a church that opposes gay marriage to force an eviction? The result would be chaos.

Clearly, whatever our politics, regardless of our personal beliefs about animal rights, we all have a stake in ensuring that animal liberation is not achieved through brutal "by any means necessary" tactics.

PART THREE

For the People

13

Animal Rights
vs. Medical Research

In 2007, PETA's Ingrid Newkirk broke her wrist. She later reported to the readers of *Animal Times* that pain-controlling drugs had alleviated her suffering. "Ooh, the pain!" she wrote. "Thank goodness for IV drips." Newkirk then turned this experience into an excuse for a diatribe against the use of animals in medical research, asking how a monkey that broke its arm in a cage "coped without pain control."[1]

Newkirk's zeal blinded her to a deep irony: As she works overtime to undermine our ability to use animals in advancing scientific knowledge and improving medical techniques, she benefited directly from past animal research in the treatment of her broken wrist. Without animal experiments, the sophisticated method of delivering pain control that brought her so much relief would not have been developed (not to mention the surgical and bone-resetting techniques from which she also undoubtedly benefited).

Given the intense suffering that a broken bone may cause, Newkirk probably received an opioid—the medical term for narcotic—to relieve her pain. Most such drugs are derived from the opium poppy, whose pain-alleviating power has been known since antiquity.[2] But until the last one hundred years or so, the quality of pain control was uneven at best. That changed with the creation of modern palliative medicine in the twentieth century, a task of immeasurable importance to humanity and one that required the use of animals. Dr. Eric Chevlen, a pain control specialist and my co-author for *Power Over Pain: How to Get the Pain Control You Need*, summed up the matter for me: "Most progress in pain relief in the last two hundred years has depended on animal research. Without it, the old person with cancer, the young woman in a difficult childbirth, the child with burn injuries, even the activist with a broken wrist—all of them would have no more pain relief available to them than did the miserable groaning wounded of the Civil War."[3]

In 1929, for example, research in mice led to a big breakthrough in pain control. First the animals were "noxiously stimulated by placing a clamp on the base of their tails to which they responded by vocalizing and biting the clamp." Then, morphine was delivered in dosages proportionate to the weight of the mice. Lo and behold, these mice did not react to the otherwise painful clamp on their tails. Yes, mice were made to feel pain, but it led to the "D'Amour-Smith tail-flick test," a breakthrough that allows doctors to predict with confidence "the potency of a new opiate ... in relation to the standard opiates."[4]

Another epochal breakthrough leading to dramatically improved palliation occurred in a study that, based on animal experiments such as those conducted with Pavlov's famous dogs—as well as observations of pain in humans—allowed scientists to hypothesize the existence of a "spinal cord mechanism that regulated the transmission of pain sensations."[5] This allowed other scientists to propose a plan "for the construction of a world of pain," resulting in the mapping of the biological mechanisms by which we feel pain.[6] The knowledge derived thereby led in turn to the creation of the International Association for the Study of Pain and the founding of the journal *Pain*, not to mention more research— mostly using animals—in increasingly sophisticated methods of pain control.

One of the countless beneficiaries of this research was Ingrid Newkirk, who roundly condemns the very kind of work that resulted in the medical protocols that brought her such welcome relief. Nobody would or should expect Newkirk to refuse the treatment she was offered, but the gratitude she expressed for it does raise an important question: Why should society heed her efforts to thwart future medical advances that will be achieved through animal research when she is so willing to receive benefits from such experimentation?

How Our Current System of Animal Research Developed

The modern system of animal research was created only in recent decades. Previously, scientists seeking cures for human diseases engaged in what today would be egregiously unethical—indeed, *criminal*—experiments, often using vulnerable humans such as prisoners and orphans as their subjects. For example, the smallpox vaccine was developed after Edward Jenner, in 1796, noticed that milkmaids who contracted a mild form of the disease known as cowpox seemed never to get smallpox. So he harvested fluid from a woman with cowpox and injected it into an eight-year-old boy. Six weeks later he exposed the boy to smallpox—an act that today would rightfully earn him a long prison sentence.[7]

The drive to protect human research subjects from such risk began in Prussia in 1898 after Albert Neisser, a German dermatologist, injected a cell-free syphilis serum into prostitutes (including a ten-year-old), without their awareness, hoping they would be immunized. Tragically, the experimental treatment instead *infected* his subjects, causing such a public uproar that Neisser was censured by the state, and the Prussian government promulgated the first detailed regulatory protections of human subjects in Western medicine.[8]

The Prussian law protected children and adults who could not legally or factually consent to being experimented upon by requiring that such research be restricted to therapeutic procedures (that is, experiments designed to help them as patients). Nontherapeutic research could only be conducted upon people capable of agreeing, and then only when their informed consent was obtained with full disclosure of the risks and hoped-for benefits of the experiment.

After World War I, the Weimar Republic passed "extraordinarily advanced"[9] national laws protecting human subjects. These also drew a sharp distinction between therapeutic and nontherapeutic research. Therapeutic research could be done without consent "only if it is urgently required and cannot be postponed because of the need to save life or prevent severe damage to health."[10] The bar against nontherapeutic research without consent was absolute.

Unfortunately, the evils of the age soon ensnared German medicine. The rising tide of eugenics undermined the Hippocratic tradition and destroyed the nation's medical ethics, like ocean waves sweeping aside a castle of sand. After the Nazi revolution brought Hitler to power, few doctors complained when the Weimar rules that protected human subjects were rescinded and replaced, not irrelevantly, by "a most stringent and research restricting law on animal protection."[11]

The rest of the story is steeped in infamy, perhaps best chronicled in Robert Jay Lifton's seminal book, *The Nazi Doctors*.[12] For example, at death camps SS doctors carried out inhumane "medical" experiments, during which mostly Jewish inmates were subjected to horrible crimes of bodily violation. Women had their cervixes injected with caustic substances in an attempt to invent sterilization-by-injection; men were subjected to intense X-ray exposure of their genitals to induce sterilization, with later castration to study the damage that radiation caused to the testes; inmates were deliberately exposed to typhus contagion, to determine the efficacy of various sera. At Auschwitz, Joseph Mengele (I refuse to dignify his name with the respectful title "Dr.") engaged in a sadistic study of identical twins, including children whom he physically examined over several months, measuring every part of their body and taking their blood, and then lethally injected them prior to dissection.[13]

Like a phoenix rising out of the ashes of the Holocaust, Hippocratic values reasserted themselves in the world-famous Nuremberg Code—in reality a judicial decision that laid down the foundations for an international framework protecting human subjects in medical and animal experimentation.[14] Among its provisions, the code sought to minimize the health dangers faced by human research subjects by requiring animal experimentation prior to any experiments in humans:

> 3: The experiment should be so designed and based on the results of animal experimentation and knowledge of the natural history of the disease or other problem under study that the anticipated results justify the performance of the experiment.[15]

Thus, animal research in scientific testing is a crucial human rights protection—not an example of human cruelty.

The Nuremberg Code was a watershed in the history of medical ethics and it led to the rules governing medical and scientific research today. Thus, in the United States, government regulations known as the "Common Rule" require that animal testing be done prior to human experimentation in areas such as drug approval, diagnostic machinery, and basic science to learn biological facts that are a condition precedent to moving forward with experimental research that may or may not one day bring human benefit. Thus, when animal rights activists rail against medical labs—and attack scientists doing animal research—they attack a system that was explicitly designed to protect the human rights of vulnerable people.

Animal Rights Arguments against Animal Research

Animal rights/liberationists mount two primary arguments against the use of animals in medical and scientific research. The first is entirely an ethical assertion: Regardless of the admitted (at least to some extent) benefits that humans receive from animal experimentation, the research must be stopped because it is immoral. The most notable proponents of this approach are Gary ("animal rights based on sentience") Francione and Tom (animals as "moral patients") Regan. In his influential *The Case for Animal Rights*, Regan put it this way (emphasis in the original):

> The rights view [asserts that] no one, whether human or animal, is ever to be treated as if she were a mere receptacle, or as if her value were reducible to her possible utility for others. We are, that is, never to harm the individual merely on the grounds that this will or just might produce "the best" aggregate consequences. To do so is to violate the rights of the individual. That is why the harm done to animals in pursuit of scientific purposes is wrong. The benefits derived are real enough; but some gains are ill-gotten, and all gains are ill-gotten when secured unjustly.... *Those who accept the rights view ... will not be satisfied with anything less than the total abolition of the harmful use of animals in science—in education, in toxicity testing, in basic research.*[16]

Francione frames the argument similarly. While charging that the benefits derived from animal research are vastly exaggerated by its supporters,

Francione avers that even though "the use of nonhumans in biomedical research may involve a plausible claim of necessity," that justification, "cannot serve to provide a satisfactory moral basis for this use of animals."[17] Why? Since (in his view) there are no distinctly human characteristics that justify in *all cases* a claim of moral superiority of every human over every animal, using them in research is as morally wrong as using supposedly inferior humans in experiments:

> We are left with one and only one reason to explain our differential treatment of animals: We are human and they are not, and species difference alone justifies differential treatment. But this criterion is entirely arbitrary and no different from maintaining that, although there is no special characteristic possessed only by whites, or no defect possessed by blacks that is not also possessed by whites, we may treat blacks as inferior to whites merely on the basis of race. It is also no different from saying that, although there is no special characteristic possessed only by men or no defect possessed only by women, we may treat women as inferior to men based merely on the basis of sex.[18]

For the "rights view" to prevail, Regan, Francione, and their colleagues will have to convince society that animals are, for all intents and purposes, morally equal to people. At the very least, they will have to convince us that it is immoral—indeed, evil—to use animals in research, regardless of the benefit we might receive, the advances in biological knowledge we could derive, the amelioration or cure of terrible human (and animal) diseases. This position is terribly misguided, in my view, but it permits an ethical debate based upon an empirically accurate understanding that animal research benefits humankind and that applying the rights view to the matter would deprive us of these results.

The other, and I must say predominant, animal rights approach to opposing animal research—let's call it the "antiscience meme"—is intellectually dishonest and factually unsupportable. Not only is animal research ethically wrong, this argument goes, but it provides no benefits to humans and actually causes us significant harm.

The animal rights group Physicians Committee for Responsible Medicine (PCRM), which is well known for opposing animal research, generally takes this approach. Contrary to its name, PCRM is not a group of physicians advocating for better medical practices. According to *Newsweek*, less than 5 percent of its members are actually doctors.[19] During PCRM's formative years, PETA donated more than a million dollars to the group—not because it supports objective science and the best medical practices, but because it promotes animal rights and argues vociferously for vegetarianism behind a façade of advocacy for responsible medical practices.[20]

PCRM's leader is Dr. Neal Barnard, a psychiatrist by training who has never actually practiced that discipline but has instead pursued animal rights activism and nutritional research.[21] Demonstrating his zeal, in 2001, Barnard co-signed hundreds of letters with Kevin Jonas, the founder of SHAC (later imprisoned for crimes not involving Barnard), urging recipients to break their links with Huntingdon Life Sciences.[22] Together with the "Christian vegetarian" and ophthalmology professor Stephen R. Kaufman, Barnard has argued that animal testing, while sometimes "intellectually seductive," is

> poorly suited to addressing the urgent health problems of our era, such as heart disease, cancer, stroke, AIDS, and birth defects. Even worse, animal experiments can mislead researchers or even contribute to illnesses or deaths by failing to predict toxic effects of drugs. Fortunately, other, more reliable methods that represent a far better investment of research funds can be employed.[23]

Misdirecting attention from the actual place of animals in the research process—and the limited purposes to which they are put—Barnard and Kaufman claim that "Animal 'models' are, at best analogous to human conditions, but no theory can be proved or refuted by analogy. Thus, it makes no logical sense to test a theory about humans using animals."[24]

This might be true—*if* animal research were the be-all and end-all of the research enterprise. But it is not. Rather, animal experimentation is merely one important tool out of many that produce biological knowledge and help determine which medical products should move forward into more advanced studies and which should be abandoned. Hence, rather than generally coming at the end of experimental processes, animal studies are important *toward the beginning*—as we saw with Dr. Edward Taub's monkeys, which proved his novel theory about the plasticity of the brain, allowing him to develop the constraint-induced movement therapy that is now—no thanks to Alex Pacheco and PETA—helping so many paralyzed people around the world.

PETA also denies that animal research provides valuable benefits. And like others of its ilk, the organization contends that superior experimental means are available for use in place of animal studies. For example, PETA states on its website:

> Animals are routinely cut open, poisoned, and forced to live in barren steel cages for years, although studies show that because of vast physiological variations between species, human reactions to illnesses and drugs are completely different from those of other animals. Today's non-animal research methods are humane, more accurate, less expensive, and less time-consuming than animal experiments, yet change comes slowly and many researchers are unwilling to switch to superior technological advances. Animal experimentation not only is preventing us from learning more relevant information, it continues to harm and kill animals and people every year.[25]

There are indeed other research methods that can and should be used in place of animals where appropriate, but these methods *cannot replace all animal research.* Thus P. Michael Conn of the Oregon National Primate Research Center, writing with James V. Parker, says in *The Animal Research War* that "animal models allow closer approximation to human response" than other forms of research, such as computer models and test tube experiments, that are also conducted prior to human trials. "They are not perfect, of course; animals host different diseases and different responses." But the "fundamentals of life are the same." Thus, "some animals are good human-like models for one thing and some for another; some have a cardiovascular system that is similar to humans while others have similar skin."[26]

Ingrid Newkirk attempted to refute the scientific arguments for animal research in an *Animal Times* article, which contained the following sidebar:

> Here are some rebuttals to vivisectors' favorite arguments:
>
> **"We must observe the complex interactions of cells, tissues and organs."**

Yes, in human beings, not by taking healthy animals from different species, artificially inducing a condition, and then trying to apply the results to us. Interactions vary enormously from species to species. For example, penicillin kills guinea pigs, aspirin kills cats, and morphine, a depressant in humans, stimulates horses.

Although tested as "safe" on animals, many drugs—including phenactin, E-Ferol, Oraflex, Zomax, Suprol, and Selacryn—had to be taken off the market after causing death or illness in thousands of people. More than half the drugs the Food and Drug Administration approved between 1976 and 1985 had to be withdrawn or relabeled because of serious side effects.[27]

Newkirk, however, "forgot" to mention a crucial point that undermines her entire thesis: These and other drugs that have been recalled or relabeled over the years didn't go straight from animal tests to your local pharmacist's shelves. In fact, no scientist claims that the results of animal testing correlate directly with effects on humans, which is why drugs that first pass animal toxicity and efficacy studies must then go through extensive human trials before they enter medicine's armamentarium. Thus, even if animal testing failed to uncover dangers that later came to the fore, so too did human testing. On the other hand, animal testing often prevents toxic drugs from ever being tried on humans. Thus, Newkirk's evidence is specious and misleading. But what else is new?

The "Science Page" on SHAC's website bears the statement "Words mean nothing, action is everything." Given the organization's irrationality and fanatical zeal, the slogan is apt; yet SHAC uses words to prevaricate and deceive, making baldly false assertions about the benefits of animal research and citing statistics that are irrelevant or misleading. For example, SHAC claims that "40% of patients suffer side effects as a result of prescription treatment." So what? Side effects from prescribed medications—which can range from the very mild, such as dry mouth, to the deadly—are hardly the result of animal experimentation. Moreover, animal testing often identifies these side effects before they reach the stage of human testing.

SHAC also repeats the oft-stated animal rights canard that animal testing impeded rather than helped the development of the polio vaccine, stating, "Polio researchers were misled for years about how we catch the disease because they had experimented on monkeys." The implication is that these tests delayed the development of the vaccine that has obliterated the disease in most of the world; but the truth is quite to the contrary.

Yes, monkeys were used early in the fight against polio and their rate of infection proved to be different from that of humans. But this did not delay the creation of the vaccine. The early monkey studies occurred during the 1920s and 1930s, before science developed the microscopic technology to view the poliomyelitis virus directly. Thus, "the only way to study the then totally invisible virus was to show its presence by the paralysis it produced on administration to the spinal cord of monkeys."[28] Had scientists not used monkeys for this purpose, they would have had to infect people in order to observe and understand the disease's progression.

More to the point, using animals did not delay the Salk and Sabin vaccines, but rather enabled these lifesaving medicines to be developed. This became possible after scientists successfully isolated and cultured the polio virus from mouse brain. It was then injected into the brains of white mice, which contracted the disease, thus verifying that the isolated virus—now observed—was indeed polio. Proof that the virus was replicating in cultures was obtained by injecting both monkeys and mice, which soon became paralyzed with the disease. The only alternative to using these animals in this way would have been to inject humans with the polio virus!

It is worth noting that these animal experiments led directly to a full understanding of the workings of the polio virus (for which the scientists won the 1954 Nobel Prize in Medicine), which in turn allowed Salk and Sabin to create their lifesaving vaccines.[29] Thanks in part to animal research, polio is today on the verge of complete eradication from the planet, a magnificent human achievement that simply would not have occurred had mice and monkeys been deemed off limits in polio research.[30]

Treating AIDS

To gauge the value of animal research in medical science, one need only consider its role in combating AIDS, the modern equivalent of the polio scourge. As Steven L. Teitelbaum—a professor at Washington University

School of Medicine and former president of the Federation of the American Societies for Experimental Biology—editorialized in *Science* magazine, "Our knowledge of the AIDS virus thus far could not have been achieved without the use of animal research."[31]

For example, research with chimpanzees determined that AIDS originated with the mutation of a virus commonly found in a subspecies of the animal in Africa—which intriguingly does not make the animals sick. As reported by *Newsweek* in 1999:

> Few things in life are more satisfying than solving a mystery—especially if it involves 14 million deaths and has stumped the world for nearly 20 years. So imagine the satisfaction of Dr. Beatrice Hahn of the University of Alabama at Birmingham. On Sunday she announced to a conference of virologists in Chicago that she'd learned the origins of HIV-1, the virus responsible for 99 percent of the world's 33 million AIDS cases. Her findings ... confirm what scientists have long suspected—that the virus came originally from an African primate. Hahn and her colleagues were able to trace it specifically to a subspecies of chimpanzee called *Pan troglodytes*.

The scientists created a genetic family tree comparing the human HIV virus with the chimpanzee SIV form of the pathogen. They next verified that the chimp subspecies lives in West Central Africa, where HIV is thought to have originated. The work also found the mode of transmission from chimp to human:

> The animals have long been hunted for food, so blood from the carcasses could easily have entered the hunters' bodies through superficial wounds. Hahn's group showed how, after jumping the species on at least three occasions, chimpanzee SIV evolved into the three families of HIV-1 strains recognized today.[32]

Monkeys and chimpanzees remain crucial in the unfinished quest for an AIDS vaccine. As two scientists writing in *Nature* reported:

> During the 1980s and 1990s, chimpanzees played a critical role in clarifying our basic understanding of HIV-1, and in the testing of potential vaccines. However, few HIV-1 infected chimpanzees progressed to a state of immunodeficiency. And the usefulness of studying the progression of AIDS was

eventually displaced by work with monkeys, in which HIV-1-like viruses produce infections and clinical signs resembling those in humans suffering from AIDS. Nevertheless, chimpanzees are the only natural animal model that can be infected with HIV-1. Thus, they are still important for testing vaccines aimed at preventing HIV-1 infection or reducing the virus loads of infected individuals.[33]

Would we prefer that human subjects had died instead? Or should this important and potentially lifesaving work not be done at all? Newkirk told us her answer back at the height of the AIDS epidemic in 1989: "Even if animal tests produced a cure for AIDS, we'd be against it."[34]

There haven't been any cures for AIDS discovered yet, but important treatments that extend lives and improve its quality have been found—and all required animals in their development. For example, Merck's protease inhibitor, brand name Crixivan, a medicine that dramatically reduces HIV levels in an infected patient's system, could not have been brought safely to market but for animal testing. As recounted in *Science*, Merck discovered the three-dimensional structure of HIV's protease (an enzyme involved in viral replication) and published the finding in 1989. This opened the way for developing "protease inhibitors" that could, in theory, prevent the HIV virus from multiplying.

Using methods that did not involve animals, Merck's scientists designed a protease inhibitor, known as L-689,502, that looked extremely promising for use in treating AIDS patients. But before it could ethically be tried in human beings, regulations required that the compound first be tested safely in large animals to predict how it would react in a living human body.

All eight dogs that were used to test the inhibitor "suffered serious liver damage," which raised concern that L-689,502 was too dangerous for human trials. Forced back to the drawing board, Merck developed a new chemical structure known as L-735,524. "The drug had high potency in the test tube and moved into animal studies that summer. No red lights flared," which opened the door for human trials. The drug became generally available in 1996 and since then has saved the lives and alleviated the suffering of millions of people who are living with AIDS.[35] Had the wrong formula been put into human testing without a prior assessment of its safety in animals, the resulting human deaths could have devastated that entire field of inquiry.

Now, look how this story was spun by animal rights activists, who claimed that rather than save human lives and help Merck get the right medicine into human trials, the dog testing slowed the progress of protease inhibitors into the medical marketplace. The animal rights activist Peter Tatchell put the charge this way:

> The initial development of these highly effective anti-HIV therapies was, it appears, seriously compromised by reliance on animal testing. In possibly one of the biggest medical scandals of recent times, there was a four-year delay in the clinical trials of protease inhibitor treatments. This may have contributed to the needless deaths of tens of thousands of people world-wide.[36]

So when animal safety testing demonstrated that the protease inhibitor needed more work before it could be used by humans, activists twisted this into the lie that the animal work unconscionably delayed the desperately needed treatments.[37] Such cruel fabrications and/or ignorant advocacy are rife within the animal rights movement, sowing confusion and misunderstanding about the integrated role that animal testing plays in the development of medical modalities.

In 2008, scientists announced they had created a technique by which animal parts and potentially even organs could be transplantable into humans—something already done with pig heart valves—without the body's immune system rejecting the tissues. The *Telegraph* reported:

> Scientists have overcome the problem of rejection, which has previously prevented animal tissues from being used in patients. It opens the way for a range of new procedures using animal parts. Children could be given pigs' heart valves that can grow with them, avoiding the need for repeated surgery; tissues such as ligaments, which have previously been difficult or impossible to repair, could be replaced; and eye patients could even be provided with new corneas.
>
> By stripping the animal tissue of its cells with a series of chemical treatments, the scientists were left with a biological scaffold that provides a structure but no longer carries the factors that can trigger a recipient's body to

reject a transplant. When the scaffold is surgically inserted into the patient's body, his or her own cells grow into it to create new tissue.

Because the patient's own cells fill the scaffold to create the tissue, scientists say there are no problems with rejection and the tissues are also able to regenerate, allowing them to last longer.[38]

Developing this technique to the point where it has advanced to the very brink of human trials unquestionably required animal research. And if it should become part of medicine's armamentarium, the lives of animals will have to be taken to save those of human beings. One can still claim, of course, that such experiments and potential lifesaving uses are unethical because it is immoral to treat animals in such an instrumental fashion. What cannot be claimed in the face of such astonishing scientific advances is that human beings do not benefit substantially from animal research.

Vilifying Researchers

Misleading the public about the scientific validity of animal research is bad enough. But some animal rights—and even welfare—activists go further, trying to undermine the public's faith in the character of scientists by denigrating animal researchers as so many sadists who cruelly subject animals to pointless suffering. Dr. Elliot Katz, the founder of In Defense of Animals, put it this way on the organization's website:

> You can't imagine the shock I felt when I first came face to face with the horrors that were befalling millions, in some cases billions, of animals in our nation's laboratories and fur and factory farms, our nation's puppy mills.
>
> As a veterinarian, I'd been trained to help animals—to relieve their pain—to heal their wounds. I had been taught not to stand by or turn my back while animals suffer and die—certainly not to purposely burn them or beat them, poison them or starve them, blind them or electrocute them, addict or infect them.[39]

Are "puppy mills" wrong? You bet! But the inhumane raising of pedigreed dogs by an unscrupulous minority within the dog breeding industry should never be conflated with the proper and humane use of animals in medical research. (We will take up the issues of fur and industrially raised meat later.) Unfortunately, depicting researchers as sadists is standard fare in animal rights advocacy.

Another case in point: The former PETA educator Gary Yourofsky used even more vivid and incendiary language in an article published in Abolitionist-Online in 2005, comparing animal research to "mentally retarded children" being kept "in tiny cages at the National Institutes of Health waiting to be mutilated, blinded, burnt, and killed by a vivisectionist."[40] And who could forget Peter Singer's prophecy that "Surely one day . . . our children's children, reading about what was done in laboratories in the twentieth century, will feel the same sense of horror and incredulity at what otherwise civilized people could do that we now feel when we read about the atrocities of the Roman gladiatorial arenas or the eighteenth-century slave trade."[41]

Even the supposedly moderate and responsible animal welfare activist Matthew Scully denigrated the ethics of medical researchers in his book *Dominion*. Scandalously depicting animal research as "the beginnings of evil," he wrote:

> In our own day, we might with justice call most animal testing and experimentation "meat science" for the researchers seem to have lost all regard for their subjects as anything more than that. The same attitude that can view wildlife as only commodities, and livestock only as production units, can see in primates, dogs, cats, rabbits, mice, and rats that dream only research tools there to serve every inquiry, however idle, repetitive, or purely commercial. It is as if every animal in our day is falling a level in the order of creation . . . laboratory animals to the level of microbes or cell cultures one need not even treat as living, feeling beings at all.[42]

This is defamatory. Talk to any animal researcher—and I have talked with many—and you will learn, contrary to Scully's baseless accusation, that researchers endure the gut-wrenching work of experimenting upon and euthanizing animals not because they don't care about the animals in their charge, but rather because they hope their work will add to human knowledge and help alleviate human (and animal) suffering. One can disagree with animal research as a matter of ethics, one can legitimately argue that animal research sometimes takes us down false paths in science's quest for cures, but it is unfair and wrong to allege or imply that these dedicated scientists are sadists who enjoy inflicting pain on helpless animals.

14

Our System of Animal Research

In late 2002, public health professionals were terrified. A new and deadly disease given the name "severe acute respiratory syndrome," or SARS, had sickened thousands of people in Vietnam and China. Hundreds had died. The threat of a worldwide pandemic was real and growing.

A crucial step in combating the disease was identifying its cause. Based on the symptoms and the tissue samples of its victims, many scientists suspected that a previously unknown coronavirus—a virus closely related to the microbe that causes the common cold—was the SARS pathogen. But they weren't sure. There was also evidence that it might be caused by the matapneumovirus, an altogether different microbe.

To find the precise cause of the deadly and fast spreading disease, scientists conducted a standard research protocol used in such cases to learn what virus or bacteria causes a particular illness. They placed the suspect coronavirus into the nostrils of monkeys to see if they would become ill. Most did. After the animals died or were euthanized, their lungs were studied microscopically to see whether the damage caused by the induced disease was similar to that suffered by its human victims. The results matched. As a direct consequence of these necessary animal studies, on April 16, 2003—only months after the disease first appeared—World Health Organization researchers announced that the "SARS-associated coronavirus" caused severe acute respiratory syndrome.[1]

Successful identification of the SARS virus empowered public health officials to move on to the next steps of combating the disease. First came a reliable diagnostic test. Efforts were also begun to develop a vaccine—a process that requires animal testing. For example, after a proposed vaccine stimulated a proper immune response in mice, it went into Phase 1 human testing (about which more below) to determine safety.[2] All in all, what could have been a catastrophe was limited to a tragedy: According to the WHO, 8,098 people worldwide became sick with SARS during the 2002–2003 crisis, of whom 774 died.[3]

If animal rights/liberationists had their way, this urgent mission of mercy to identify SARS would have been hampered significantly because researchers would not have been able to use animals in their work. Moreover, the alternatives that animal liberationists promote in lieu of animal work—computer simulations, human cell lines, autopsy reports, case studies, and the like—would simply not have been sufficient to get the job done. Indeed, the swift and accurate identification of the cause of SARS aptly illustrates why animals are so important to medical and scientific progress and the alleviation of human suffering.

On an altogether different front, monkeys may be paving the way for paralyzed people to use their brains to control mechanical arms with just their thoughts. As the *New York Times* reported:

> The researchers . . . used monkeys partly because of their anatomical similarities to humans and partly because they are quick learners. In the experiment, two macaques first used a joystick to gain a feel for the arm, which had shoulder joints, an elbow and a grasping claw with two mechanical fingers.
>
> Then, just beneath the monkeys' skulls, the scientists implanted a grid about the size of a large freckle. It sat on the motor cortex, over a patch of cells known to signal arm and hand movements. The grid held 100 tiny electrodes, each connecting to a single neuron, its wires running out of the brain and to a computer. The monkeys learned to hold the grip open on approaching the food, close it just enough to hold the food and gradually loosen the grip when feeding.

Why not use humans now in the research instead of monkeys? "Scientists have to clear several hurdles before this technology becomes practical, experts said. Implantable electrode grids do not generally last more than a period of months, for reasons that remain unclear."[4] Thus, it is either subject humans to repeated brain surgery, use monkeys, or abandon this promising field altogether.

An Integrated Approach to Science

Animal experimentation is a multilayered process within an integrated system of scientific advancement and medical progress. It involves both basic research, meaning investigations into how organisms behave or function, and applied research, meaning experiments that look for solutions to identified problems. Dr. Edward Taub—the researcher unjustly accused of abusing the Silver Spring monkeys, who nevertheless succeeded in bringing constraint-induced movement therapy (CIMT) to the world—told me that animals are essential to obtaining biological knowledge in preparation for more advanced work that sometimes culminates in new medical therapies. "When you start out," he told me, "there is no light at the end of the tunnel, that is, you don't have the knowledge needed to move your work forward."

The first step in the process is to formulate the research project and write a proposal that convinces the researcher's peers that the project deserves support. Then, the researcher must obtain funding, which requires the submission of a specific research protocol. Assuming all goes well—and most proposals do not get this far—experimentation begins. Often, the protocol will include research with animals to learn whether the hypotheses being investigated are actually worth pursuing in more advanced studies.

In many ways, this is a process of elimination: "Most ideas turn out to be wrong," Taub said, "but once in a while something comes through."[5] It certainly did for Taub, as we saw in Chapter 2, when he proved that the primate brain exhibits plasticity, opening the door to his eventual development of CIMT. Moreover, the basic research that Taub conducted on monkeys garnered new knowledge from which other scientists might be inspired to new brainstorms that could improve the human condition. Basic research explains more of life's mysteries, and its benefits are multiplied as the knowledge derived is put to uses that may not have been contemplated when the initial experimentation began.

A more recent example of basic research comes in the emerging field of nanotechnology. Nanotech, as it is known, involves the engineering of functional systems on a very tiny scale, perhaps at the molecular level. These extremely tiny mechanisms, much smaller than the width of a human hair, may have wonderful medical applications, but they are also potentially dangerous if injected into the body. Learning whether and how nanotech may become medically useful thus cannot progress without the use of animals.

One such experiment looked into whether nanotech could become useful as a diagnostic tool to find cancer tumors at a very early stage when the lesions are far smaller than can be detected by current imaging methods. Determining the feasibility of this approach cannot be done on computers or with tissue cultures. It requires a living, breathing organism with a circulatory system—hence, animals.

The earliest animal work involved rodents, specifically mice, as the *San Francisco Chronicle* reported:

> Stanford scientists are blending the latest in nanotechnology with a quirky light effect discovered in the 1920s to create a new way to scan for tumors— a process that is potentially safer and more sensitive than current cancer screens....
>
> Today's most advanced cancer diagnostic tools, such as PET scans, can pick up a tumor about 5 millimeters wide—containing tens of millions of cancerous cells. The new technique, called Raman imaging, has the potential to detect microscopic clumps of only a few hundred cancer cells.
>
> A more precise test for cancer such as this one might pick up the disease more quickly and give surgeons a more complete picture of where the tumors are that need to be removed. The experimental Raman imaging system has been tested only on mice, but it could be ready for human clinical trials in a year.... The goal will be to detect colon cancer.[6]

If this nanotechnology works, not only will colon cancer be detected at earlier stages, but many people who are squeamish about having colonoscopies will be more likely to accept preventive screening.

Given the tremendous lifesaving potential of this area of study, activists against animal research should be forced to answer a simple question: How could this fruitful work have proceeded without animals? In order to test the new technique, the scientists first needed to know that the animals had cancer, and thus the cancer was induced. The scientists also needed to know if the technology detected the tumors, requiring that the mice be euthanized and their tissues studied to gauge how the imagers performed. The safety of injecting nano-imagers into the body also had to be observed, since if they caused harm, the entire concept of nano-imagery would have to be rethought or abandoned.

This was work that couldn't have been done adequately with tissue lines, cadavers, or computer programs. It required living organisms, either animals or humans. Inducing cancer in humans and then euthanizing and dissecting them would be a serious violation of human rights. Thus, we had the same simple choice that faces us in much of the life sciences: Either we eschew this potential boon to human health "for the animals"— the position of animal rights activists—or we use animals as research subjects "for the people." What we cannot do with intellectual integrity is assert that animal research offers no scientific benefit.

Basic research with animals has also been essential in the field of regenerative medicine, a new approach to medicine that offers great hope for some of humankind's most intractable medical conditions. According to the National Institutes of Health,

> Regenerative medicine is the process of creating living, functional tissues to repair or replace tissue or organ function lost due to age, disease, damage, or congenital defects. This field holds the promise of regenerating damaged tissues and organs in the body by stimulating previously irreparable organs to heal themselves.[7]

Parkinson's disease is an example of a degenerative medical condition that scientists hope to alleviate or cure with regenerative medical methods. Parkinson's is caused when certain brain cells become diseased, interfering with the production of a substance called dopamine that helps control bodily movements. At present there is no cure, and while current treatments can slow down the disease progress, eventually the condition results in serious disability.

The suffering caused by degenerative diseases such as Parkinson's is not a mere abstraction, but a tragedy that afflicts the actual lives of real people. Animal research is essential to finding efficacious treatments—

perhaps even a cure for Parkinson's—through regenerative medical techniques.

One emerging field of research toward this end involves stem cells, with animal studies an essential component. For example, many scientists hoped that embryonic stem cells (ESC) could be used to rebuild the areas of the brain afflicted by Parkinson's.[8] But thanks to early animal work, they soon learned that while embryonic stem cells may offer the potential to treat Parkinson's symptoms, their use also poses significant risks. As reported in the *Proceedings of the National Academy of Sciences* in December 2000, researchers at Harvard Medical School and McLean Hospital in Belmont, Massachusetts, injected mouse embryonic stem cells into rats in an attempt to alleviate Parkinson's-like symptoms. Of the twenty-five rats receiving the injections, fourteen showed modest improvement while six showed no benefit and five died of brain tumors caused by the embryonic stem cells. In other words, the hoped-for treatment actually *killed one-fifth of the animal subjects.*[9] Because animal research disclosed that embryonic stem cells cause tumors, human trials have not been allowed.

The exciting possibility that adult stem cells—which would come from the patient's own body rather than from embryos—could offer hope for the development of a Parkinson's treatment has been demonstrated in animal studies by researchers at Griffith University in Australia:

> Project leader Professor Alan Mackay-Sim said researchers simulated Parkinson's symptoms in rats by creating lesions on one side of the brain similar to the damage Parkinson's causes in the human brain. "The lesions to one side of the brain made the rats run in circles," he said. "When stem cells from the nose of Parkinson's patients were cultured and injected into the damaged area the rats re-acquired the ability to run in a straight line.
>
> "All animals transplanted with the human cells had a dramatic reduction in the rate of rotation within just 3 weeks," he said. "This provided evidence the cells had differentiated to give rise to dopamine-producing neurons influenced by being in the environment of the brain. In-vitro tests also revealed the presence of dopamine."
>
> "Significantly, none of the transplants led to formation of tumors or teratomas in the host rats as has occurred after embryonic stem cell transplantation in a similar model."[10]

Animal research was clearly indispensable in the invention of "induced pluripotent stem cells" (IPSCs), which may provide all the hoped-for benefits of ESCs while avoiding the moral controversy raised by ESC research with its destruction of human embryos. IPSCs were first developed by a Japanese scientist named Shinya Yamanaka when his team inserted four genes into the skin cells of rats, and thereby "reprogrammed" these cells into a new kind of stem cells. To prove that IPSCs were pluripotent—that is, theoretically capable of being transformed into every type of tissue—Yamanaka then transplanted the cells into mice. Upon dissection, the team found that tumors had formed in all three basic tissue types of the body—a big breakthrough that would clearly have been impossible without the animal experimentation.[11]

Because this approach worked in mice, it was subsequently tried successfully in making human IPSCs, which were found to "meet the defining criteria we originally proposed for human ES cells (14), with the significant exception that the IPS cells are not derived from embryos."[12] This human work in the test tube and in cultural medium was followed up with further animal research, demonstrating that IPSCs alleviated the symptoms of a Parkinson's-like disease in rats. As *Forbes* reported:

> A novel and untested stem cell therapy has significantly improved the symptoms of Parkinson's disease in rats, according to a study released Monday. Researchers at the Whitehead Institute for Biomedical Research in Cambridge, Massachusetts, used a relatively new technique to re-engineer stem cells from skin cells and then treat rats with the debilitating neurological disease. When the rats were tested weeks after the cell transplant, their Parkinson's symptoms were significantly reduced, confirming that these substitutes for embryonic stem cells, so-called reprogrammed stem cells, can replace lost or damaged neurons.[13]

Animal research also disclosed that IPSCs, like ESCs, cause tumors.

Regenerative medicine is still in its infancy and only time will tell whether it transforms clinical medical practice as its proponents hope. But this much is sure: Without animal testing—and the knowledge thereby derived—regenerative medicine would die aborning.

Drug Testing

During the postwar period, the United States developed a method of testing pharmaceuticals and medical appliances that requires the use of animals. This field is governed by the Federal Food, Drug, and Cosmetic Act, which granted the FDA the authority to make rules and regulations and to develop policies that control how drugs, vaccines, treatments, and medical devices are brought from initial concept to the medical clinic.[14]

The rules, regulations, and policies required of scientists in bringing new medical products, vaccines, and drugs to the clinic involve the use of animals as an early part of a very complex, time-consuming, and expensive process that also includes other modalities such as computer models and cell lines as well as human trials—all of which are designed to protect human safety and promote human well-being.[15] The U.S. Food and Drug Administration describes several stages in drug approval. First, scientists "probe the effects of chemical compounds on enzymes, cell cultures or other substances" affected by the disease that the drug is intended to treat. Then, the chemicals shown to be potentially effective must be applied in "two or more species of animals to determine whether they can be safely used in humans."

No more than five in five thousand tested compounds pass these preclinical trials allowing human testing to begin. There are three stages of human trials that usually take several years to complete, with the progress to the next stage of experimentation depending on the successful outcome of the previous one:

+ Phase I studies test the product for adverse effects on a small number of healthy volunteers.
+ Phase II studies prove the drug's effectiveness in patients who have the disease or condition that the product is intended to treat.
+ Phase III studies determine the drug's safety, effectiveness, and dosage. In these trials, hundreds or thousands of patients are randomly assigned to be treated with either the tested drug or a control substance, usually a placebo.
+ The results of Phase III are then submitted to the FDA for review by a team of chemists, physicians, epidemiologists, and other specialists.[16]

If after all this it is found that the product's health benefits outweigh the risks, then the drug may be approved for marketing. Thus, while animal testing is a crucial link in drug testing—essential to reduce the potential for harm to human trial participants—it is only one link. The fact that despite all this effort some drugs still cause harm demonstrates the complexity of the problem of developing efficacious and safe medicines, not the inaptness of animal testing.

Toxicology Testing

The field that animal rights activists make the most hay about (sometimes righteously) is testing the safety of finished products, ranging from household cleansers and pesticides to cosmetics and food additives, as well as pharmaceuticals. The hyperbole over this issue makes it difficult to differentiate fact from fiction in judging the propriety of using animals in this way. For example, PETA stated in one of its publications that "tests on animals don't make hazardous products safe. Bleach isn't safe to drink just because it was forced down rats' throats."[17] This accusation goes without any supporting citation, no doubt because testing labs are not actually forcing any animals to drink bleach.

This isn't to say that all the toxicology and safety testing done today is necessary. But it is to say that testing is not done because companies want to be cruel. Rather, such toxicology studies are generally performed because they are legally required or are deemed necessary to ensure that human consumers are not harmed.

The test that is most often complained about by animal rights activists is the "Draize" method of checking to see whether a product might harm the human eye. There is no question that the Draize test is not pleasant to consider: a small amount of the product being tested is dripped into the eye or on the skin of an albino rabbit to see whether there is a serious adverse reaction. Animal rights activists are fond of publishing vivid and stomach-churning pictures of rabbits with puffed-up red eyes, coupled with the allegation that the damage was caused by researchers pouring bleach or some other known toxic substance into the animals' eyes.

Don't believe it. What animal rights/liberationist propaganda doesn't disclose is that the Draize method *is no longer used to identify corrosive or irritating materials.* Rather, *non-animal testing is used first* to determine whether the product is corrosive or irritating. *Only* if a product is found to be nonirritating is it put into the eyes or on the skin of rabbits, to make sure.[18] And even this modern Draize method contains safeguards. Thus the Research Defense Society points out: "In its current form it is a very mild test, in which small amounts of substances believed to be non-irritants are used, and are washed out of the eye at the first sign of any irritation."[19]

Still, there is no question that it would be preferable to do away with the Draize method altogether if it could be done consistent with public safety. A major international effort to find substitutes is under way—in part, it must be admitted, because of the public concern raised by animal rights advocacy, even though it is often misleading. But until these new approaches are developed, the current mild test will still have to be used, and animal rights activists will continue to mislead the public about caustic materials being poured into rabbits' eyes in labs all over the world, even though they know that it is no longer true.

Acute toxic testing uses rats and mice to determine the amount of a substance that could cause death or serious harm to humans. The National Academy of Sciences describes how this is done:

> The test animals, typically rodents (rats or mice) are observed for a period of several days to 2 weeks after dosing, and observations of deviant behavior, growth, or mortality are recorded. Historically, the primary focus of an acute toxicity test was to determine a chemical's median lethal dose (LD_{50}), the dose that causes death in 50% of the test animals. Today, acute toxicity tests are used also to determine dosing regimens for longer-term toxicity tests and to evaluate more fully the effects of acute exposure.[20]

Acute toxicity testing in rats and mice reveals much valuable information beyond the immediate effect of the toxic substance. For example, "Acute studies reveal whether frank toxicity [obvious, strong, or direct toxicity] is sudden, delayed, time-limited, or continuous." They also provide "insight into the time course of absorption, distribution, and clearance of a toxicant." For the time being, such tests offer "at least one relatively quick and inexpensive tool in testing schemes that screen large numbers of chemicals and identify chemicals that warrant further toxicity testing."[21] While it would certainly be nice if tests could be developed that didn't take the lives of mice and rats, at present they just don't exist.

Animals are also necessary for chronic toxicity and to determine the propensity of a substance to cause cancer (carcinogenicity). In the United States, the Environmental Protection Agency's guidelines specify that "testing should be performed with two mammalian species, one a rodent and the other a nonrodent. The rat is the preferred rodent species and the dog is the preferred nonrodent species."[22] Again, it must be stressed that such tests are not conducted to be cruel but to protect human health and safety.

Similarly, the cancer risk a substance may pose is tested "for a minimum of 24 months (rats) and 18 months (mice)," and the tests "are designed to provide data for cancer-hazard identification and dose-response evaluation."[23] After the testing, the animals are euthanized and their tissues extensively tested to determine whether any cancers have formed. Such testing is required by law and government regulation. And because cancer testing depends on living organisms in which cancers can develop, there simply is no substitute for using animals—as unpleasant as that may be.

❧•☙

Space does not permit a full exploration of all the purposes and methods of animal testing. But it is clear that animal testing is necessary to protect human health and promote human welfare, and it will be so for the foreseeable future. Moreover, much of the work that is done is legally required, meaning that activists who protest against particular labs are spitting into the wind. This doesn't mean that we should not explore ways to reduce the need for animals wherever we can. But it does mean that all the hue and cry of animal rights activists about how animal testing is unnecessary and/or harmful is so much bunk. And ask yourself this: If the activists are mendacious about this crucial matter, where else are they not telling the whole truth?

15

Ensuring the Proper Care of Lab Animals[1]

U nless one accepts Gary Francione's belief that animals have the absolute right not to be property, and hence not to be used instrumentally, animal research will continue in the quest to gain biological knowledge, develop medical treatments and cures, and protect the safety of patients. But this doesn't mean that we may treat animals in any way we choose. To the contrary, medical researchers understand their solemn obligation to conduct their important work in ways that minimize pain and discomfort to animals.

This moral obligation is also a legal requirement throughout most of the world. Different countries have developed different legal and regulatory standards to govern animal testing—some more and some less protective. In the United States, the primary law governing the use of animals is the Animal Welfare Act, first passed in 1966 and expanded several times thereafter, which allows the United States Department of Agriculture (USDA) to regulate the use of many warm-blooded animals in experiments (among other provisions).[2]

Under the Animal Welfare Act, medical researchers must give animals drugs to prevent pain and suffering (unless measuring pain is the purpose of the experiment). Each research facility has to have an Institutional Animal Care and Use Committee (IACUC) to approve and monitor each experiment involving animals, and inspect the facilities semiannually. Each IACUC is required to ensure that the researchers actually need to use animals in their experiments and that the animals are adequately housed and fed. To deter "rubberstamping," the committees are required to have at least three members, including one from the local community not affiliated in any way with the research facility and one veterinarian. Any practice that could cause pain to the animals requires that a veterinarian be consulted and that the animals receive tranquilizers, analgesics, anesthetics, and pre- and postsurgical care. If pain must be inflicted as part of the experiment, it can last only as long as necessary to accomplish the scientific purpose.

To ensure that these committees do their jobs properly, the federal government's Animal and Plant Health Inspection Service (APHIS) conducts surprise inspections to monitor the treatment of animals. Moreover, the Animal Welfare Act applies whether or not the experiment receives federal funding.

Animal rights activists dismiss these protections and note that they do not apply to mice, rats, or birds—which constitute well over 90 percent of the tens of millions of animals used in biomedical research each year. But there are good reasons for this approach. First, because the rats and mice are expensive—generally costing between ten and thirty dollars each—it would be economic folly to treat them poorly. Second, requiring that rats, birds, and mice receive the same protections as monkeys, dogs, and sheep would impose an undue burden on the scientific enterprise. According to Sally Satel, a psychiatrist and senior fellow at the American Enterprise Institute, extending coverage of the AWA and its attendant regulations to these animals would be prohibitively expensive, would reduce the ability to ensure that primates and other animals are protected, and in the end would serve no substantial purpose:

> According to the journal *Science* (Nov. 23), the USDA regulates about 2400 animal facilities. Adding rodents, the department estimates, would almost double the number of total research sites for inspection. The facilities themselves would also be hit hard. An analysis by the National Association for Biomedical Research estimates expenditures anywhere from $80 to $290 million a year for the paperwork burden alone. The Association of American Medical Colleges, which represents teaching hospitals and their large research enterprises, warns that reporting requirements will soar while animal welfare will not be improved "one iota."

Moreover, Satel points out correctly that abusing lab rats and mice would harm the research enterprise itself and go against the economic grain:

> Any facility getting research funds from the U.S. Public Health Service (e.g., NIH, all medical schools, teaching hospitals and major research-intensive universities) must take care of any rats, mice or birds according to the PHS`s Policy on Humane Care and Use of Laboratory Animals. They must also adhere to the Guide for the Care and Use of Laboratory Animals....
>
> What's more, regulations notwithstanding, it serves no one's interest to mistreat research animals. After all, stress upsets their immune, nervous and cardiovascular systems, thus skewing experimental results. Moreover, many mice now used in labs are "knockout mice," meaning a specific gene has been deleted or knocked out. Expensive and valuable, these mice take about 24 months to develop and play a key role in decoding the function of the specific genes (scientists compare the physiologic function of genetically intact mice with ones missing a given gene). To ensure their health and longevity, such mice are housed under germ-free conditions in climate-controlled rooms, given optimal nutrition and ready access to veterinarians.

So, what is the purpose of all the agitation? Satel nails the actual agenda squarely on the head: "The campaign to put rats, mice and birds under the AWA is not about their protection, it is a cynical ploy to liberate animals, no matter the toll on medical inquiry and, ultimately, on human suffering and disease."[3]

Even so, most rats, mice, and birds receive voluntary protection by being part of programs accredited by a private, nonprofit organization called the Association for Assessment and Accreditation of Laboratory Animal Care International. AAALAC grants or denies accreditation based upon the National Research Council's published criteria in *Guide for the Care and Use of Laboratory Animals* (1996), which generally follows the NIH formula, as well as other resources. With more than 750 programs in 29 countries having subjected themselves to AAALAC jurisdiction, the organization has undoubtedly brought wide improvement in the treatment of research animals.[4]

This is a record for which the AAALAC is justifiably proud. The organization's executive director, John G. Miller, told me:

It is my best scientific estimate that 90 percent-plus of all animals used in research—including rats, mice, birds, and other animals not covered by the AWA—are at facilities that have received full AAALAC accreditation. This includes all major pharmaceutical companies, all major contract research organizations (such as Huntingdon Life Sciences, Covance, etc.), most major biotech companies, and all major commercial producers of lab animals. Indeed, ninety-nine of the top 100 NIH (grant) awardees conducting animal research are accredited.[5]

This is above and beyond what the government requires by law or regulation, with the exception of Veterans Administration laboratories that use animals, which must be accredited by the AAALAC according to VA regulations.

Many of these rules are similar to those governing human experimentation. However, *animals actually enjoy greater protection* than do human subjects, since unlike federal regulations over human experimentation, the Animal Welfare Act applies *whether or not federal funding supports the experiment.* Moreover, experiments using people are not subject to surprise government inspections but must rely exclusively on institutional review boards (IRBs) for oversight. Further, there is no government agency equivalent to the Animal and Plant Health Inspection Service created explicitly to protect human subjects, no matter how vulnerable or defenseless the people being experimented upon may be, nor is there an organization that provides inspection and accreditation services equivalent to the AAALAC. As a consequence, according to Carl Cohen, a professor of philosophy at the University of Michigan,

> Opportunities to increase human safety ... are commonly missed; trials in which risks may be shifted from humans to animals are often not devised, sometimes not even considered. Why? For the investigator, the use of animals as subjects is often more expensive, in money and time, than the use of human subjects. Access to suitable human subjects is often quick and convenient, whereas access to appropriate animal subjects may be awkward, costly, and burdened with red tape.[6]

One can agree or disagree with Professor Cohen, but it is unreasonable to contend that scientists and laboratories do not exert great efforts to treat laboratory animals humanely. Of course, adherents to animal rights ideology regard any use of animals in research as abuse by definition. And in some places—particularly in Europe—they are gaining alarming traction. For example, a Swiss court outlawed research on macaques that was designed to learn how the brain adjusts to change.[7] But for those who believe that substantial benefit to humans (and animals) comes through such research, the efforts to ensure proper care are laudable and in keeping with the uniquely human moral obligation not to cause any animal gratuitous pain or unnecessary suffering.

The Three Rs

The vast majority of animals used in research today are "purpose-bred," meaning that they are raised, and in some cases genetically altered, for specific research purposes. There is also a pronounced emphasis on using small animals, with some 95 percent of animals used being rodents, frogs, or fish. But sometimes larger animals are required, such as dogs, cats, and primates. Some people may find it especially disturbing to learn that dogs are used in research, but there are reasons for it. First, government regulations require testing in animals other than rodents in many cases. And according to Frankie Trull, president of the Foundation for Biological Research, a nonprofit (and partially industry-funded) educational organization, many drug studies use dogs, especially purpose-bred beagles, "because they need animals that are of a manageable size, all from a known gene pool—to rule out extraneous variables—and because scientists have learned that dogs and humans metabolize compounds that pass over their gums in a very similar manner."[8] That isn't a pleasant thought, but using these dogs—none of which has been a pet—is a necessary part of some drug testing. Moreover, despite what some animal rights activists might tell you, few shelter animals end up in research, and those that do would otherwise have been euthanized.

Still, while the benefits derived from animal research are really beyond dispute and it is highly doubtful that animals can ever be eliminated totally from the research enterprise, where we can reduce the number of animals subjected to experimentation, we should. To that end, ethicists and the scientific community have developed an advocacy program known as the "Three Rs," for refinement, reduction, and replacement:

1. The goal of "refinement" is to encourage the modification of research protocols in order to minimize the pain and distress that research animals might feel in the experiment.
2. "Reduction" signifies the creation of strategies that will lead to fewer animals being used to obtain the same amount of research data, or increasing the amount of information obtained per animal so that fewer animals need to be used.
3. The idea behind "replacement," as the name implies, is to stimulate researchers to create alternatives to using animals in experiments at all.

The Three Rs are laudable, so long as the program's implementation does not interfere unduly with the research enterprise and is not perceived as an acknowledgment by research scientists that there is something wrong or immoral with using animals in the goal of reducing human suffering.

The good news, from an animal welfare perspective, is that scientists have developed several research methods that require fewer animals to advance knowledge without harm to humans. The increasing sophistication of computers now permits much theoretical research to be done in cyberspace rather than on laboratory operating tables. Similarly, using human cell lines instead of animals often provides researchers with valuable information that obviates the need to use animals. For example, a European scientific panel has approved 34 alternatives to using animals in toxic testing, with about 170 more on the way. (According to the *Washington Post*, a similar panel in the United States has moved much more slowly in approving alternatives.)[9] These techniques may work better than using animals in many specific research circumstances; and as long as they promote effective research, they should be vigorously pursued.

In the last one hundred years—because scientists humanely study, manipulate, and yes, kill and dissect research animals in the cause of gaining biological insights, curing disease, and promoting the greater human good—vaccines have been created, scientific knowledge has advanced, new lifesaving medical and surgical techniques have been developed, diseases have been cured, with more to come. And all this has alleviated human suffering and promoted human thriving. It also has served animals, for example in the development of vaccines against distemper, rabies, and feline leukemia. This scientific process will continue to provide great benefits to humankind and animals alike—unless ideologues in the animal rights movement succeed in bringing the research enterprise to its knees.

So, the next time you hear vapid movie stars and other celebrities supporting PETA (as they paradoxically wear red ribbons for AIDS awareness or pink for breast cancer), or you are subjected to gruesome and often anachronistic or staged pictures of animals supposedly being made to suffer unnecessarily in research laboratories, or you hear the histrionic moans from animal liberationists denying the benefits of using animals in research, or you read of ALF terrorists comparing themselves to Martin Luther King or Gandhi as they seek to rationalize their attacks on researchers, consider the bleak alternatives to animal testing. In the end, there are only two: impeding scientific progress across a wide stretch of medical and biological endeavors, or using vulnerable humans instead of animals. Both are unacceptable if we wish to improve the human condition and maintain our claims of being a good and compassionate moral community.

16

Meat Is Not Murder

Next to animal research, activists' primary target of protest is the meat industry. Animal rights believers loathe meat eating—even condemn it as "murder," although this term is applicable only to the killing of human beings—because it requires the raising and slaughter of food animals.[1] Arguments mounted by animal rights activists against eating meat range from the ethically based, to the scientific, to the pseudoscientific, to the environmental (which are beyond our scope here), to the outright ignorant. In considering some of their arguments, remember that even if meat eating extended the human life span to 150 years, animal rights/liberationists would still liken it to murder—or even, as we saw in our discussion of PETA's Holocaust on Your Plate campaign, to genocide.

Are We Omnivores or Herbivores?

Some activists argue that meat eating is not a natural human activity, asserting that rather than being omnivores, we are actually herbivores somehow gone terribly wrong. One such advocate is Dan Piraro, the fabulously successful author of the syndicated cartoon *Bizarro*. A fervent self-described animal rights believer, Piraro often advocates on behalf of his cause in his cartoons and has a special section boosting the ideology on his

Bizarro website. Supporting his thesis that humans are natural plant eaters, Piraro claims:

> The teeth of a carnivore are long and pointed, for tearing. Ours are blunt and flat by comparison.... The jaws of carnivores move up-and-down, but not side-to-side. This is because they tear off meat and swallow it whole. They don't chew. An herbivore's jaws move up-and-down AND side-to-side for grinding vegetation. The intestines of carnivores are short and simple, 3 to 6 times their body's length.... An herbivore's intestines are long and complex, 8 to 13 times their body's length.... A carnivore can eat rotting, bacteria-ridden meat completely raw without getting sick.... Ever try to eat road kill?... A carnivore is quick, cunning and without sympathy so that it can catch and kill other animals efficiently and without remorse. For the vast majority of human history we have been without tools, weapons, or fire. During this period, how many animals do you suppose we successfully caught, ate, and kept down?[2]

Piraro's argument relies heavily on misdirection and the ignorance of his readers. It is certainly true that we are not "carnivores" strictly speaking, but like our closest genetic cousin, the chimpanzee—which hunts and eats monkeys and other small animals—we naturally consume both vegetative food and animal flesh.

This scientific truth was set forth clearly by John McArdle, a professor of psychology at the University of Southern California, in "Evidence of Humans as Omnivores," a paper published by the Vegetarian Resource Group, a *pro-vegetarian* nonprofit organization that also publishes the *Vegetarian Journal.* "As far back as it can be traced," Dr. McArdle notes, "clearly the archeological record indicates an omnivorous diet for humans that included meat. Our ancestry is among the hunter/gatherers from the beginning. Once domestication of food sources began, it included both animals and plants."[3]

One look at the famous and beautiful cave drawings in France, such as those at Lascaux and Chauvet, proves Dr. McArdle's point. Thought to be 25,000 to 30,000 years old, the drawings vividly depict the animals that early man hunted for sustenance. But that is nothing compared with other evidence that meat has been a natural food for humans probably for as long as we have existed as a species. Humans have consumed animal flesh—either as scavengers or as hunters—for well over one million years. Some scientists theorize that we became directed meat eaters in part because we learned how to cook; others posit that our eating of meat resulted from improved hunting techniques.[4]

But what about the biology of our jaws and intestines? McArdle states, "Evidence on the structure and function of human hands and jaws, behavior, and evolutionary history ... either support an omnivorous diet or fail to support strict vegetarianism." The best evidence, he claims, comes from our teeth. "The short canines in humans are a functional consequence of the enlarged cranium and associated reduction of the size of the jaws.... Interestingly, the primates with the largest canines (gorillas and gelada baboons) both have basically vegetarian diets. In archeological sites, broken human molars are most often confused with broken premolars and molars of pigs, a classic omnivore."

Moreover, our guts are just not like those of herbivores: "Nearly all plant eaters have fermenting vats (enlarged chambers where food sits and microbes attack it). Ruminants like cattle and deer have forward sacs derived from remodeled esophagus and stomach. Horses, rhinos, and colobine monkeys have posterior, hindgut sacs. Humans have no such specializations."[5]

It is so clear that meat is a natural food for human beings that the matter is not worth belaboring further. That being so, it means, as McArdle states, that arguments against the meat industry must rest on morality (if it has a face, don't eat it), or welfare premises (ban the factory farm!), or health (meat is unwholesome), or environmental (meat eating is "destroying the planet").

"Humane Meat"

At one time, having meat whenever one desired would have been considered proof of extraordinary prosperity. No more. Meat is generally inexpensive and readily available to even the poorest among us in the United States. Today, many in and out of the animal rights movement disdain the ready availability of inexpensive meat because of the industrial methods developed in recent decades known as "concentrated animal feeding operations" (CAFOs).

Most pigs and poultry in the United States are not raised on the modern-day equivalent of Old McDonald's Farm, with an oink-oink here and a cluck-cluck there. Rather, a CAFO permits a large number of animals to be housed together, with specialization of techniques and greater efficiency. (Beef and lamb are not raised in this manner.) Animal rightists and most animal welfare advocates are united in their disgust for CAFOs, labeling them pejoratively as "factory farms." In PETA's lament,

> The green pastures and idyllic barnyard scenes of years past, which are still portrayed in children's books, have been replaced by windowless metal sheds, wire cages, gestation crates, and other confinement systems—what is now known as "factory farming."
>
> Farmed animals have no federal legal protection against horrific abuses that would be illegal if they were inflicted on dogs or cats: neglect, mutilations and drug regimens that cause chronic pain and crippling transports through all weather extremes, and inhumane slaughter. Yet farmed animals are no less sensitive, intelligent, or capable of feeling pain than are the dogs or cats whom we cherish as companions.[6]

Representatives and supporters of the meat industry vehemently deny this oft-made charge, asserting that modern methods keep the animals safer and healthier, as well as protecting the public from diseased meat. Thus, the nonprofit, pro-industry Animal Agriculture Alliance states on its website:

> Animals are generally kept in barns and similar housing, with the exception of beef cattle, to protect the health and welfare of the animal. Housing protects animals from predators, disease, and bad weather or extreme climate. Housing also makes breeding and birth less stressful, protects young animals, and makes it easier for farmers to care for both healthy and sick animals. Modern housing is well-ventilated, warm, well-lit, clean, and scientifically-designed to meet an animal's specific needs, including temperature, light, water and food. Because it is designed to meet specific needs, a hog barn wouldn't be used for cows, any more than an adult would sleep in a child's crib. Housing is designed to allow the farmer to provide the best animal care possible.[7]

But the greatest benefit of CAFOs—at least from industry and many consumers' perspectives—is that they allow many meat products to be produced inexpensively and thus fit well within most families' food budgets.

There is no question that the animals raised with industrial methods are not kept in natural environments; but it is also true that these animals have *never been* in natural settings and so cannot know what they are missing. Nevertheless, some animal welfare advocates urge consumers to restrict their meat eating to what is known as "humane meat," from animals raised on farms that permit more natural settings.

One of the chief proponents of organic meat is Michael Pollan, author of *The Omnivore's Dilemma: A Natural History of Four Meals*.[8] In this thoughtful book, Pollan searches for ethical ways to eat a variety of foods. Along the way, he makes a pertinent point that would cause animal rights true believers' blood to boil:

> As humans contemplating the suffering or pain of animals we do need to guard against projecting onto them what the same experience would feel like to us. Watching a steer force-marched up the ramp to the kill-floor door, as I have done, I have to forcibly remind myself this is not Sean Penn in *Dead Man Walking*, that the scene is playing very differently in the bovine brain, from which the concept of nonexistence is thankfully absent.[9]

Nor does Pollan believe it would ever be possible to cease killing animals even if we were all to become vegetarians, since clearing extra land for crops would merely involve the killing of different animals such as field mice and birds and animals that would eat the harvested crops:

> If America was suddenly to adopt a strictly vegetarian diet, it isn't at all clear that the total number of animals killed each year would necessarily decline, since to feed everyone animal pasture and rangeland would have to give way to more intensively cultivated row crops.

Indeed, he asserts that if the goal is to kill as few animals as possible, "people should probably try to eat the largest possible animal that can live on the least cultivated land: grass-finished steaks for everyone."[10] (More on this matter below.)

However, Pollan unequivocally loathes the CAFO, writing that "for all its technological sophistication," it is a place where animals "are treated as machines—'production units'—incapable of feeling pain. Since no think-ing person can possibly believe this anymore, industrial animal agriculture depends on ... a willingness to avert one's eyes."[11] The answer to this (in his view) abuse is to eat "humane meat": either animals that are hunted or those that are raised on a traditional farm.

These options still result in dead and butchered animals, Pollan is honest enough to admit—and he doesn't mince words about what the experience is like. Having purchased a humanely raised chicken, he watches as Daniel the farmer gathers and crates it. The next stop is the farm abattoir:

> I stacked several chicken crates in the corner of the killing cones and, while Daniel sharpened his knives, began lifting chickens from the crates and plac-ing them, head first, into the killing cones, which have an opening at the bot-tom for the chicken's head. Taking the squawking birds out of the crate was actually the hard part; as soon as they were snug in the cones, which kept their wings from flapping, the chickens fell silent. Once all eight cones were loaded, Daniel reached underneath and took a chicken head between his first finger and thumb, holding it still. Gently, he gave the head a quarter turn and then quickly drew his knife across the artery running alongside the bird's windpipe. A stream of blood erupted after the cut, pulsing slightly as it poured down into a metal gutter that funneled into a bucket. Daniel explained that you wanted to sever only the artery, not the head, so that the heart would continue to beat and pump out the blood. The bird shuddered in its cone, its yellow feet dancing spastically.[12]

Later in the book, Pollan shoots a wild pig and vividly describes the expe-rience of watching Angelo, his guide, butcher it, finding it "disgusting." But he assuages his feelings with the knowledge that he had just participated in "one of the food chains that have sustained life on earth for a million years made visible in a single frame, one uncluttered and most beautiful example of what is."[13]

Don't tell that to most animal rights activists. While HSUS considers humane meat to be an acceptable temporary way station en route to vege-tarianism or veganism,[14] most animal rights adherents believe humane meat to be "murder" just like meat obtained through any other type of animal husbandry. Farm Sanctuary speaks for most co-believers when it states:

Farm Sanctuary opposes the slaughter, consumption and commodification [*sic*] of farm animals. Those who are sincere in their concern for animals and for the environment make a knotty compromise if they choose to eat ostensibly crate-free or free-range meat instead of a vegan diet. The degree to which so-called humane meat is more sustainable than factory-farmed meat is negligible; plant-based agriculture is far more environmentally sound than animal agriculture—whether "humane" or factory-farmed. . . . Farm Sanctuary has never and will never support so-called "humane" meat. We maintain that the words "humane" and "slaughter" are mutually exclusive.[15]

There's another problem with "humane meat" that advocates like Pollan and Matthew Scully, the author of *Dominion*—a fervent animal welfare book that reads much like an animal rights tract—tend to ignore or downplay: It is more a way for empathetic people with disposable income to feel good about themselves than a way to make the CAFO obsolete through market forces. Thus, Pollan writes about the satisfaction of preparing and eating a meal in which the food—both meat and plant— was prepared nonindustrially.

To compare my transcendently slow meal to the fast food meal I "served" my family at that McDonald's in Marin, the one that set me back fourteen bucks for the three of us and was consumed in ten minutes at sixty-five miles per hour, is to marvel at the multiplicity of a world that could produce two such different methods of accomplishing the same thing: feeding ourselves, I mean.[16]

But for many families, the ability to feed everyone for fourteen dollars is more than a mere convenience; it is a tremendous benefit.

Scully—who unlike Pollan is a vegetarian—doesn't wish to leave the matter up to consumers but advocates outlawing all CAFOs. He acknowledges that industrial methods allow meat and dairy products to be brought to market at a far lower cost. (In my local supermarket, for example, eggs labeled as coming from uncaged chickens—the kind I prefer to buy for ethical reasons—cost more than two dollars extra per dozen than eggs from caged hens. Skinless, boneless chicken breasts labeled as coming from cage-free chickens cost three dollars more per pound than those not so labeled.)[17] But Scully all too casually dismisses, with a wave of his pen, the impact that considerably higher meat costs would have on struggling families. "Yes," he writes, "it will mean paying higher prices for meat and dairy products, and therefore, for many consumers, consuming less of both. But the meat you buy, when you eat it, will not have the taste of a bitter life."[18]

I'm sorry, that just isn't adequate. Access to nutritious, inexpensive food is a great benefit to people on limited budgets. Thus, although CAFOs clearly do not provide animals with an optimal environment, they do promote a substantial human good by bringing affordable meat to hundreds of millions of people. This may be sufficient to justify CAFOs as they currently exist, or perhaps with reforms like regulating the number of animals that can be kept in the facilities. But working out such issues requires extensive research and empirical analysis—not the hyperemotionalism of animal rights activists—so that the benefit to humans and alleged harm to animals can be assessed and balanced.

Promoting Humane Slaughter

Animal rights activists seek to persuade the public that slaughtering methods are cruel, with terrified animals often killed slowly or butchered by sadistic or mind-numbed workers before they are dead. For example, PETA claims:

> At the slaughterhouse, cattle may be hoisted upside-down by their hind legs and dismembered while still conscious. The kill rate in a typical slaughterhouse is 400 animals per hour and "the line is never stopped simply because an animal is alive," according to one slaughterhouse worker.[19]

Given the inaccuracy of animal rights propaganda about the place of animals in medical and scientific research, it seems unwise to trust any such assertion to be accurate regarding the actual practice in slaughterhouses.

But there are more reliable sources of information than PETA. One particularly trustworthy writer is Temple Grandin, a professor at Colorado State University who is professionally dedicated to promoting animal welfare in general and proper slaughter methods in particular. She is one of the world's premier experts on animal management. Professor

Grandin is also autistic. In her splendid book, *Animals in Translation: Using the Mysteries of Autism to Decode Animal Behavior*, she writes that her autism—which causes her to think more in pictures than words—allows her to understand how animals perceive the world.[20] This understanding has enabled her to design systems for slaughter that are both humane and efficient. She writes that she is successful because she doesn't anthropomorphize animals but instead strives to see things as they do. Then, animal husbandry techniques can be developed based on what will work *for them*, rather than what would work for us if we were in the same situation.

As one example, Professor Grandin tells of the time she was consulted by a feed lot to find out why its cattle were balking and acting scared before being herded down the squeeze chute, which permits them to be held still for the injection of medications. Grandin looked at it from the cattle's perspective and discovered that the problem involved the animals walking from the bright sunlight into a darkened barn:

> That might seem a little surprising, since prey animals, like cattle, deer, and horses, usually like the dark. They can hide in the dark and feel safe, or at least safer than they feel during the day. But the problem wasn't the dark, it was the contrast of going from bright to dark. They don't like that kind of experience that temporarily blinds them and that includes looking into a bright light when they're standing in relative darkness. . . .
>
> The answer was right in front of them. I really do mean directly in front of them, because the people who built the barn in the first place had installed a big sliding garage door on the front of the barn that the owner had left closed. . . . [T]hey got a couple of guys to put their shoulders up against the door, and after a few minutes of straining and grunting they got the thing opened. That was the end of the problem. The cows all walked into the chute as nice as could be.[21]

Grandin's empathy for animals' perspectives enabled her to create slaughter mechanisms and procedures that are more humane than those previously in use. Not only does death come quickly, but the animals do not know it is coming and so they are not afraid.

Toward this end, Grandin innovated by applying a Hazard Analysis Critical Control Point (HACCP) method to animal welfare for the U.S.

Department of Agriculture. Grandin's welfare audit recognizes that no human endeavor is perfect, including the slaughter of food animals, but works to keep mistakes to an absolute minimum. She explains:

> For my animal welfare audit, I came up with five key measurements inspectors need to take to ensure animals receive humane treatment at a meatpacking plant:
> + Percentage of animals stunned, or killed, correctly on the first attempt (this has to be at least 95 percent of the animals).
> + Percentage of animals who remain unconscious after stunning (*this must be 100 percent*).
> + Percentage of animals who vocalize (squeal, bellow, moo, meaning "ouch" or "you're scaring me!") during handling and stunning . . . (no more than 3 cattle out of 100).
> + Percentage of animals who fall down (animals are terrified of falling down, and this should be no more than 1 out of 100) . . .
> + Electric prod usage (no more than 25% of the animals).[22]

Grandin also created a list of five acts of abuse that are grounds for automatic failure of an audit: dragging a live animal with a chain, running cattle on top of each other on purpose, sticking prods and other objects into sensitive parts of animals, deliberately slamming gates on animals, and losing control and beating an animal.[23]

The efforts of Professor Grandin and other animal welfarists—and also, credit where credit is due, animal rights advocacy—have brought about changes in attitudes that have materially influenced the slaughterhouse industry. For instance, the *Los Angeles Times* reported how one hog-processing plant had made its entire approach to the distasteful job of killing pigs more humane:

> Hogs are unloaded as soon as they arrive, into cool pens with long troughs of water. If they can't walk, they are euthanized on the spot. . . . On the kill floor, workers no longer shoot the hogs in the brain with retractable bolts. Instead, they clap a harness over the animal's head and back and deliver an electric charge. A computerized display lets them know if they're getting a "good stun" or if they need to reposition the harness.
> Some hogs squeal when the stun is applied. Others jerk. All go rigid in seconds as the electrical impulse induces cardiac arrest. When the harness is

lifted, the animals slump, flaccid and unblinking, and roll down onto a con-
veyor belt. A second worker checks for signs of consciousness and then
quickly slits the throat. Everyone on the kill floor knows they could be fired if
they let a hog suffer.[24]

None of this is pleasant, but we have become so removed from the
reality of how we obtain our food that honesty compels an honest
recounting. And while most of the slaughterhouse abuses that animal
rights activists bring to light are the exception rather than the rule—the
meat industry spends much time and effort raising and slaughtering their
animals humanely—all meat eaters should understand that the slaughterhouse is a reality required by their diets.

Meat as Nutrition

As we have seen, meat is a natural part of the human diet. But is it good
for us? As with many controversies in our society, it depends on whose
opinion is cited. Since entire sections of libraries could be devoted to the
many books that have been written on both sides of this issue, we will not
be able to resolve it here. But there is no question that meat provides nutri-
ents that the human body needs for optimal health, including:

+ Protein
+ Minerals such as iron
+ Vitamins, such as vitamin B12, an essential element for brain develop-
  ment in children
+ Fatty acids
+ Calories

This is not to say that a nutritionally adequate vegetarian or vegan diet
cannot be derived through a combination of careful eating choices and
supplements. As a United Nations study of the nutritional needs of people in developing countries concluded:

> Meat is not an essential part of the diet but without animal products it is nec-
> essary to have some reasonable knowledge of nutrition in order to select an
> adequate diet. Even small quantities of animal products supplement and

complement a diet based on plant foods so that it is nutritionally adequate, whether or not there is informed selection of foods.[25]

Animal rights activists see the consumption of *any* animal product—even milk, cheese, and eggs—as anathema. They urge people to become vegan, eschewing all products derived in whole or in part from animals. Veganism, however, does not seem to be healthy for children. Several studies have found that a meat-free diet for pregnant women increases the risk of birth defects.[26] Moreover, vitamin B12 is an essential human nutrient supplied almost exclusively by animal products. It is necessary for the formation of red blood cells, for example, so those who consume an insufficient quantity are prone to anemia. Prolonged deficiency can cause nerve damage, and babies breast-fed by vegan mothers have been known to suffer neurological problems due to a deficiency of vitamin B12.[27]

As the Vegetarian Society notes on its website, "The only reliable unfortified sources of vitamin B12 are meat, dairy products and eggs." But what about supplements? "The current nutritional consensus is that no plant foods can be relied on as a safe source of vitamin B12." Thus, the society recommends: "Good sources of vitamin B12 for vegetarians are dairy products or free-range eggs. ½ pint of milk (full fat or semi skimmed) contains 1.2 µg. A slice of vegetarian cheddar cheese (40g) contains 0.5 µg. A boiled egg contains 0.7 µg." The society urges vegans to take yeast extract, textured vegetable protein, soya milk, and other such foods, even though it explicitly warns that these may not deliver all the B12 needed by the human body, and they have not been proven adequate to the task.[28]

Balance is the key to good nutrition, essential for optimal health. The U.S. Department of Agriculture's "Food Pyramid" includes grains, vegetables, fruits, milk, and meat/beans. The foods under the meat/beans category are lean cuts of "meat, poultry, fish, dry beans, eggs, and nuts."[29]

Veganism Is "Murder" Too

When the actress Jessica Simpson wore a T-shirt bearing the words "Real Girls Eat Meat" in 2008, PETA went apoplectic. "Jessica Simpson might have a right to wear what she wants," a PETA spokesperson said, "but she doesn't have a right to eat what she wants—eating meat is about suffering and death."[30] Listening to animal rights activists bray about the wrongness of slaughtering animals for food—summarized by their advocacy phrase "meat is murder"—one would think that the choice we have is either a diet in which animals are killed or a strictly vegan diet involving no animal deaths.

But life is never that simple. As Michael Pollan acknowledges in *The Omnivore's Dilemma*, plant agriculture results in the mass slaughter of countless animals each year—rabbits, gophers, mice, birds, snakes, and other field animals killed during the harvest and by other mechanized farming methods in the production of wheat, corn, rice, soybeans, and other staples of vegan diets. And that doesn't include the rats and mice poisoned in grain elevators or animals that die from loss of habitat cleared for agricultural use.

What's an animal rights activist to do? Not mention this inconvenient fact in advocacy materials, to be sure. But if the matter comes up in debate, the animal rightists have a problem: They believe it is "speciesist" to grant some sentient animals—including humans—greater value than others; or as PETA's Ingrid Newkirk so famously put it, "a rat is a fish is a dog is a boy." Thus, they cannot contend that it is more wrong to kill a pig than a rabbit. Nor can they argue, as we shall see, that field animals experience less agonizing deaths from plant agriculture than do food animals. No question: They hold a weak intellectual hand.

I asked Gary Francione what he thought. He responded that the main focus shouldn't be on the animals being killed but on the *intent* behind the killing:

> Forget about animals. The very same situation exists with respect to humans. We build roads knowing that people will die; we raise speed limits knowing that an additional 10 miles means X deaths. Humans are killed every year refining oil. Humans are killed and maimed incidental to all human activities. There is an enormous difference between harm that happens that we do not intend to occur and that which we intend. We should obviously endeavor to commit as little harm as possible but we cannot eliminate harm. We can, however, eliminate intentional harm. And eating animals involves an intentional

decision to participate in the suffering and death of nonhumans where there is no plausible moral justification.

But when farmers sow and reap their crops, they know that rabbits, gophers, mice, and snakes living in the ground are going to be made as predictably dead as the pig that becomes bacon. Moreover, these "collateral damage" deaths (as they are sometimes called) are often far more excruciating than those inflicted in a modern slaughterhouse. After all, field animals may flee in panic as the great rumbling harvest combines approach, only to be shredded to bits by the merciless blades. Or they may be burned to death when field leavings are set afire. Or, poisoned by pesticides. Or fall to predators when their plant cover has been removed—and unlike humans, these predators will not care a whit about the suffering they cause.

Francione also claimed that omnivores cause a far greater animal toll than vegans. "It takes three and a quarter acres to feed an omnivore for a year," he said. "Twenty vegans can be fed from that same space. Therefore, to the extent that there is harm caused to sentient beings by the production of plants, that harm is only multiplied by the omnivore."[31]

But that isn't the issue. The argument made by animal rights activists is not a utilitarian comparison of the carnage, but rather the claim that meat is murder while veganism is supposedly cruelty-free. Moreover, if the lowest number of animals killed is what matters morally, veganism may not offer the most ethical approach.

In 2001, S. L. Davis of the Department of Animal Sciences at Oregon State University in Corvallis wrote a paper claiming that the diet most likely to result in the deaths of the fewest animals would be beef, lamb, and dairy—not vegan. Davis found a study that measured mouse population density per hectare in grain fields both before and after harvest and estimated a harvest casualty rate of ten mice per hectare. Then, he multiplied that figure by 120 million hectares of farmland in the United States, meaning that 1.2 billion mice would die each year in food production if America became a wholly vegan country. Next, he estimated the number of animals that would be killed if half our fields were dedicated to raising grass-eating forage animals (cows, calves, sheep, lambs, etc.) for meat and other products. He found that there would be 300,000 fewer animal deaths annually from such an omnivorous diet than would be caused by a universal vegan diet. "In conclusion," Davis wrote, "applying the Least Harm Principle ... would actually argue that we are morally obligated to move to a ruminant-based diet rather than a vegan diet."[32]

We are not obligated to do any such thing, of course. And while the number of animals killed in plant agriculture is impossible to quantify with any accuracy, I think Davis's somewhat tongue-in-cheek study made an important point: Contending that meat eating is murder while veganism is morally pristine—even though it predictably involves the killing of animals—is pretense. Otherwise, animal rights believers would mount mass protests seeking to reform farm practices that they know result in painful death for countless animals.

This much is clear: No matter your diet, no matter whether you pork out on prime rib and mashed potatoes or restrict your intake to tofu on toast, animals surely died that you might live.

So this is the moral of the tale: Each of us should consider carefully what we put into our bodies. Those who think it is wrong to eat anything that once had a face should by all means become vegetarian or vegan, and more power to them. Anyone who believes that CAFOs are unacceptably cruel and who can afford the extra cost should limit their flesh intake to "humane meat" or become an ovo-lacto-vegetarian, consuming only cage-free eggs and other animal products that don't come from dead animals. Many will probably choose to disregard the whole issue and stoke up the barbeque. But since meat is a natural part of the human diet, and given the great efforts that are made to reduce or eliminate the suffering of most food animals, it seems clear to me that nobody is morally superior to anyone else based simply on what they eat.

17

Fur, Hunting, and Zoos

 since animal rights activists believe that animals should be free from human exploitation in any form, it is not surprising that protests plague almost every form of animal use today. These include commercial and recreational fishing, pet stores, dog breeding, horse racing, beekeeping, animals in circuses, the practices of animal shelters, including euthanasia (about which the movement is divided), spaying and neutering pets, keeping birds in cages, horse-drawn carriages, rodeos, the managing of wild horses and urban pigeons, down pillows, silk (yes, PETA even opposes the exploitation of silkworms, actually moth larvae, which it calls "feeling beings")[1]—the list is almost endless. Here we will examine just a few of the more controversial animal uses.

Wearing Fur

Everyone who watches the news or reads a newspaper knows that animal rights activists are in an unremitting war against the fur industry, with activities ranging from legitimate efforts to dissuade people from buying fur products—epitomized by PETA's provocative ads of beautiful actresses or models who pose in the nude "rather than wear fur"—to illegal direct actions such as burglarizing fur farms or throwing red paint on people's fur apparel. But animal rightists also peddle a lot of disinformation in support of the cause. For example, PETA's website states:

Those who wear fur trim and fur coats have the blood of minks, raccoons, foxes, beavers, and other animals on their hands. Animals on fur farms spend their lives in tiny cages only to be killed by anal or genital electrocution, which causes them to have a heart attack. Some are skinned alive. Animals in the wild may languish for days in traps before they die or are killed.[2]

In their zeal to destroy the fur industry, however, animal rightists typically don't tell the whole story.

First, let's look at the method by which farmed fur animals are killed. PETA denounces the electrocution of large fur animals, asserting that this practice is opposed by the American Veterinary Medical Association in the 2000 report of its Panel on Euthanasia. PETA's reliance on the opinions of the AVMA is profoundly ironic. While the association *explicitly supports* carbon monoxide poisoning as an "acceptable" method of killing small fur animals,[3] PETA decries the practice as inhumane, claiming falsely that the animals are "poisoned with hot, unfiltered engine exhaust from a truck. Engine exhaust is not always lethal, and some animals wake up while they are being skinned."[4]

But PETA's statement about electrocution is also misleading. Whatever the 2000 report may have said, the *AVMA Guidelines on Euthanasia*, published in 2007, *do not* unequivocally condemn electrocution as a method of euthanasia for fur animals such as fox, but rather label it "conditionally acceptable,"[5] so long as the euthanasia is a two-step process during which the animal "is first rendered unconscious," for example by electric stunning.[6]

I spoke with a mink farmer about all this. Paul Westwood sells about 15,000 mink pelts per year and has good reason to be knowledgeable about the tactics of animal liberationists: His farm was broken into in the 1990s and 1,100 animals were "liberated"—although most decided to refuse freedom. "All but two or three hundred stayed in their cages," Westwood recalled. "Of those, all but fifty were caught. Twenty-five of those fifty were killed on the roads by cars, ten were later rounded up, and about fifteen escaped into the wild, either becoming predators, prey, or starving to death."

Westwood forcefully denies the charge of earning a cruel living, stating that treating his animals properly is both an ethical imperative and a commonsense matter of business practicality. "With fur animals, the quality of their care is directly related to the quality of the pelt that is obtained. Mink require pristine conditions or you will not obtain pristine pelts. And since the quality of the fur impacts the price received, it would not only be wrong to treat your animals poorly, but it would cost you money."

The mink, generally weighing from three to ten pounds, are kept in well-bedded cages in sheds with the sides open so that the animals experience natural light and temperatures. Those that are not used for breeding (Westwood keeps about three thousand breeding females) live for about nine months, being born in April or May, reaching their full growth in September, and being dispatched after they grow their winter coats around December.

PETA and other anti-fur activists tell the public that the fur animals experience severe suffering in captivity and become so agitated that they chew on themselves. But Westwood notes that mink spend most of their days sleeping. Moreover, it isn't as if wild mink were trapped and put in cages; captivity is all the fur mink know, and they are selectively bred for placidity. As a consequence, "Very few mink clip their own fur, and when they do it is akin to someone biting their fingernails. It is very rare—maybe one in ten thousand—for mink to actually injure themselves."

I asked about the killing part of the business. Westwood assured me that the animals do not suffer, just as the American Veterinary Medical Association says. "We use carbon monoxide gas [*not*, as PETA claims, from truck engine exhaust]. It has no scent. The animals do not get agitated. They simply fall asleep."[7]

Animal rights activists like to argue that animal industries are not environmentally friendly, but that isn't true about fur farming. "Mink is green," Westwood said. The garments are not made from synthetics and they are biodegradable. Along with grain and vitamins, mink eat the offal left over from beef, chicken, and turkey operations that would otherwise end up in landfills. Mink manure is used in fertilizer and the oil is blended into perfumes and cosmetics.

The hue and cry against farm-raised fur such as mink appears to have had relatively little impact. According to the National Agricultural Statistical Service, 2.83 million mink pelts were produced in 2007, a number that has essentially held steady for nearly a decade, although down from a peak of about 4.6 million pelts produced and sold in 1989. But the prices that farmers received were way up, with the 2007 auction paying $185.8 million to growers—a record year.[8]

What about trapping? Surely that's inexcusably cruel, right? One would certainly think so if the only information on the matter came from animal liberationists. Based on claims of these groups, trapping seems positively barbaric. For example, FurIsDead.com luridly tells Web surfers: "Animals can languish in traps for days. Up to 1 out of every 4 trapped animals escapes by chewing off his or her own feet, only to die later from blood loss, fever, gangrene, or predation."[9] PETA's website similarly depicts a vivid picture of cruelty, stating: "When an animal steps on the spring of a steel-jaw trap, the trap's jaws slam on the animal's limb. The animal frantically struggles in excruciating pain as the trap cuts into his or her flesh often down to the bone, mutilating the animal's foot or leg."[10]

As with so many claims of animal rights groups, these charges are overstated, archaic, or simply untrue—at least when modern trapping methods are employed. Trapping technology has vastly improved over time. The old steel jaws of death that PETA wants you to envision have long since been replaced with a modern offset foothold trap that does not cause the same serious damage to limbs.

Here's an interesting fact: Readers may recall that several years ago, Canadian gray wolves were reintroduced into Yellowstone National Park. Many were captured with the same type of "offset" foothold trap that is used in modern fur trapping! Rather than being crippled by the traps, or chewing off their own feet and dying of gangrene, the wolves were transported and released back into the wild none the worse for wear. The modern foothold trap is frequently used by environmentalists and government wildlife management professionals in their efforts to help ecosystems thrive.

Herb Bergquist, a biologist for the U.S. Fish and Wildlife Service, Northwest Region, verified that today's foothold traps do not cause the kind of injuries claimed by PETA. "Yes, it is true," Bergquist told me, "foothold traps have been and are consistently used to restrain and hold animals later to be released unharmed. Fox, coyote, lynx, bobcat, otter, beaver, and the list goes on."[11] Independent studies have also shown that such offset traps cause few injuries to animals.[12] Thus, as is true about so much that is contained in PETA's "fact sheets," its description of contemporary leg-trapping methods is a canard.

I asked Bergquist, "But what about the charge that animals are forced to linger for days in traps? Are there any rules about that?" His answer was unequivocal:

> You bet there are! No one wants to see an animal suffer—and that includes, *above all*, trappers and regulators! Given the easy target that traps and trappers are to the animal rights groups, trappers go to great lengths to put the welfare of the animal first, and they are the first to condemn any method or event that caused an animal unnecessary stress or harm while being restrained. These are the facts: Almost all of the states in the U.S. have strict rules that traps must be checked every twenty-four hours (I think up to forty-eight hours in a couple of states). In general, based on when furbearers are most active, if caught in a live restraint device, designed to hold the animal alive, it is held for two to eight hours. After the first few minutes they stop fighting the trap, settle down and are extremely calm.[13]

That, of course, is why these traps are so useful in relocation efforts.

Granted, the point of fur trapping is not to relocate animals; and anyone who wears raccoon, coyote, or beaver pelts and worries about the ethics of wearing fur should certainly consider where their clothing came from and how it was obtained. To learn more, I spoke with Donnie MacLeod of Nova Scotia, who supplements his income as an engineer— and paid for his children's college expenses—by trapping bobcat, raccoon, fox, mink, coyote, and other furbearing animals.

MacLeod told me that while "trapping does not lead to an aesthetic death," it also "is not a cruel death." He explained that "the kind of trap used depends on the kind of animal you are after." Sometimes trappers use offset foothold traps. "That holds the animal without injuring them. They then are killed very quickly, usually with a .22 caliber gunshot to the head, or perhaps a quick clubbing" (thus giving groups like PETA gory pictures with which to raise funds and vilify trappers). Some animals are killed outright by the traps:

> "Killer snares" catch the animal around the throat. They don't strangulate, but rather the animal dies when their jugular vein is compressed, quickly

rendering the animal unconscious on the way to death. Water animals may be taken with "drowning wires," but these animals don't experience the same stress you or I would under the same circumstances. Their mouths and nostrils reflexively close when under water and they don't drown in the sense of breathing water into their lungs. Rather, being underwater they don't breathe and their deaths come from a buildup of carbon dioxide in the bloodstream that causes them to fall into unconsciousness.[14]

After the animal is harvested, it is taken to the fur shed and skinned—dead, not alive. Sometimes the meat is consumed or sold, or it may be used for bait. Otherwise, it is put out as food for hawks, eagles, and other scavengers.

This is not to say that trapping doesn't occasionally cause pain to animals before they are killed. But it is fair to state that, contrary to assertions by animal rightists, trapping is not a barbaric activity. And it is highly regulated. As Bergquist told me, "The activity of trapping is regulated and enforced on the state level. Every state in the country has a fish and wildlife division in which methods for capture, species limits, and seasons are determined based on scientific study. The time and duration of the season depends on the estimated size harvest that would be optimal for the health of that species."[15]

As with many of the issues discussed in these pages, there is also an oft-neglected human side to the story: Trapping sustains many rural and wilderness communities, where attacks on fur harvesting can have devastating economic consequences. This was made clear in a story in the *New York Times* in February 2003 about the effect that banning the import of wild fur to many European countries had on indigenous communities in Canada—causing poverty and forcing residents to open their lands to industrial uses in order to survive:

> "I'm still bitter about what was done to us," said Stephen Kakfwi, the premier of the Northwest Territories. "We pleaded with Greenpeace and the others. We told them we will have to turn to oil and gas and minerals for jobs if they took such a hard stance." . . .
>
> Nine Cree settlements around James Bay recently voted in a referendum to allow the provincial government to flood 115 square miles of traditional

hunting lands for hydroelectric development in exchange for millions of dollars in aid and greater autonomy. Among the strongest supporters of the agreement were trappers who could no longer make a good living off the area's foxes and beavers, said Bill Managoose, the executive director of the Grand Council of the Quebec Cree. "By saying don't kill the animals," Mr. Managoose said, "they killed the economy."[16]

The Wildlife Society probably got it right in noting that "much opposition to trapping is associated with urban-oriented cultures," while "those who approve of, practice, or benefit from trapping are primarily from rural cultures or are from areas where primary (land-based) employment predominates." As the society remarks, "This dichotomy of lifestyles and values, combined with a general lack of objective information about trapping, creates barriers to understanding and resolving controversial issues associated with trapping." The organization approves of correct trapping as a legitimate tool of wildlife management and much more:

> Trapping is part of our cultural heritage that provides income, recreation, and an outdoor lifestyle for many citizens through use of a renewable natural resource. It is often vital to the subsistence or self-sufficiency of peoples in remote regions who have few other economic alternatives. Trapping is a primary tool of most animal damage control programs and an important technique in wildlife research. In some situations, trapping is important in furbearer management and the management of other species and can be effective in reducing or suppressing wildlife diseases.[17]

Given the environmental credentials of the Wildlife Society, it seems to me that the core question about fur trapping is this: Since it is not an intrinsically cruel and sadistic activity, why should (mostly) city slickers decide how residents of rural areas live upon the land they love?

Hunting

Needless to say, animal rights activists detest hunting. Frankly, I don't much like it either, even when the animals are used as food. I recall going with my father to see what we thought was a nature documentary about thirty years ago. Much to our unpleasant surprise, it actually concerned trophy hunting, which I consider killing for ego. To this day I remember one particular line of dialogue justifying the kill as the hunters held up the dead head of a beautiful elk destined to be put on a wall: "He was an old bull who probably would have starved during the winter anyway." Appalled, we walked out—and my dad grew up in Idaho, where as a youth he hunted to help feed his family.

Then again, like most people who are uncomfortable with hunting, I have lived my entire life in urban environments, and while I have fished extensively—another activity opposed by animal rightists—I have no experience with shooting and dressing animals as food. Besides, the idea of shooting any living thing makes me squirm. But that doesn't mean my values should prevail. Hunting culture is very important in much of rural America, and hunting supplements the diet of many families; in fact, it remains a matter of survival in some parts of the world.

Animal liberationists, however, refuse to acknowledge the benefits of hunting. Some even attempt to thwart hunters by harassing them as they seek their prey or warning animals of the human presence so they will run away. This could be dangerous, even foolhardy, given that the hunters have guns and may not be able to see the hunting opponents clearly as they move through the underbrush. Moreover, the potential for heated conflict between the hunter and the thwarter is very real.

As a consequence, most states have outlawed the harassment of hunters, to the chagrin of Wayne Pacelle, who when he worked for the Fund for Animals (now merged with HSUS) told the New York Times, "We believe we have the same right to protect wildlife as they do to shoot wildlife. These laws make it a crime to shout at an animal but it is legal to shoot an animal. This is a strange priority."[18] Pacelle once called for the total outlawing of hunting, telling an animal rights publication, "We are going to use the ballot box and the democratic process to stop all hunting in the United States. . . . We will take it species by species until all hunting is stopped in California. Then we will take it state by state."[19] But as the head of HSUS, Pacelle has lowered his sights to argue more reasonably for the legal ban of certain types of hunts that would be found objectionable by many who do not oppose hunting in principle. For example, HSUS supports the Sportsmanship in Hunting Act, which would prohibit closed-range ranches from importing "exotic" animals not indige-nous to the United States to be hunted by paying customers (a practice called "canned hunting"). HSUS also seeks to outlaw bear baiting, pheas-ant stocking, and hunting contests that involve killing as many animals as possible.[20]

In light of the forces arrayed against them, hunters have organized to defend their "right to hunt." They point out correctly that hunting licenses help support national wildlife preserves and environmental conservation. As one article in defense of hunting notes, hunters and hunting organiza-tions contribute more than one billion dollars annually in licenses and public land access fees, plus voluntary contributions by hunting advocacy organizations. In fact, sportsmen's licenses account for more than half of all funding for state natural resource agencies.[21] This level of fees would never be collected from photographers and hikers. The same is true of tro-phy hunting, in which license fees help support ecosystems. In Africa and elsewhere, these fees are invaluable in enabling poor countries to police and protect wild areas. In addition, the meat of trophy kills is often con-sumed, especially in poor countries.

Considering the cost to the animals relative to the human benefit, there seems little justification for hunting techniques that are akin to shooting fish in a barrel, such as killing animals over the Internet. But hunting will probably never be totally banned, nor should it be. Even sport hunting for trophies should be allowed until it expires from natural causes. Times are changing and the "Great White Hunter" culture epitomized by Ernest Hemingway is thankfully on the wane.

Zoos and Animal Parks

Animal liberationists consider it exploitive to hold animals in captivity for purposes of display or human recreation. They also believe that exhibiting animals is by definition cruel. Here is how PETA describes that evil insti-tution, the zoo:

> Despite their professed concern for animals, zoos can more accurately be described as "collections" of interesting "specimens" than as actual havens or

homes. Even under the best of circumstances at the best of zoos, captivity cannot begin to replicate wild animals' habitats. Animals are often prevented from doing most of the things that are natural and important to them, like running, roaming, flying, climbing, foraging, choosing a partner, and being with others of their own kind. Zoos teach people that it is acceptable to interfere with animals and keep them locked up in captivity, where they are bored, cramped, lonely, deprived of all control over their lives, and far from their natural homes.[22]

On the other hand, zoological park professionals believe their work offers great value to the public and also to animals. An article in the *Journal of the American Veterinary Medical Association*, asking if it's "ethical to keep animals in zoos," explained the benefits succinctly:

> Zoos support conservation by educating the public, raising money for conservation programs, developing technology that can be used to track wild populations, conducting scientific research, advancing veterinary medicine, and developing animal handling techniques.
>
> By studying animals in captivity and applying that knowledge to their husbandry, zoos can provide valuable and practical information that may be difficult or impossible to gather in the wild.... Zoos also help by participating in collaborative efforts with other zoos and conservation groups, or directly supporting a wildlife reserve by contributing expertise, training, funding, and other resources.[23]

To which I would add that zoos, aquariums, water theme parks, and the like may also be the only opportunity children have to see firsthand and up close the magnificence of animals in their awesome diversity and complexity. The recreational benefits—particularly as a family activity—should not be discounted, and indeed would seem to justify the existence of zoos (assuming humane practices).

Of course, there are zoos and then there are zoos. It is clearly our human duty to ensure that zoological parks and other such institutions treat the animals in their care with proper regard for their individual needs. Part of this obligation is legally required. For example, the Animal Welfare Act applies to zoos. But merely meeting a legal minimum is insufficient. The best zoos and aquariums demonstrate their commitment to their public responsibilities and the animals in their care by belonging to the Association of Zoos and Aquariums (AZA). Among its many programs, the AZA develops high standards of husbandry, offers professional training to its members, participates in conservation efforts, educates the public, and accredits members as meeting the highest ethical standards for the housing and care of their animals. In its 2008 *Guide to Accreditation of Zoological Parks and Aquariums*, the AZA set forth how important it considers its accreditation function:

> In developing its accreditation program, AZA has been especially concerned with the need for assuring the highest standards of animal management and husbandry. It is our belief that this objective is paramount in the operation of collections of living creatures and that good conscience permits no higher priority. It also accords special attention to the use of the living collections and the nature of their management for conservation, education, scientific studies, and recreational purposes, thus justifying the maintenance of such collections.[24]

Toward this end, a study touted by the AZA, funded by the National Science Foundation, showed that "zoos and aquariums are enhancing public understanding of wildlife and the conservation of the places animals live. We believe these results will help institutions develop even more effective exhibitions and educational programs that help connect people with nature and encourage attitude and behavioral changes that help conservation."[25]

None of this matters to animal rights believers. But for the 143 million people who visited the 218 AZA-accredited institutions in 2005 (such as the splendid Monterey Bay Aquarium and the Smithsonian National Zoological Park in Washington, D.C.), it is good to know that the dollars they spend support facilities that care enough about their role in society to walk the extra mile by adhering to the AZA's standards for animal care.[26]

There are many other uses of animals around which activists have stoked controversy, sometimes justified, sometimes not—so many, in fact, that even a general discussion could take up several chapters. But this book is not intended to resolve every disagreement over the protection of animals.

Rather, my primary purpose is to analyze the ideas and principles that shape the moral issues surrounding our use of animals. Thus, the time has come to shift our discussion to the principle that is ultimately at stake in the debates over animal rights: the importance of being human.

18

The Importance
of Being Human

How should we think of animals? Animal rights activists, as we have seen, believe that sentience or the ability to feel pain grants animals a moral status equivalent to that of human beings, meaning they have what might be called natural rights that have heretofore been reserved to us.

Peter Singer's utilitarianism rejects the entire concept of unequivocal rights. Rather, this theory holds that animals and humans should be given "equal consideration" in determining the propriety of actions as measured by utilitarian outcomes. Equal consideration is really a euphemism to describe the establishment of a new moral hierarchy in which individual capacities are what matter morally. This means, among other things, that humans (and animals) possessing higher capacities would be allowed to benefit from the instrumental use of humans (and animals) with lower capacities as measured by "personhood" criteria, according to what Singer calls the "quality of life" ethic.

At the other extreme, several hundred years ago the French philosopher René Descartes asserted that we could treat animals just as we please because, he philosophized, they are akin to automatons and hence cannot really experience either pleasure or pain. Science and common sense have obliterated this crass view, but even today some commentators assert that regardless of our contemporary knowledge that animals do indeed feel pain and suffer and experience emotions, people should still be allowed to treat their own animals in any way they see fit.

Ilana Mercer, a columnist for *WorldNetDaily*, took this view when writing "in defense of Michael Vick," the football star imprisoned for engaging in inexcusably cruel dog-fighting activities. "Human beings ought to care for and be kind to animals," she said, "but a civilized society is one that never threatens a man's liberty because of the callousness with which he has treated the livestock he *owns*."[1] In a follow-up piece, denying (correctly, in my view) that animals have rights because they lack moral agency, Mercer went even further off the rails:

> Like PETA, I don't distinguish between the pig farmer and the dog fighter. Unlike PETA, I believe all animals are property. Man is the only top dog. Although people will go to great lengths to distinguish their preferred form of animal use from Vick's the distinction is nebulous. One either owns a resource or one doesn't. Whether one kills animals for food or for fun, the naturally licit basis for large-scale pig farming or game hunting is the same: ownership of the resource.[2]

Perhaps, but should we really be reducing everything to market principles? To rely on "animals are our property" absolutism is as wrong from its end of the spectrum as animal rights ideology is from the other extreme. Adopting Mercer's views would permit people to torture puppies for pleasure and starve horses to death if they failed to win a race. It would allow dog fighting and cock fighting, inhumane slaughter of food animals, putting chimps in cramped cages for their whole lives, and doing away with all legal protections for lab animals.

Surely we can find a middle ground that doesn't grant unwarranted rights to animals but does permit robust protection of their welfare. What basis is there for such an approach? The human attribute that Mercer mentions as lacking in animals: moral agency. We as humans—*and we alone*—have moral agency, which means that we have not only rights, *but also duties*. As the only truly moral species in the known universe, we must determine the extent and scope of our obligations to our fellow creatures. It would be absurd to expect any animal to respect the "rights" of another animal or of human beings. Since no other species can even comprehend the concept, animal rights would necessarily be enforced by humans. So those who argue vociferously for animal rights are actually calling for the highest level of human duties toward animals.

Animals Don't Have Rights; Humans Do Have Duties

The concept of "rights" permeates modern political and cultural discourse, but sometimes the word is bandied about far too loosely. Many in the media and the wider public use the term "animal rights" to mean being kind to animals and treating them humanely. The animal rights movement, however, is not really about improving the way people treat animals; rather, it asserts that animals literally have rights equivalent to those enjoyed by people. This usage turns the principle of rights on its head, because "rights" properly understood are distinctly and exclusively a human concept that can only apply to human actions.

Without getting too bogged down in philosophy, let's take a few moments to consider how we should understand the concept of "rights." Carl Cohen, a professor of philosophy at the University of Michigan, defines a right as "a valid claim, or potential claim, that may be made by a moral agent, under principles that govern both the claimant and the target of the claim."[3] This means that for animal "rights" to exist, they must govern the behavior of humans—the targets of the claim in Cohen's definition—and animals—the purported claimants of rights. In other words, for animals to have the right to life, that right would have to apply not only from people to animals, but also from animals to people, as well as from animals to each other.

Cohen illustrates these points with the example of a lion hunting down and eating a baby zebra. He writes cogently (emphasis added):

> Do you believe the baby zebra has the *right* not to be slaughtered? Or the lioness has the right to kill that baby zebra to feed her cubs? Perhaps you are inclined to say, when confronted by such natural rapacity (duplicated in various forms millions of times each day on the planet earth) that neither is right or wrong, that neither zebra nor lioness has a right against the other. Then I am on your side. Rights are pivotal in the moral realm and must be taken seriously, yes; but *zebras and lions and rats do not live in a moral realm*—their lives are totally *amoral*. There is no morality for them; animals do no moral wrong, ever. *In their world there are no wrongs and there are no rights.*

Hence:

> The concept of wrongs, and of rights, are totally foreign to animals, not conceivably within their ken or applicable to them.[4]

David S. Oderberg, a philosophy professor at the University of Reading, describes this two-way-street concept of rights somewhat differently, but with the same result (emphasis added):

> [W]hat matters in the having of rights is twofold: a) knowledge; b) freedom. More precisely, a right holder must first *know that he is pursuing a good*, and secondly, *must be free to do so*. No one can be under a duty to respect another's right if he cannot know what it is he is supposed to respect. Similarly, no one can call another to account over respecting his right if the former cannot know what it is the latter is supposed to respect. By "call to account" I mean making a conscious demand on them, even without speaking a word. How can a right holder make a conscious demand on another if he cannot know what he is demanding?[5]

Let's ponder an illustration that may ease understanding: If I intentionally ran you down with my car as you walked across the street, would I have violated your right to life? Absolutely. You have a valid claim that I not kill you, simply on the basis of being human, and I have the same right not to be killed by you. Since we are both moral beings, we are both rights bearers who have the concomitant obligation to respect each other's rights.

Now, if I went jogging in the hills and a cougar ran me down and killed me, would the cat have violated my right to life? The very idea is ludicrous. She has no duty toward me and I have no claim against her. If she killed me to feed her cubs, for example, she would merely have been behaving like a cougar. If she were then hunted down and killed, it would not be as a punishment for having committed a moral wrong, but as a prophylactic to guard the public safety.

We can now see the absurdity of the whole concept of animal rights. According to animal rights thinking, humans could not make any claim to any right against any animal—nor, obviously, would animals have rights among each other. On the other hand, not only would we humans have rights in relationship to each other, but animals would have rights against us—except that the animals' claims against us would be enforced only by other humans acting on behalf of the animals, which would have no idea what was going on. It's enough to make one dizzy. The whole thing is so preposterous that it borders on being a sham.

"Wait just a darned minute!" animal liberationists may be saying as they pound the table. "What about infants and cognitively disabled human beings who similarly cannot understand rights? Based on your argument, they too would not possess rights because the concept is 'foreign' and beyond their 'ken.'"

Not so. Moral agency is inherent and exclusive to human *nature*, meaning it is possessed by the *entire species*, not just individuals who happen to possess rational capacities. Robert P. George and Christopher Tollefsen of Princeton put the matter this way in the context of the human embryo:

> We are members of a certain animal species—Homo sapiens. Any whole living member of that species is a human being. His or her nature is a *human* nature. Such a nature is a *rational* nature. Human beings are *rational animals*. No, a human (rational) nature is not something that a human being *acquires* at some point after he or she comes into existence, or can lose prior to ceasing to exist.... [T]he basic natural capacity is inherent in human nature.[6]

Since almost all human beings at some level either inhabit, have inhabited, or possess the inherent potential to inhabit the moral realm, then each of us bears at least fundamental rights, such as the right to life and bodily integrity. Otherwise, there is no such thing as universal human rights. In contrast, *no* animal has *ever* possessed *any* of these capacities, nor do any have the present potential to develop them.

This means that the entire issue of animal rights isn't actually about "rights" at all. Rather, it is an exclusively human debate about the nature and scope of our responsibilities toward animals—responsibilities that are *predicated solely on our being human*. (Animals, as amoral beings, bear neither rights nor responsibilities toward us or each other.) Thus the animal rights controversy is ironic proof of the unique nature of the human species, or what some call "human exceptionalism."

A Distinction with a Difference

Some might ask: What difference does it make if we say that animals possess rights, or instead, that they are *objects* of our duties? Isn't this just a matter of semantics?

A notable animal protectionist says it makes no difference. In *Dominion: The Power of Man, the Suffering of Animals, and the Call to Mercy*, a fiery diatribe against abuses (and most uses) of animals, Matthew Scully argues that the terminology we use is not crucial:

> Turning to the question of animal rights, I confess that I could hardly care less whether any formal doctrine or theory can be adduced for these creatures. There are moments when you do not need doctrines, when even rights become irrelevant, when life demands some basic response of fellow-feeling mercy and love.[7]

But this is very wrong. As moral creatures, we human beings need principles by which to gauge our conduct. Only then can we truly judge what is right, what is wrong, and why. Without "doctrines," life could become totally erratic, based only on expediency, self-indulgence, or the emotions of the moment.

So philosophy, doctrines, ideology, principles *do matter* in determining moral propriety in human affairs. As an illustration, let us digress for a moment and consider the problem faced by Abraham Lincoln during the Civil War. Were we one nation facing a rebellion, as Lincoln insisted in his call to save the Union? Or instead, were there two nations, with one—the United States of America—engaged in a war of aggression against the other—the Confederate States of America—to deny the South's right to establish itself as an independent nation? Lincoln understood that if he lost the intellectual struggle over what the fight was really about, the North would also lose the war. Thus, when General Robert E. Lee retreated south toward Virginia after his army's 1863 loss at Gettysburg (as the historian Allen C. Guelzo recounts), the pursuing General George Gordon Meade issued an order that drove Lincoln up the wall precisely because it confirmed the South's definition of the cause of the war:

> But that [Lincoln's post-Gettysburg] jubilation crested when Lincoln learned that Meade had issued a congratulatory order to the army, urging them to

"greater efforts to drive from our soil every vestige of the presence of the invader." *Drive from our soil?* Lincoln erupted. . . . "Will our generals never get that idea out of their heads? The whole country is our soil."[8]

Similarly, in judging the morality of our interactions with animals, it matters a lot whether we invoke the purported "rights" of animals or think of our human "duties" to animals, primarily because the animal rights meme degrades humankind from the exceptional species on earth into merely another animal. Indeed, should we personalize fauna (if you will), the consequences to humankind would be as profound as they would be deleterious. In contrast, by debating animal protection issues on the basis of our uniquely human duties, we confirm our status as the earth's most morally important species—a necessary predicate both to the care of animals and to the maintenance of universal human rights.

What justifies the presumption that human life matters most? Some see the issue as religious, since virtually all major faith traditions promote the proper care of animals but also assert that humans have greater worth than animals. For example, in Matthew 10:29–31, Jesus tells his disciples:

> Are not two sparrows sold for a penny? Yet not one of them will fall to the ground apart from the will of your Father. And even the very hairs of your head are all numbered. So don't be afraid; you are worth more than many sparrows.

St. Francis of Assisi is rightly celebrated for loving animals, yet he never claimed that animals were equal to people, nor was he a strict vegetarian, but consumed meat when offered it as a guest. As David Grumett noted, "Francis's dietary practices should be seen in light of his hierarchical view of creation, according to which every living being praises God but is also available for human use and consumption as food, at least in the present age."[9] And while the Catholic Church commemorates the great saint's deep love for animals with the annual "Blessing of Pets," acknowledging them as God's creatures, it does not maintain that humans and animals are moral equals, nor does it require the faithful to "liberate" their animals.

Even religions that doctrinally require vegetarianism do so because they believe it is our duty not to cause animals to suffer, and they warn that we will suffer a karmic penalty for abusing animals. Indeed, I think it is fair to say that no major world religion supports the explicit human/animal moral equivalency that is promoted by animal rights ideology, much less the Peter Singer–style utilitarianism that opens the door to infanticide and medical experiments on the cognitively disabled.[10]

An embrace of human exceptionalism does not depend on religious belief, however. Whether our distinctive moral characteristics flow from the processes of blind evolution, or the mind of God, or some other mechanism, the unique importance of being human can be robustly supported by a rational examination of the differences between humans and all other known life forms.

The idea that human beings stand at the pinnacle of the moral hierarchy of life should be—and once was—uncontroversial. After all, what other species in the known history of life has attained the wondrous capacities of human beings? What other species has transcended the tooth-and-claw world of naked natural selection to the point that, at least to some degree, we now control nature instead of being controlled by it? What other species builds civilizations, records history, creates art, makes music, thinks abstractly, communicates in language, envisions and fabricates machinery, improves life through science and engineering, or explores the deeper truths found in philosophy and religion? What other species has true freedom? Not a one. David Oderberg gets to the heart of why humans are exceptional:

> No experiment that has ever been conducted into animal behavior has demonstrated that animals know *why* they do what they do, or are *free* to choose one course of action over another. From insects to apes, all kinds of complex behaviors have been demonstrated, such as deception, tool making, social group formation, mutual assistance. But nothing has been found which sets apes apart from insects in any qualitative sense bearing on freedom and knowledge of purpose. The "gee whiz" articles that appear in the popular press on a regular basis, revealing the latest trickery or intelligence on the part of some animal (usually an ape), are therefore useless as forming an empirical justification for regarding animals as metaphysically, in their nature, the same as human beings.[11]

Can anyone really argue that our species is not unique and, as far as we know, unprecedented? Who can reasonably deny that human life is lived in mental and moral realms never before seen in the known history of life? Only humans have the capacity to intentionally embrace the good—or engage in the worst evil. It was from a profound understanding of these facts that Thomas Jefferson wrote the immortal words declaring humanity's natural right to freedom: "We hold these truths to be self evident, that all men are created equal, that they are endowed by their Creator with certain inalienable rights, among which are life, liberty, and the pursuit of happiness."[12]

Moreover, as the only truly moral species known to exist, we alone have the ability to comprehend the grandeur and beauty of the natural world. The elephant is incapable of looking at a cheetah or a zebra with awe. Nor can the cat appreciate the beauty of the blue jay or the butterfly. Yet even small children can appreciate the value and beauty of animals, as the little boy on the boat I mentioned in the introduction did when he responded with heartfelt exuberance to Fungi the dolphin.

Perhaps the most important distinction between us and the beasts of the field—as animals were once called—is our moral agency. Only we have duties. As the philosopher Hans Jonas put it so well, "something like an 'ought to' can issue only from man and is alien to everything outside him."[13] Charles S. Nicoll, a physiologist at the University of California, Berkeley, made the same point in "A Physiologist's Views on the Animal Rights/Liberation Movement":

> The belief that there are no morally relevant differences between us and animals ignores ... significant and uniquely human qualities. We are the only species that has developed moral codes to judge our behavior, especially our behavior toward each other and toward animals. We are the only species that can make moral judgments and enter into moral contracts with other reasoning beings who understand the concept of morality and rights. We are moral agents: animals are not. The difference between us and animals is clearly a morally relevant one.[14]

Thus, the sow that permits the runt of her litter to be excluded from suckling to the point of starvation is not a negligent parent, while a human mother who did the same thing would be branded a monster. The cat that plays with the baby bird that falls out of the nest before consuming it is not sadistic. In contrast, any human who tortured an animal would be rightly seen as pathological.

On a related note, Professor Nicoll also noted that humans uniquely empathize with other species:

Ours is the only species that can prevent and cure diseases in ourselves and other animals, and only we show concern about the welfare of other species. Indeed we frequently expend great effort and expense to preserve the habitats of animals and to save some from extinction. There are no animal societies for the prevention of cruelty to humans or animals. We would suggest that our concern for other species is another morally relevant difference between us and other animals.[15]

Thus, unlike the orca that tosses a hapless seal through the air without a moment's consideration of the agony her prey is experiencing, only humans have the capacity to recoil in revulsion when we see our fellow creatures suffer. In fact, it is our humanity, *and only our humanity*, that permits us to recognize and care that—Descartes notwithstanding—"animals are not stones; they feel."[16] This uniquely human capacity to empathize with and appreciate "the other" is one of the best things about us. It is why we harshly judge cruel actions toward animals such as those committed by Michael Vick to the fighting dogs he tortured. It is this same empathy that drives Temple Grandin to devise humane methods of cattle slaughter and impels Ingrid Newkirk to promote animal rights extremism.

Animal rightists try to fudge these differences—for example, by noting that chimps use rudimentary tools—but in the end they cannot deny that we are an exceptional species and that the differences between humans and any other animal are vast in both degree and kind. This is precisely why they insist on using the lowest common denominators, such as mere sentience or the ability to feel pain, as the measuring sticks by which to assess moral value.

When, however, the debate finally reaches the point where enough uniquely human attributes have been identified to persuade reasonable people that they matter in determining moral status, animal rightists pull out what they think is their trump card—the game of the philosopher and the dupe:

PHILOSOPHER: What makes human beings different from animals?

DUPE: Only humans create. Only humans are rational. Only humans project abstractly into the future.

PHILOSOPHER: True, but not *every* human can do those things. By your reasoning, individuals who do not have the capacities to create, rationalize, or think abstractly should be treated like animals, because you have claimed that it is these capacities that matter morally.

Thus, Peter Singer has written that if we are to treat animals differently from humans based on membership in the human species alone, there must be a "relevant characteristic that distinguishes *all humans* from *all members* of other species." (My emphasis.) And because there are "some humans who quite clearly are below the level of awareness, self-consciousness, intelligence, and sentience, of many non-humans," and hence do not individually possess the characteristics that are deemed to grant humans special value, then the only rational course is to reject mere humanity as the measuring stick for moral value and find alternative criteria.[17]

Singer has it 180 degrees backward. Moral value should not be based on the *capacities of each individual,* since that standard would obliterate universal human rights, but upon the *intrinsic natures* of species. Reasoning, using language, inventing, projecting out into the future, creating—the list is long—are capacities that flow from the *nature* of humans and are absent from the natures of all animals.

The philosopher Carl Cohen explains why rights belong to all humans as members of a moral community:

Objections of this kind [that some human individuals don't possess the morally relevant capacities] badly miss the point. It is not individual persons who qualify (or are disqualified) for the possession of rights because of the presence or absence in them of some special capacity, thus resulting in the award of rights to some but not to others. Rights are universally human; they arise in the *human moral world,* in a moral *sphere.* In the human world moral judgments are pervasive; it is the fact that all humans including infants and the senile are members of that moral community—not the fact that as individuals they have or do not have certain special capacities, or merits—that makes humans bearers of rights.[18]

More to the point, no animal, *not one*, can be held morally accountable for its actions, which is to say that no animal has duties. Duty bearing—like rights bearing—is a uniquely human attribute, a fundamental difference from all animals, and part of what makes us the only known truly moral beings. Or as Cohen puts it, humans possess *"moral autonomy*—that is, *moral self-legislation,"* which "is for all animals out of the question."[19]

The game of the philosopher and the dupe is clever sophistry. The point of the exercise is to change the issue from differing natures of humans and animals, to the consequences of treating some humans as if they were animals. The game is won for the animal rightist when her antagonist is convinced that in order to avoid dehumanizing some people, we must treat animals as if they were human.

Let us now take the defense of human exceptionalism one step further: Without the conviction that humankind has unique worth based on our nature rather than our individual capacities, universal human rights are impossible to sustain philosophically. As the noted philosopher Mortimer J. Adler wrote, if we ever came to believe that humans do not all possess a unique moral status, the intellectual foundations of our liberties collapse:

> Those who now oppose injurious discrimination on the moral ground that all human beings, being equal in their humanity, should be treated equally in all those respects that concern their common humanity, would have no solid basis in fact to support their normative principle. A social and political ideal that has operated with revolutionary force in human history could be validly dismissed as a hollow illusion that should become defunct.[20]

Adler then explained why knocking humans off the pedestal of exceptionalism could lead to tyranny:

> On the psychological plane, we would have only a scale of degrees in which superior human beings might be separated from inferior men by a wider gap than separated the latter from non-human animals. Why, then, should not groups of superior men be able to justify their enslavement, exploitation, or even genocide of inferior human groups, on factual and moral grounds akin to those that we now rely on to justify our treatment of the animals we

harness as beasts of burden, that we butcher for food and clothing, or that we destroy as disease-bearing pests or as dangerous predators?[21]

I don't see how Adler's analysis can be disputed. Indeed, the effect of denying humans a special status is easily perceived in Peter Singer's utilitarianism, with its sanction of infanticide and the use of cognitively devastated humans in place of animals in medical experiments. Moreover, granting sacred liberties to animals would degrade the importance of rights altogether, just as wild inflation devalues money.

But animal rights supporters, in their zeal to elevate animals into rights-bearing creatures, are blind to this reality. Rather than embrace the uniqueness of human beings, they bitterly reject the notion that humans have greater value than animals, even to the point of blatant misanthropy. A writer for the *New Yorker* reported that Ingrid Newkirk told him "the world would be better without humans in it." When he expressed reservations about her antihuman attitude, she wrote him a furious follow-up e-mail:

> There are a billion mean tricks of Nature. And human beings, who aren't a "thing apart" but part of nature are cruel, out of sheer obliviousness if nothing else, but often out of malice or selfishness. A few clothes and a Jag and being able to read the NYT [*New York Times*] don't separate "us" from or elevate "us" above the other species![22]

In this view, believing in human exceptionalism shows hubris, a disdainful pride that leads us to believe we are entitled to treat animals as cruelly as we desire. Along this line, the Animal Liberation Front (ALF) claims that anthropocentrism—a human-centered ethical system—reflects a "misguided perception that humans are the only species of import on the planet, rather than just one among many who have intrinsic value and who contribute to the equilibrium and beauty of the Earth." The purported result of this arrogance is a "profound sense of disconnection from nature and other life forms—with an attendant callous disregard for their wellbeing and the consequent erosion of our own characters."[23]

Actually, the opposite is true. Because we *are* unquestionably a unique species—the only species capable of even contemplating ethical issues and assuming responsibilities—*we uniquely are capable of apprehending the difference between right and wrong, good and evil, proper and improper con-duct* toward animals. Or to put it more succinctly, if being human isn't what requires us to treat animals humanely, what in the world does?

Beyond this, if our goal is to protect animals from human exploitation and cruelty, we don't need to convey sham "rights" upon them. Rather, our approach can come exclusively from the self-imposition of human duties. Indeed, Matthew Scully's *Dominion* calls for an end to nearly all uses of animals, including "factory farms," whaling, most animal research, and the use of animal organs to save human lives. Scully supports the Great Ape Project, promotes vegetarianism, and advocates removing the tax-exempt status of the Safari Club International because he disagrees with its position on trophy hunting, an activity he hyperbolically condemns as "pure evil."[24]

I disagree with much of what Scully writes, because in my view his advocacy is hyperemotional and overly strident—for example, castigating a supporter of veal consumption as "doing what he pleases and getting what he wants, the whims of man in their familiar guise of the will of God"[25]—as well as outrageously anthropomorphic. Most glaringly, *Dominion* fails to consider the good that humans receive from animals, an omission this book, in part, has strived to rectify. But in calling for society to adopt radical animal welfare policies, Scully at least comes at the issue (mostly) from an appropriate appeal to human duty and conscience. "Even if we do not attach the same moral importance to human welfare as to animal welfare," he writes, "it is still human conduct we are talking about, and one wonders ... that there cannot be at least a few universally accepted standards to govern human conduct towards animals."[26] Thus, *Dominion* proves, if nothing else, that a "rights" approach is unnecessary for supporting the most stringent prohibitions on the human use of animals.[27]

Do Plants Have Rights?

Once we knock ourselves off the pedestal of exceptionalism, once we conclude that animals are also somehow rights bearers within the "community of equals"—that is, once we start personalizing the natural world and project into it attributes formerly reserved to humankind—where do we stop? How about at plants? After all, plants feel no pain, they are not sentient, they have no interests that a utilitarian would suggest be given equal consideration. Right?

Maybe not. Switzerland recently undertook a government-sanctioned process that could be construed as the beginning step in establishing "plant rights." A few years ago, the Swiss added to their national constitution a provision requiring that "account to be taken of the dignity of creation when handling animals, plants and other organisms." No one knew exactly what that meant, so officials asked the Swiss Federal Ethics Committee on Non-Human Biotechnology to figure it out. The resulting report, "The Dignity of Living Beings with Regard to Plants," is enough to short-circuit the brain.[28]

A "clear majority" of the committee adopted what it called a "biocentric" moral view, meaning that "living organisms should be considered morally for their own sake because they are alive."[29] (Think about the potential ramifications: Pond scum is alive. Bacteria are alive.) Thus, the committee determined that *individual plants*—quite apart from ecosystems—have intrinsic value, requiring that we should never "harm or destroy plants arbitrarily." The reasoning behind this conclusion reflects a dramatic expansion of the moral relativism that permeates animal rights ideology (emphasis added):

> This opinion was justified either by arguing *that plants strive after something,* which should not be blocked without good reason, or that recent findings in natural science, such as the many *commonalities between plants, animals and humans at molecular and cellular level,* remove the reasons for excluding plants in principle from the moral community.[30]

Hence, the committee determined, we cannot claim "absolute ownership" over plants and "we may not use them just as we please, even if the plant community is not in danger, or if our actions do not endanger the species, or if we are not acting arbitrarily."[31]

The report offers this illustration of an immoral action against an individual plant: A farmer mows his field (apparently an acceptable action, perhaps because the hay is intended to feed the farmer's herd—the report doesn't say). But then, his work done, he casually "decapitates flowers with his scythe on his way home without a rational reason." The committee frowned upon the hypothetical scything, though its members could not agree why, precisely, it was wrong. The report states, opaquely: "At this point it remains unclear whether this action is condemned because it expresses *a particular moral stance of the farmer toward other organisms* or because something bad is being done *to the flowers themselves*." (Emphasis in the original.)[32]

Such bizarre thinking has real-world impact. As discussed in the *Wall Street Journal*, declaring plant dignity could impede important research. When a scientist wanted to investigate whether he could introduce barley genes into wheat to determine whether that would make it more resistant to fungus, he was forced to argue that "he was actually helping the plant, not violating its dignity," in order to get the okay for his research to proceed.[33]

Switzerland's enshrining of "plant dignity" is a symptom of a cultural disease that has infected Western civilization, causing us to lose the ability to think critically and distinguish serious ethical concerns from frivolous musings. It also reflects the triumph of a radical anthropomorphism in which elements of the natural world are viewed as morally equivalent to people. One of the prime culprits behind this growing phenomenon is the *reductio ad absurdum* of animal rights. And frankly, it is driving us crazy.

On Intrinsic Human Dignity

Why is this happening? Why seek to breach the species barrier separating humans from animals and even begin to erase the moral distinction between fauna and flora? What is really behind these and the many other concerted movements within Western society to demolish the unique moral status of humankind?

Bringing animals, and perhaps even plants, into the moral community with human beings would break the spine of Judeo-Christian ethics, which hang on the belief that all humans are entitled to equal moral worth regardless of individual capacities, age, or state of health—that all have "intrinsic human dignity." Discarding the concept of intrinsic human dignity would humble—nay, degrade—the human self-image to the point where people would willingly sacrifice their own well-being "for the animals" or to "save the planet." An ethic that upholds the sanctity and equality of human life would give way to a utilitarianism that countenances the discarding of unwanted human ballast, much as we get rid of unwanted animals today. (Consider that Peter Singer is the world's foremost proponent of infanticide.) In the world that would rise from the ashes of human exceptionalism, moral value would be subjective and rights temporary, depending on each animal's individual capacities at the time of measuring. Worse, if current trends continue, nature itself could be personalized and given "rights." Don't laugh; the preamble to the new constitution of Ecuador states: "Persons and people have the fundamental rights guaranteed in this Constitution and in the international human rights instruments. Nature is subject to those rights given by this Constitution and Law."[34]

The assault on the unique importance of being human has the potential to cause great harm, as the primatologist and evolutionist Frans de Waal points out in *Good Natured: The Origins of Right and Wrong in Humans and Other Animals*. De Waal believes that chimpanzees have a rudimentary understanding of morality and that "science can wrest morality from the hands of philosophers,"[35] yet he makes a case for the importance of a human-centered morality:

> No matter how well intentioned the concerns of animal rights advocates, they are often presented in a manner infuriating to anyone concerned about *both* people and animals. Human morality as we know it would unravel very rapidly indeed if it failed to place human life at its core. Again, there is no judgment here about the objective value of our lives compared to the lives of other creatures. Personally, I don't feel superior to a butterfly, let alone a cat or a whale. But who can deny our species the right to construct a moral universe from a human perspective?[36]

This means eschewing the notion of animal rights and instead analyzing ethical issues involving animals from the standpoint of duty—both to animals and to ourselves:

> Unfortunately for the animals, they are not the only ones hanging in the balance. Human lives are also at stake. Anyone who enters a hospital or picks up a prescription at the pharmacy makes use of animal testing. Few people

consider it trivial to fight diseases such as AIDS, that affect millions. If a vaccine could be developed without using animals, of course that would be preferable. But there are no signs that this stage will be reached anytime soon. Choices must be made.... Phrasing the issue, as I do here, in terms of our *responsibilities* to other life forms, leaves the moral pyramid intact, and may lead to less radical conclusions than phrasing it in terms of rights.[37]

The issue of human exceptionalism is not, as De Waal seems to think, merely about feeling superior to butterflies—although we are unquestionably a higher life form. And it may seem abstract. But it is a matter of crucial importance: How we think about ourselves determines how we act—toward ourselves, each other, animals, and the environment. I believe that if we ever ceased thinking of ourselves as the apex of evolution/creation, the deleterious impact on our society would be profound. After all, if we are merely animals, why should we alone bear the sometimes onerous moral responsibilities that we have heretofore assumed along with our privileged status among species?

***

I hope it is now very clear that the animal rights movement is not simply about being nicer to animals. Its adherents, while certainly not monolithic, share a dangerous ideology that sometimes amounts to a quasi religion, the central dogma of which is that domesticating any animal is evil.

In this, they are deeply wrong. Human slavery was (and is) evil. Keeping elephants and zebras in properly designed and maintained zoos and animal parks is not. The Rwandan and Cambodian genocides were acts of evil. Humanely slaughtering millions of animals to provide the multitudes with nourishing and tasty food and durable clothing is not. Mengele's lethal experimentation on identical twins at Auschwitz was truly heinous. Testing new drugs or surgical procedures on animals to save children's lives and promote human (and animal) thriving is both morally beneficent and ethically justified. That animal liberationists don't see this, and can't even tell the ethical difference between eating meat and murder, means they have no business preaching morality to anyone.

For the rest of us who love animals, recognize their nobility, and believe that as human beings we owe them respect and kindness—but also understand that our obligation to humanity matters even more—let us strive continually to improve our treatment of animals as we also promote human prosperity and health. First and foremost, this means rejecting out of hand all moral equivalences between human beings and animals, as we embrace with humility and gratitude the intrinsic importance of human life.

Supplement

For those who want more information pro and con about animal rights than could be provided in one book, the following are a few of the resources available.

Books

Hundreds of books have been published on the issue of animal rights. Most of these—far too many to list—are decidedly on the pro side, with very few books written in explicit opposition. Here is a sampling:

Con

The Animal Research War, by P. Michael Conn and James V. Parker (Palgrave Macmillan, 2008). Conn, an animal researcher, tells what it is like to be the target of animal rights ideologues. He and Parker also explain the importance of animals in medical research, what is done to assure proper and humane care, and the consequences to science of shutting down animal research labs.

An Odyssey with Animals: A Veterinarian's Reflections on the Animal Rights and Welfare Debate, by Adrian R. Morrison (Oxford University Press, 2009). Morrison has been a prominent opponent of animal rights ideology from the earliest days of the movement. The animal researcher and professor of veterinary medicine crafts a multifaceted argument in favor of using animals humanely in research, the center of which is his staunch belief that human interests must be the primary concern of science and society.

Pro

Dominion: The Power of Man, the Suffering of Animals, and the Call to Mercy, by Matthew Scully (St. Martin's Griffin, 2001). *Dominion* is a screed against virtually all uses of animals from a near-absolutist animal welfare position. Scully, a political conservative, makes a special point of attempting to persuade Christians that their faith requires his prescription for radical changes in the use of animals. On the plus side, he supports his beliefs from the perspective of human duty rather than animal rights. Many of the problems Scully addresses are real, but he stacks the deck by making virtually no attempt to explain the human good received from the practices he criticizes. Still, *Dominion* is probably the most influential book published about animal protection in recent times.

Animal Liberation, by Peter Singer (Avon Books, 1975, 1990). Singer is a utilitarian philosopher, not an animal rights adherent. But this book, perhaps more than anything else, is responsible for unleashing the forces that transformed animal protection advocacy from the welfare approach to the belief that animals have human-style rights.

The Case for Animal Rights, by Tom Regan (University of California Press, 1983). Regan is a very influential philosopher among people who accept animal rights ideology. If you want to understand fully how people came to believe that animals should literally possess rights, this 400-page treatise is essential reading.

The Great Ape Project: Equality Beyond Humanity, edited by Paola Cavalieri and Peter Singer (St. Martin's Griffin, 1993). Cavalieri and Singer proposed that great apes be brought into a "community of equals" with human beings as a method of "breaking the species barrier" and undermining human exceptionalism. The Great Ape Project is supported by several authors, including the primatologist Jane Goodall, the biologist Richard Dawkins, and the animal rights philosopher Tom Regan, as well as Cavalieri and Singer. Spain adopted the Great Ape Project into its public policy in 2008.

Terrorists or Freedom Fighters? Reflections on the Liberation of Animals, edited by Steven Best and Anthony J. Nocella (Lantern Books, 2004). This book, with chapters by animal rights notables such as Steven Best,

Ingrid Newkirk, Tom Regan, and the convicted arsonist Rodney Coronado, is an apologia for the use of terroristic tactics and criminality in the name of animal liberation. *Terrorists or Freedom Fighters?* vividly illustrates the significant part played by hyper-radicals in the animal rights movement and belies its claim to be peaceable.

Websites

Secondhand Smoke. For those interested in the broader concept of human exceptionalism as well as the specific issue of animal rights, my blog *Secondhand Smoke* may be worth a visit. SHS considers a wide array of subjects including assisted suicide/euthanasia, bioethics, human cloning, and radical environmentalism, as well as the dangers of animal rights/liberation. My views expressed at SHS reflect my understanding that the philosophy of human exceptionalism is the bedrock of universal human rights. Or to put it another way, human life matters.

http://www.wesleyjsmith.com

Animal Industry Supporters
Americans for Medical Progress. This organization is dedicated to protecting society's investment in research by nurturing public understanding of and support for the humane, valuable, and necessary use of animals in medicine. Americans for Medical Progress (AMP) is a 501(c)3 nonprofit charity supported by the nation's top universities, private research facilities, research-related businesses, scientific and professional societies, as well as by foundation grants and contributions from individuals.

http://www.amprogress.org

Animal Agriculture Alliance. Established in 2001, the Animal Agriculture Alliance includes individuals, companies, and organizations interested in helping consumers better understand the role that animal agriculture plays in providing a safe, abundant food supply to a hungry world. By speaking with a common voice, the alliance will ensure that consistent and accurate messages based on sound science are communicated to the public. Activities focus on bringing truthful information to consumers so the role of animal agriculture in the food sector can be appreciated.

http://www.soundagscience.org

Center for Consumer Freedom. A nonprofit organization financed by the food industry, the CCF could be fairly described as "PETA's worst nightmare." It is edgy and aggressive, for example in its anti-PETA campaign, "PETA Kills Animals," which exposed the number of dogs and cats, some adoptable, that PETA euthanizes at its headquarters in Norfolk, Virginia. But what makes the CCF especially valuable is the depth of its resources pertaining to organizations and individual animal rights activists.

http://www.consumerfreedom.com

Foundation for Biomedical Research. The FBR is the nation's oldest and largest organization dedicated to improving human and animal health by promoting public understanding and support for humane and responsible animal research. The FBR works to inform the news media, teachers, students and parents, pet owners and others about the essential need for lab animals in medical and scientific research and discovery. FBR also monitors and analyzes the actions of animal rights activists. Its "Illegal Incidents Report" is a record of criminal activities committed in the name of animal rights.

http://www.fbresearch.org

Fur Commission USA. Representing some 400 mink-farming families on over 300 farms in more than two dozen states, the Fur Commission USA works to ensure superior standards of animal husbandry through its own certification program and to educate the public about responsible fur farming and the merits of fur. The FCUSA gives the side of the fur controversy that is not usually presented in the media or by animal rights activists and animal welfare organizations.

http://www.furcommission.com

National Animal Interest Alliance. The NAIA is an association of business, agricultural, scientific, and recreational interests dedicated to promoting animal welfare, supporting responsible animal use, and strengthening the bond between humans and animals. The NAIA members are pet owners, dog and cat clubs, obedience clubs and rescue groups, as well as breeders, veterinarians, research scientists, farmers, fishermen, hunters, and wildlife biologists.

http://www.naiaonline.org

Animal Rights Sites

Websites promoting animal rights are numerous and ubiquitous. Here is a representative sample:

People for the Ethical Treatment of Animals. PETA's websites are sophisticated and often misleading. They include information about PETA's ideology, current projects in animal rights advocacy, and a section telling activists how to "get involved."

http://www.peta.org

Of special concern is the PETA site aimed at children called "PETA Kids," which proselytizes children with animal rights dogma through celebrities, contests, games and products.

http://www.petakids.com

Abolitionist-Online. This online magazine is dedicated to promoting animal rights/liberation ideology. It includes interviews with activists and articles on veganism, and it promotes the views of people ranging from the responsible, such as Gary Francione, to the most radical Animal Liberation Front criminals.

http://www.abolitionist-online.com

The North American Animal Liberation Press Office. Animal rights radicalism at its most raw, the NAALPO is a conduit for terrorist press releases from criminal enterprises such as the Animal Liberation Front. The site also has a newsletter; a list of "Informers, Infiltrators, Snitches, and Agents," with pictures and information on law enforcement agents investigating animal rights crimes and on people who have cooperated with them, for potential targeting; and links to the most radical animal rights and environmental groups.

http://www.animalliberationpressoffice.org/index.htm

Animals Used in Nobel Prize Experiments

Animal research is the prime target of animal liberationists, some of whom falsely claim that animal research is useless in the advancement of medical science. The truth is 180 degrees to the contrary, as is amply demonstrated by the vast body of Nobel Prize–winning work in physiology and medicine that required the use of animals to succeed Although great strides have been made in computer modeling and cell cultures, animal research remains essential to medical progress: seven of the last ten Nobel Prizes in medicine have relied at least in part on animal research.

Year	Scientist(s)	Animal(s)	Contributions Made
2007	Capecchi*, Evans, Smithies	Mouse	Discovery of principles for introducing specific gene modifications in mice by the use of embryonic stem cells
2006	Fire, Mello	Round-worm	RNA interference, or gene silencing by double-stranded RNA
2005	Marshall, Warren	Gerbil	Discovery of a bacterium that leads to gastritis and peptic ulcer disease
2004	Axel, Buck	Mouse	Odorant receptors and the organization of the olfactory system
2003	Lauterbur, Mansfield	Clam, rat	Imaging of human internal organs with exact and non-invasive methods (MRI)
2002	Brenner, Horvitz, Sulston	Round-worm	Genetic regulation of organ development and programmed cell death
2000	Carlsson, Greengard, Kandel	Mouse, guinea pig, sea slug	Signal transduction in the nervous system

1999	Blobel	Various animal cells	Proteins have intrinsic signals that govern their transport and localization in the cell.
1998	Furchgott, Ignarro, Murad	Rabbit	Nitric oxide as signaling molecule in cardiovascular system
1997	Prusiner*	Hamster, mouse	Discovery and characterization of prions
1996	Doherty, Zinkernagel	Mouse	Immune-system detection of virus-infected cells
1995	Lewis, Wieschaus, Nusslein-Volhard	Fruit fly	Genetic control of early structural development
1992	Fischer, Krebs	Rabbit	Regulatory mechanism in cells
1991	Neher, Sakmann	Frog	Chemical communication between cells
1990	Murray*, Thomas*	Dog	Organ transplantation techniques
1989	Varmus, Bishop	Chicken	Cellular origin of retroviral oncogenes
1987	Tonegawa	Mouse	Basic principles of antibody synthesis
1986	Levi-Montalcini, Cohen	Mouse, chick, snake	Nerve growth factor and epidermal growth factor
1984	Milstein, Kohler, Jerne	Mouse	Techniques of monoclonal antibody formation

1982	Bergstrom, Samuelsson, Vane	Ram, rabbit, guinea pig	Discovery of prostaglandins
1981	Sperry, Hubel*, Wiesel*	Cat, monkey	Processing of visual information by the brain
1980	Benacerraf, Dausset, Snell	Mouse, guinea pig	Identification of histocompatibility antigens and mechanism of action
1979	Cormack, Hounsfield	Pig	Development of computer assisted tomography (CAT scan)
1977	Guilemin, Schally, Yalow	Sheep, swine	Hypothalamic hormones
1976	Blumberg, Gajdusek	Chimpanzee	Slow viruses, and new mechanisms for dissemination of diseases
1975	Baltimore*, Dulbecco, Temin	Monkey, horse, chicken, mouse	Interaction between tumor viruses and genetic material
1974	de Duve, Palade, Claude	Chicken, guinea pig, rat	Structural and functional organization of cells
1973	von Frisch, Lorenz, Tinbergen	Bee, bird	Organization of social and behavioral patterns in animals
1972	Edelman, Porter	Guinea pig, rabbit	Chemical structure of antibodies
1971	Sutherland	Mammalian liver	Mechanism of the actions of hormones
1970	Katz, von Euler, Axelrod	Cat, rat	Mechanisms of storage and release of nerve transmitters

1968	Holley, Khorana, Nirenberg	Rat	Interpretation of genetic code and its role in protein synthesis
1967	Harttline, Granit, Wald	Chicken, rabbit, fish, crab	Primary physiological and chemical processes of vision
1966	Rous, Huggins	Rat, rabbit, hen	Tumor-inducing viruses and hormonal treatment of cancer
1964	Bloch, Lynen	Rat	Regulation of cholesterol and fatty acid metabolism
1963	Eccles, Hodgkin, Huxley	Cat, frog, squid, crab	Ionic involvement in excitation and inhibition in peripheral and central portions of the nerve
1961	von Bekesy	Guinea pig	Physical mechanism of simulation in the cochlea
1960	Burnet, Medawar	Rabbit	Understanding of acquired immune tolerance
1957	Bovet	Dog, rabbit	Production of synthetic curare and its action on vascular and smooth muscle
1955	Theorell	Horse	Nature and mode of action of oxidative enzymes
1954	Enders, Weller, Robbins	Monkey, mouse	Culture of poliovirus that led to development of vaccine
1953	Krebs, Lipmann	Pigeon	Characterization of the citric acid cycle
1952	Waksman	Guinea pig	Discovery of streptomycin

1951	Theiler	Monkey, mouse	Development of yellow fever vaccine
1950	Kendall, Hench, Reichstein	Cow	Antiarthritic role of adrenal hormones
1949	Hess, Moniz	Cat	Functional organization of the brain as a coordinator of internal organs
1947	Carl Cori, Gerty Cori Houssay	Frog, toad, dog	Catalytic conversion glycogen; role of pituitary in sugar metabolism
1945	Fleming, Chain, Florey	Mouse	Curative effect of penicillin in bacterial infections
1944	Erlanger, Gasser	Cat	Specific functions of nerve cells
1943	Dam, Doisy	Rat, dog, chick, mouse	Discovery of function of vitamin K
1939	Domagk	Mouse, rabbit	Antibacterial effects of prontosil
1938	Heymans	Dog	Role of the sinus and aortic mechanisms in regulation of respiration
1936	Dale, Loewi	Cat, frog, bird, reptile	Chemical transmission of nerve impulses
1935	Spemann	Amphibian	Organizer effect in embryonic development
1934	Whipple, Murphy, Minot	Dog	Liver therapy for anemia

1932	Sherrington, Adrian	Dog, cat	Functions of neurons
1929	Eijkman, Hopkins	Chicken	Discovery of antineuritic and growth stimulating vitamins
1928	Nicolle	Monkey, pig, rat, mouse	Pathogenesis of typhus
1924	Einthoven	Dog	Mechanism of the electrocardiograph
1923	Banting, Macleod	Dog, rabbit, fish	Discovery of insulin and mechanism of diabetes
1922	Hill, Meyerhof	Frog	Consumption of oxygen and lactic acid metabolism in muscle
1920	Krogh	Frog	Discovery of capillary motor regulating system
1919	Bordet	Guinea pig, horse, rabbit	Mechanisms of immunity
1913	Richet	Dog, rabbit	Mechanisms of anaphylaxis
1912	Carrel	Dog	Surgical advances in the suture and grafting of blood vessels
1910	Kossel	Bird	Knowledge of cell chemistry through work on proteins including nuclear substances
1908	Metchnikov, Ehrlich	Bird, fish, guinea pig	Immune reactions and functions of phagocytes

1907	Laveran	Bird	Role of protozoa as cause of disease
1906	Golgi, Cajal	Dog, horse	Characterization of the central nervous system
1905	Koch	Cow, sheep	Studies of pathogenesis of tuberculosis
1904	Pavlov	Dog	Animal responses to various stimuli
1902	Ross	Pigeon	Understanding of malaria life cycle
1901	von Behring	Guinea pig	Development of diphtheria antiserum

Source: Foundation for Biomedical Research, http://www.fbresearch.org/ Education/nobels.htm

Text of the Nuremberg Code

The Nuremberg Code is one of the great human rights documents in recent history. Issued by the Nuremberg Tribunal in the wake of the medical abuses of the Holocaust, the code explicitly requires animal experiments before testing on human subjects as a crucial matter of protecting the safety of humans.

Permissible Medical Experiments

The great weight of the evidence before us to effect that certain types of medical experiments on human beings, when kept within reasonably well-defined bounds, conform to the ethics of the medical profession generally. The protagonists of the practice of human experimentation justify their views on the basis that such experiments yield results for the good of society that are unprocurable by other methods or means of study. All agree, however, that certain basic principles must be observed in order to satisfy moral, ethical, and legal concepts.

1. The voluntary consent of the human subject is absolutely essential. This means that the person involved should have the legal capacity to give consent; should be so situated as to be able to exercise free power of choice, without the intervention of any element of force, fraud, deceit, duress, overreaching, or other ulterior form of constraint or coercion; and should have sufficient knowledge and comprehension of the elements of the subject matter involved as to enable him to make an understanding and enlightened decision. The latter element requires that before the acceptance of an affirmative decision by the experimental subject there should be made known to him the nature, duration, and purpose of the experiment; the method and means by which it is to be conducted; all inconveniences and hazards reasonably expected; and the effects upon his health or person which may possibly come from his participation in the experiment.

   The duty and responsibility for ascertaining the quality of the consent rests upon each individual who initiates, directs, or engages in the experiment. It is a personal duty and responsibility which may not be delegated to another with impunity.

2. The experiment should be such as to yield fruitful results for the good of society, unprocurable by other methods or means of study, and not random and unnecessary in nature.

3. The experiment should be so designed and based on the results of animal experimentation and knowledge of the natural history of the disease or other problem under study that the anticipated results justify the performance of the experiment.

4. The experiment should be so conducted as to avoid all unnecessary physical and mental suffering and injury.

5. No experiment should be conducted where there is an a priori reason to believe that deaths or disabling injury will occur; except perhaps, in those experiments where the experimental physicians also serve as subjects.

6. The degree of risk to be taken should never exceed that determined by the humanitarian importance of the problem to be solved by the experiment.

7. Proper precautions should be made and adequate facilities provided to protect the experimental subject against even remote possibilities of injury, disability, or death.

8. The experiment should be conducted only by scientifically qualified persons. The highest degree of skill and care should be required through all stages of the experiment of those who conduct or engage in the experiment.

9. During the course of the experiment the human subject should be at liberty to bring the experiment to an end if he has reached the physical or mental state where continuation of the experiment seems to him to be impossible.

10. During the course of the experiment the scientist in charge must be prepared to terminate the experiment at any stage, if he has probable cause to believe, in the exercise of good faith, superior skill and careful judgment required of him, that a continuation of the experiment is likely to result in injury, disability or death of the experimental subject.

Acknowledgments

No author of a book of this kind is an island onto himself. We need help from others who are informed in the subjects about which we write. We also need the support of friends and family, who encourage us in the endeavor and forgive us for the time we take away from them toiling in front of the computer screen to put together a cogent and readable book.

I am deeply in the debt of many for their help and assistance in this regard. First, to the Discovery Institute in Seattle, whose management recognized the importance of the moral and ethical issues raised in this book and brought me on as a senior fellow in human rights and bioethics, in part to help support this work. Thanks in particular to my DI colleagues present and past, including Bruce Chapman, Steve Buri, Jay Richards, Mark Ryland, Robert Crowther, Anika Smith, Keith Pennock, Seth Cooper, Alex Lykken, Patrick Bell, and to all the helpful staff for all they have done and continue to do in my behalf and in the struggle to defend human exceptionalism.

The seed funding for this work was provided by a grant to the Discovery Institute from the Searle Freedom Trust. Without this early support, it is unlikely that this book would ever have been written, and I am very grateful to the trust.

My deep and continuing appreciation go to my publisher, Encounter Books, which has been so supportive of my writing. Special thanks to the publisher, Roger Kimball; to my wonderful editor, Carol Staswick, and to Heather Ohle, Emily Pollack, Sam Schneider, Lauren Miklos, Nola Tully, and Erin Pursell.

Thanks also to the anonymous sources and helpers who asked not to be identified, for reasons that will become clear to readers of this book. It is remarkable and disturbing in a free society that the animal rights movement is so feared that many good and knowledgeable people are intimidated against speaking their minds publicly about the uses of animals.

A singular thank you to the animal rights activist and philosopher Gary L. Francione for sharing his ethical perspectives freely with me, despite knowing that we profoundly disagree about animal rights and that I would criticize his views. I have strived earnestly to present his perspectives fairly and in proper context, and I hope that I have done them justice.

Sincere thanks for the invaluable contributions of the activists who work personally and professionally against the animal rights agenda—perhaps at great risk to themselves—including: Jacquie Calnan of the Americans for Medical Progress; P. Michael Conn, animal researcher and author; Jane Mackta of the New Jersey Association of Biomedical Research; David Martosko of the Center for Consumer Freedom; Professor Adrian R. Morrison of the Department of Animal Biology, School of Veterinary Medicine, University of Pennsylvania; Teresa Platt of the Fur Commission USA; Patti Strand of the National Animal Interest Alliance; and Frankie Trull of the Foundation for Biomedical Research.

Muchas gracias to sources in and out of animal industries who selflessly gave of their time: Bonnie Bergin and the staff of the Assistance Dog Institute, Herb Berquist, Eric Chevlen, Criss Davis, Sarah Llewellyn-Evans, Guillermo Gonzalez, William Hurlbut, David Juday, Richard L. Lobb, Donnie MacLeod, John J. Miller, Melanie Morgan, David Oderberg, Richard Sternberg, Andreas-Solomon Sussmilch, Dr. Edward Taub, and Paul Westwood.

My profound appreciation to the novelist Dean Koontz for his thoughtful and eloquent preface.

Finally, my deepest love and gratitude to friends and family who put up with me in patience and good cheer, with encouragement and affection, especially Mark and LaRee Pickup, Rita and Mike Marker, John and Kathi Hamlon, William and Erica Hurlbut, Dean and Gerda Koontz, Fr. Leo and Denise Arrowsmith, Pal Steve and Allison Hayward, Colin Smith and the late Casie Fillio-Smith, Peter and Lexie Demirali, Terrie and Rick Davies, Tom Lorentzen, Daniel and Jennifer Lahl, and James and Patricia Shinn, My love to the Saunders family, South Carolina, Connecticut, New York, and Rhode Island branches: Jerry, Barbara, Jim, Vickie, Jennifer, Jeremiah, Sara, Patrick Ryan, Stephen, Leslie, Rebecca, Eric, and Joshua. Undying devotion and gratitude to my dearest mother,

Leona Smith, and most of all, to the joy of my life and the source of so much laughter and fun, Debra J. Saunders, my wife and total sweetheart.

Notes

Introduction

[1] The Assistance Dog Institute is a nonprofit educational organization that is part of the Bergen University of Canine Studies. For more information, its website is www.assistancedog.org.

[2] E-mail correspondence from Lisa to Pam Hogle, dated February 15, 2007, distributed by Assistance Dog Institute.

[3] Canine Companions for Independence is a nonprofit 501(c)(3) organization that offers dogs to disabled clients without charge.

[4] Quoted in Katie McCabe, "Who Will Live, Who Will Die?" *Washingtonian*, August 1986, p. 21.

Chapter 1: Animal Advocacy Isn't What It Used to Be

[1] Patrick Range McDonald, "Monkey Madness at UCLA," *LA Weekly*, August 8, 2007.

[2] Communiqué from ALF Activists, "Animal Liberation Front Strikes UCLA Vivisection. Waterfront Property in Beverly Hills for Sale!" November 13, 2007.

[3] "Fire Set at UCLA Scientist's House," *Los Angeles Times*, February 6, 2008.

[4] Communiqué from ALF, "UCLA Vivisector Gets Return Visit from Animal Liberationists," Animal Liberation Press Office, February 6, 2008.

[5] David Epstein, "Throwing in the Towel," *Inside Higher Ed*, August 22, 2006.

[6] Nicola Woolcock, "Animal Activists Face Jail over Plot to Steal Body," *Times* (London), April 11, 2006.

[7] Nick Britten, "Animal Rights Gang Jailed for 12 Years to Deter 'Lunatics,'" *Telegraph*, December 5, 2006.

8 Steve Morris, David Ward and Riazat Butt, "Jail for Animal Rights Extremists Who Stole Body of Elderly Woman from Her Grave," *Guardian*, May 12, 2006.

9 Woolcock, "Animal Activists Face Jail."

10 Morris et al., "Jail for Animal Rights Extremists."

11 BBC News, "Hammond Police Discover Remains," May 3, 2006.

12 Michael Schau, "Animal Law Research Guide," *Barry University Law Review*, vol. 2 (Summer 2001), p. 148.

13 Gary L. Francione, "Animal Rights and Animal Welfare," *Rutgers Law Review*, vol. 48 (1996), p. 401.

14 Some of the following material first appeared in Wesley J. Smith, *Culture of Death: The Assault on Medical Ethics in America* (San Francisco: Encounter Books, 2001).

15 Peter Singer, *Ethics into Action: Henry Spira and the Animal Rights Movement* (Lanham, Md.: Rowman & Littlefield, 1998).

16 Ibid., p. 54.

17 Ibid., p. 81.

18 Kathy Guillermo, interview with author, March 13, 1999.

19 Frederick K. Goodwin, interview with author, October 28, 1998.

20 Katie McCabe, "Beyond Cruelty," *Washingtonian*, February 1990.

21 Richard D. Ryder, "All Beings That Feel Pain Deserve Human Rights," *Guardian*, August 6, 2005.

22 Peter Singer, *Animal Liberation*, rev. ed. (1975; New York: Avon Books, 1990), p. 6.

23 Ibid.

24 YouTube video, "Dawkins on Speciesism and Saving the Gorilla," in which Dawkins decries speciesism and makes the claim, based on what he calls "an emotional argument," that we have a duty to preserve the great apes. I don't dispute the duty but assert that it arises from the unique status of humans that Dawkins has repeatedly decried as speciesist.

Chapter 2: "All Animals Are Equal"

1 Peter Singer, *Animal Liberation*, rev. ed. (1975; New York: Avon Books, 1990), p. 1.

2 Ibid., p. ix.

3 Ibid., p. 1.

4 Gary L. Francione, "Peter Singer Supports Vivisection: Why Are You Surprised?" *Animal Rights: The Abolitionist Approach* (blog of Gary Francione), November 29, 2006, http://www.abolitionistapproach. com/?p=5.

5 Paola Cavalieri and Peter Singer, "The Great Ape Project—and Beyond," in *The Great Ape Project: Equality Beyond Humanity*, ed. Paola Cavalieri and Peter Singer (New York: St. Martin's Press, 1993), p. 308.

6 I disagree with most of Joseph Fletcher's perspectives, including his views quoted here. For a fuller description of Fletcher's beliefs and my criticisms of them, see Wesley J. Smith, *Culture of Death: The Assault on Medical Ethics in America* (San Francisco: Encounter Books, 2001).

7 Joseph Fletcher, *The Ethics of Genetic Control: Ending Reproductive Roulette* (Buffalo: Prometheus Books, 1988), p. 170.

8 Ibid., pp. 172–73.

9 Singer, *Animal Liberation*, pp. 4–5.

10 Ibid., p. 19.

11 See, for example, Peter Singer, *Rethinking Life and Death: The Collapse of Our Traditional Ethics* (New York: St. Martin's Press, 1994).

12 Peter Singer, *Practical Ethics*, 2nd ed. (Cambridge, UK: Cambridge University Press, 1993), p. 87.

13 Ibid., p. 132.

14 Singer, *Rethinking Life and Death*, p. 220.

15 John Harris, "The Concept of the Person and the Value of Life," *Kennedy Institute of Ethics Journal*, vol. 9, no. 4 (December 1999), p. 307.

16 Thomas Beauchamp, "The Failure of Theories of Personhood," *Kennedy Institute of Ethics Journal*, vol. 9, no. 4 (December 1999), pp. 309–24.

17 R. G. Frey, "Use of Animals and Low Quality Humans," *Between the Species*, vol. 4, no. 1 (1988), p. 196.

18 R. G. Frey, "Moral Community and Animal Research in Medicine," *Ethics and Behavior*, vol. 7, no. 2 (1997), p. 131.

19 Joseph P. Shapiro, *No Pity: People with Disabilities Forging a New Civil Rights Movement* (New York: Times Books, 1993), p. 273.

20 Jill Neimark, "Living and Dying with Peter Singer," *Psychology Today*, January/February 1999, p. 58.

[21] Gareth Walsh, "Father of Animal Activism Backs Monkey Testing," *Sunday Times* (London), November 26, 2006.

[22] Arkangel: For Animal Rights, "Peter Singer Endorses Animal Experiments," November 27, 2006, http://www.arkangelweb.org/international/uk/20061127singer.php.

[23] Francione, "Peter Singer Supports Vivisection."

Chapter 3: Animals Are People Too

[1] Richard Ryder, "All Beings That Feel Pain Deserve Human Rights," *Guardian*, August 6, 2005.

[2] Richard D. Ryder, "Painism: Some Moral Rules for the Civilized Experimenter," *Cambridge Quarterly of Healthcare Ethics*, vol. 8 (1999), p. 41.

[3] Ryder, "All Beings That Feel Pain Deserve Human Rights."

[4] As quoted in Katie McCabe, "Beyond Cruelty," *Washingtonian*, February 1990.

[5] Michael Specter, "The Extremist," *New Yorker*, April 14, 2003, p. 57.

I requested an interview with Ingrid Newkirk in the preparation of this book. She refused by way of an e-mail dated October 16, 2007, from a woman identified as Starza Kolman, Newkirk's executive assistant, who wrote: "Dear Mr. Smith, Thank you for your request to interview Ms. Newkirk for your latest book. Unfortunately, Ms. Newkirk must decline your request at this time. You can find all the information you need from one of Ms. Newkirk's many books which can be purchased through PETACatalogue.com."

[6] PETA has taken the Holocaust on Your Plate Campaign off its website, but examples of PETA press releases about the campaign are available in abundance. For example, as part of an effort to convince the Holocaust Museum of Virginia to showcase its perspective in an exhibit, PETA issued a press release on September 30, 2003, that included this statement:

"During the Holocaust, the Nazis used cattle cars to transport people to concentration camps," says PETA Campaign Coordinator Matt Prescott, members of whose family were murdered by the Nazis. "Animals today are powerless to stop the long, painful trip to their deaths, as were victims of the Holocaust. The Virginia Holocaust Museum can help people understand that peace begins on the plate."

Available at http://www.peta.org/mc/NewsItem.asp?id=2946.

Some of the images from Holocaust on Your Plate may be found in "PETA Cheapens the Holocaust," Frontpagemag.com, October 16, 2003, http://www.frontpagemag.com/Articles/Read.aspx?GUID= 7957D75C-B051-4E6B-BD77-D94BCEA8EFA7.

[7] Holocaust on Your Plate color brochure, "To Animals, All People Are Nazis," PETA, masskilling.com.

[8] Ibid.

[9] Anti-Defamation League press release, February 24, 2003.

[10] Open correspondence from Ingrid Newkirk to "the Jewish Community," May 5, 2005, see http://web.israelinsider.com/views/5475.htm.

[11] Ibid.

[12] Charles Patterson, *Eternal Treblinka: Our Treatment of Animals and the Holocaust* (New York: Lantern Books, 2002), p. xi.

[13] Ibid., p. 53.

[14] Ibid., p. 81.

[15] Ibid., p. 73.

[16] Ibid., p. 129.

[17] As of August 16, 2008, some of the Animal Liberation Project's images could still be accessed at the PETA/UK website, http://www.peta. org.uk/animalliberation/aboutImages.asp.

[18] Maria Garriga, "Outrage on the Green," *New Haven Register*, August 9, 2005.

[19] Claudette Vaughan, "The Abolitionist Theory of Gary Francione," Abolitionist-Online, http://www.abolitionist-online.com/interview_gary. francione.shtml.

[20] "Gary Francione: Questions and Answers on Introduction to Animal Rights: Your Child or the Dog? (an interview done in 2000)," Abolitionist-Online, http://www.abolitionist-online.com/interview-issue03_gary. francione_march.2006.shtml.

[21] Peter Singer and James Mason, *The Way We Eat: Why Our Food Choices Matter* (Emmaus, Penn.: Rodale Press, 2006).

[22] Gary L. Francione, "Abolition of Animal Exploitation: The Journey Will Not Begin while We Are Walking Backwards," Abolitionist-Online, www.abolitionist-online.com/article-issue05_gary.francione_abolition. of.animal.exploitation.2006.shtml.

23 Ibid.

24 The term "veganism" is defined by the Vegan Society as "a philosophy and way of living which seeks to exclude—as far as is possible and practical—all forms of exploitation of, and cruelty to, animals for food, clothing or any other purpose; and by extension, promotes the development and use of animal-free alternatives for the benefit of humans, animals and the environment." http://www.vegansociety.com/html/downloads/ArticlesofAssociation.pdf.

25 Gary L. Francione, "A Comment on Violence," *Animal Rights: The Abolitionist Approach* (blog of Gary Francione), August 13, 2007, http://www.abolitionistapproach.com/?p=92#more-92.

26 Gary L. Francione, e-mail interview with author, November 15, 2007.

27 Some of the following material first appeared in Wesley J. Smith, *Culture of Death: The Assault on Medical Ethics in America* (San Francisco: Encounter Books, 2000).

28 Tom Regan, *The Case for Animal Rights* (Berkeley: University of California Press, 1983), p. xiii.

29 Ibid., p. 77.

30 Ibid., p. 193.

31 Ibid., p. 320.

32 Ibid., p. 327.

33 Ibid., p. 328.

34 Carl Cohen and Tom Regan, *The Animal Rights Debate* (Lanham, Md.: Rowman & Littlefield, 2001), pp. 217–18.

35 Ibid., p. 218.

Chapter 4: Let It Begin with Apes

1 Sinikka Tarvainen, "Spain May Grant Rights to Great Apes," *Nature News*, April 29, 2006.

2 "A Declaration on Great Apes," in *The Great Ape Project: Equality Beyond Humanity*, ed. Paola Cavalieri and Peter Singer (New York: St. Martin's Griffin, 1996), p. 4.

3 John L. VandeBerg and Stuart M. Zola, "A Unique Biomedical Resource at Risk," *Nature*, vol. 437 (September 1, 2005), pp. 30–32.

4 "A Declaration on Great Apes," p. 5.

5 Ibid., p. 4.

[6] Jane Goodall, "Chimpanzees—Bridging the Gap," in *The Great Ape Project*, p. 10.

[7] Ibid., pp. 10–11.

[8] "Anthropomorphism," Merriam-Webster OnLine, www.merriam-webster.com/dictionary/anthropomorphism.

[9] Goodall, "Chimpanzees—Bridging the Gap," p. 12.

[10] Ibid., p. 15.

[11] Ibid., p. 17.

[12] Barbara Noske, "Great Apes as Anthropological Subjects," in *The Great Ape Project*, p. 266.

[13] Ibid., p. 267.

[14] Richard Dawkins, "Gaps in the Mind," in *The Great Ape Project*, p. 82.

[15] "Fossil Find Pushes Human-Ape Split Back Millions of Years," Breitbart.com, August 24, 2007, http://www.breitbart.com/print.php?id=070824121653.65mgd37f&s.

[16] Jon Cohen, "Relative Differences: The Myth of 1%," *Science*, vol. 316 (June 29, 2007), p. 1836.

[17] Artemy Beniaminov et al., "Distinctive Structures between Chimpanzee and Human in a Brain Noncoding RNA," *RNA*, vol. 14, no. 7 (July 2008), pp. 1270–75.

[18] James A. Shapiro and Richard von Sternberg, "Why Repetitive DNA Is Essential to Genome Function," *Biological Reviews*, vol. 80 (2005), pp. 227–50.

[19] William B. Hurlbut, interview with author, August 22, 2008.

[20] David Biello, "Scientist Identifies Gene Difference between Humans and Chimps," *Scientific American*, August 17, 2006.

[21] Alvin Powell, "Chimp Genome Effort Shines Light on Human Evolution," *Harvard Gazette*, September 15, 2005.

[22] Cohen, "Relative Differences: The Myth of 1%."

[23] Dawkins, "Gaps in the Mind," p. 85.

[24] Ibid., pp. 86–87.

[25] Paola Cavalieri and Peter Singer, "The Great Ape Project—and Beyond," in *The Great Ape Project*, ed. Cavalieri and Singer, p. 311.

[26] See Neil Wells, "The Great Ape Project: Legislating for the Control of the Use of Non-human Hominids in Research, Testing and Teaching—*Animal Welfare Act 1999* (New Zealand)," paper delivered at the Fourth

World Congress on Alternatives and Animal Use in the Life Sciences, August 2002, published in *ATLA (Alternatives to Lab Animals)*, vol. 32, Supplement 1 (2004), pp. 329–33.

[27] "Spanish Islands Extend 'Human Rights' to Great Apes," Institute for Ethics and Emerging Technologies, March 23, 2007, http://ieet.org/index.php/IEET/more/balearicapes200703.

[28] Martin Roberts, "Spanish Parliament to Extend Rights to Apes," Reuters, June 25, 2008.

Chapter 5: Here Comes the Judge

[1] Center for the Expansion of Fundamental Rights, http://www.cefr.org.

[2] Steven M. Wise, *Drawing the Line: Science and the Case for Animal Rights* (Cambridge, Mass.: Perseus Books, 2002), p. 26.

[3] Ibid., p. 32.

[4] Ibid., p. 34.

[5] Ibid.

[6] Ibid., p. 235.

[7] Ibid., p. 240.

[8] Ibid., p. 239.

[9] Ibid., p. 81.

[10] The Humane Society of the United States, "Federal Court to Hear Lawsuit against New York Foie Gras Factory Farm," January 9, 2008, http://www.hsus.org/press_and_publications/press_releases/cwa010908.html.

[11] Ibid.

[12] "Humane Society Loses Lawsuit against Foie Gras Farm," *North County Gazette*, May 17, 2007, http://www.northcountrygazette.org/news/2007/05/17/foie_gras_suit.

[13] Cass R. Sunstein, "Standing for Animals (with Notes on Animal Rights)," *UCLA Law Review*, vol. 47 (2000), p. 1335.

[14] Ibid., p. 1349.

[15] Cass R. Sunstein, "Can Animals Sue?" in *Animal Rights: Current Debates and New Directions*, ed. Cass R. Sunstein and Martha C. Nussbaum (Oxford, UK: Oxford University Press, 2004), p. 260.

[16] David Favre, "Integrating Animal Interests into Our Legal System," *Animal Law*, vol. 10 (2004), pp. 95–96.

[17] Laurence H. Tribe, "Ten Lessons Our Constitutional Experience Can Teach Us About the Puzzle of Animal Rights: The Work of Steven M. Wise," *Animal Law*, vol. 7 (2001), p. 5.

[18] Ibid., p. 3.

[19] *Cetacean Community v. Bush*, 386 F. 3d 1169 (9th Circuit, 2004).

[20] *Sarah, Keeli, Ivy, Sheba, Darrell, Harper, Emma, Rain, Ulysses, Henry Melvyn Richardson et al. v. Primarily Primates, Inc.*, Texas Court of Appeals No. 04-06-00868-CV, January 16, 2008.

[21] Claire Cooper, "Pets Suing Their Masters? Stay Tuned, Advocates Say," *Sacramento Bee*, May 13, 2000.

[22] Ciro Brigham, "Historic Decision Recognizes Chimpanzee as Legal Subject," *Correio da Bahia*, October 6, 2005.

[23] "European Court Agrees to Hear Chimp's Plea for Human Rights," *Evening Standard*, May 21, 2008.

Chapter 6: The Silver Spring Monkey Case

[1] The term "true believer" was coined by the philosopher Eric Hoffer. According to the *The Eric Hoffer Resource*, "*The True Believer*, though, is … concerned with the … origination of all mass movements, destructive or creative. And more importantly, it is concerned with the main ingredient of such movements, the frustrated individual. The book probes into the psychology of the frustrated and dissatisfied, those who would eagerly sacrifice themselves for any cause that might give their meaningless lives some sense of significance. The alienated seek to lose themselves in these movements by adopting those fanatical attitudes that are, according to Hoffer, fundamentally 'a flight from the self.'" http://www.erichoffer.net.

[2] Some of the material on the Silver Spring Monkey Case first appeared in Wesley J. Smith, *Culture of Death: The Assault on Medical Ethics in America* (San Francisco: Encounter Books, 2001).

[3] PETA, "PETA's History: Compassion in Action," PETA website, 2007, http://www.peta.org/factsheet/files/FactsheetDisplay.asp?ID=107.

[4] Katie McCabe, "Beyond Cruelty," *Washingtonian*, February 1990. This article claimed that Pacheco had "staged" the unsanitary conditions found in the lab. That claim was later retracted by the magazine under threat of litigation.

[5] ActivistCash.Com, "Alex Pacheco Biography," www.activistcash.com/biography.cfm/bid/1459, quoting from Associated Press, January 3, 1989.

[6] Dr. Edward Taub, interview with author, November 16, 2007.

[7] Ibid.

[8] Dr. Edward Taub, interview with author, February 12, 2000.

[9] Edward Taub, "Somatosensory Deafferentation Research with Monkeys: Implications for Rehabilitation Medicine," in *Behavioral Psychology in Rehabilitation Medicine: Clinical Applications,* ed. L. P. Ince (Baltimore: Williams & Wilkins, 1980), p. 398.

[10] Taub interview, 2000.

[11] Taub interview, 2007.

[12] Taub interview, 2007.

[13] Taub interview, 2000.

[14] Taub interview, 2007.

[15] American Stroke Association, "Constraint-Induced Movement Therapy," www.strokeassociation.org/presenter.jhtml?identifier=3029931# 2006.

[16] Steven L. Wolf et al., "Effect of Constraint-Induced Movement Therapy on Upper Extremity Function 3 to 9 Months after Stroke," *Journal of the American Medical Association,* vol. 296, no. 17 (November 1, 2006), p. 2095.

[17] Brian Hoare et al., "Constraint-Induced Movement Therapy in the Treatment of the Upper Limb in Children with Hemiplegic Cerebral Palsy: A Cochrane Systematic Review," *Clinical Rehabilitation,* vol. 21, no. 8 (August 2007), p. 685.

[18] Taub interview, 2007.

[19] Ibid.

[20] Ibid.

[21] Ibid.

[22] Ibid.

[23] "2004 Award Winners," *American Psychologist,* vol. 59, no. 8 (2004), p. 690.

[24] Taub interview, 2007.

Chapter 7: The Death of a Thousand Cuts

[1] Stephen M. Wise, *Drawing the Line: Science and the Case for Animal Rights* (Cambridge, Mass.: Perseus Books, 2002), pp. 10–11, citing

Verlyn Kinkenborg, "Cow Parts," 22 *Discover* 52, 53–62 (August 2001).

[2] Ibid.

[3] Some of this material first appeared in Wesley J. Smith, "Peta-Fried," *National Review Online*, July 11, 2003.

[4] American Veterinary Medical Association, *AVMA Guidelines on Euthanasia*, June 2007, p. 17.

[5] Correspondence from Ingrid Newkirk to Cheryl Bachelder, President of KFC, Inc., May 8, 2003, as reproduced on PETA website.

[6] *AVMA Guidelines on Euthanasia*, p. 10.

[7] PETA Media Center, "Inside the Fur Industry: Animal Factories," http://www.peta.org/mc/factsheet_display.asp?ID=56.

[8] Theresa Platt, e-mail interview with author, December 11, 2007.

[9] *AVMA Guidelines on Euthanasia*, p. 18.

[10] Amendment 10, November 2002 Florida ballot.

[11] "Resolution on Pregnant Sow Housing OK'd," *Journal of the American Veterinary Medical Association*, September 2, 2002.

[12] Farm Sanctuary, "About Us," http://www.farmsanctuary.org/about/index.htm.

[13] Farm Sanctuary, "Humane Meat," http://www.farmsanctuary.org/about/humane_meat_position.htm.

[14] Humane Society of the United States, *Charging Forward for Animals*, 2006 HSUS Annual Report.

[15] Catherine Clyne, "(R)Evolution from Within? A New Direction for the Humane Society," *Satya*, June 2005, http://www.satyamag.com/jun05/pacelle.html.

[16] *Animal People*, May 1993, as cited by the American Animal Welfare Society, http://www.americananimalwelfare.com/rights.html.

[17] Doug J. Swanson, "Guerillas Say They Fight to Help Liberate Animals; FBI Considers Group's Members Domestic Terrorists," *Dallas Morning News*, February 15, 1998.

[18] As cited by the Center for Consumer Freedom, a nonprofit education organization supported by the food industry, http://www.activistcash.com/biography_quotes.cfm/bid/3364.

[19] As reported in "Humane Society of the United States," Center for Consumer Freedom, http://www.activistcash.com/organization_overview.cfm/oid/136.

[20] Farm Sanctuary Campaigns, "The Welfare of Sows in Gestation Crates," http://www.farmsanctuary.org/campaign/gestation_evidence. htm.

[21] Amendment 10, November 2002 Florida ballot.

[22] Marc Kaufman, "Largest Pork Processor to Phase out Crates," *Washington Post,* January 26, 2007.

[23] Joe Vansickle, "Defending Farm Animal Care," *National Hog Farmer,* August 15, 2001.

[24] Alicia Caldwell and Anita Kumar, "Smoking Limited, Hog Crates Enlarged," *St. Petersburg Times,* November 6, 2002.

[25] State of Florida Elections Commission, *In re: Farm Sanctuary and Gene Bauston, President,* "Consent Order," Case FEC 02-093, filed November 25, 2002.

[26] Wes Allison, "Amendment Is Final Straw for Pig Farmer," *St. Petersburg Times,* December 13, 2002.

[27] Jerry W. Jackson, "Florida's Pig Amendment Puts Pressure on Farmers—in Other States," *Orlando Sun-Sentinel,* November 9, 2002.

[28] *Born Free USA, et al., v. Gale Norton, Secretary, Department of the Interior, et al.,* Memorandum of Opinion, United States District Court, Civil Action No. 03-1497 (JDB), August 8, 2003.

[29] Charles Abbott and Christopher Doering, "California Packer Makes Largest U.S. Beef Recall," Reuters, February 17, 2008.

[30] Bryan Denson, "Federal Inspectors Clear Oregon Primate Center after Complaint," *Oregonian,* December 4, 2007.

[31] Washington State Department of Agriculture, "Investigation into Alleged Violations of State Law by IBP, Inc., Summary Report," April 2001, p. 5.

[32] Ibid., p. 6.

[33] Ibid., p. 12.

[34] State of Washington, "IBP Investigation: Comparison of Edited Video to Unedited Video Footage," April 18, 2001.

[35] PETA Media Center press release, December 22, 2004, http://www.peta.org/mc/NewsItem.asp?id=5574.

[36] Ibid.

[37] See, for example, Co-operative Animal Health, Ltd., "Blowfly Strike in Sheep," http://www.cahl.ie/seasonalinfo/blowfly.htm.

38 PETA, "Inside the Wool Industry," http://www.peta.org/MC/factsheet_display.asp?ID=55.

39 PETA UK, "Inside the Wool Industry," quoting a "witness" to sheep shearing, http://www.peta.org.uk/factsheet/files/FactsheetDisplay.asp?ID=129.

40 Sarah Llewellyn-Evans, interview with author, January 11, 2005.

41 Australian Veterinary Association, "AVA Applauds Industry Decision on Sheep," November 17, 2004.

42 Royal Society for the Prevention of Cruelty to Animals, Australia, "Statement of RSPCA Australia Regarding Mulesing of Sheep," October 15, 2004.

43 "Pink Blames Misinformation over Australian Wool Slur," Reuters, January 18, 2007.

44 PETA website, http://getactive.peta.org/campaign/pink_wool_video?qp_source=pinkpetagen.

45 Between Australian Wool Innovation and People for the Ethical Treatment of Animals, Federal Court Litigation No: 1630, Settlement Agreement, June 29, 2007.

46 Peter Munro, "Wool Crisis as Europe Deal Unravels," The Age (Melbourne), February 17, 2008.

47 Australian Associated Press, "Wool Growers Call Euro Boycott a Beat Up," The Age (Melbourne), March 27, 2008.

Chapter 8: Proselytizing Children

1 For more details of Peter Singer's views on infanticide, see Peter Singer, Rethinking Life and Death: The Collapse of Our Traditional Ethics (New York: St. Martin's Press, 1994), p. 130.

2 Melanie Morgan, interview with author, January 8, 2008.

3 FOX News Channel, December 19, 2003.

4 Paul Watson, "The Beginning of the End for Life on Planet Earth," Sea Shepherd Conservation Society website, http://www.seashepherd.org/editorials/editorial_070504_1.html.

5 Ask Carla, "What Is Wrong with Beeswax," PETA, http://www.askcarla.com/answers.asp?QuestionandanswerID=474.

6 PETA, "Remarkable Animal Facts," http://www.peta.org/mc/amazing.asp?page=6.

[7] PETA Comics, *Your Mommy Kills Animals*, November 2003.

[8] http://www.petakids.com.

[9] http://www.petakids.com/stencils.html.

[10] http://www.petakids.com/mission_enews.html.

[11] http://www.petakids.com/celebs.html, downloaded by the author, January 24, 2008.

[12] http://www.peta.org/feat/alicia_psa/index.asp. The site also has Silverstone advocating for veganism and other animal rights agendas.

[13] Ingrid Newkirk, MySpace page, http://www.myspace.com/ingrid-newkirk.

[14] Center for Consumer Freedom, *Your Kids, PETA's Pawns: How the Animal "Rights" Movement Hurts Children*, Washington, D.C.

[15] Ibid., p. 9.

[16] Ibid.

[17] ActivistCash.com, "Gary Yourofsky Biography," http://www.activist-cash.com/biography.cfm/bid/3369.

[18] Center for Consumer Freedom, *Your Kids, PETA's Pawns*, p. 10.

[19] Ibid.

[20] Farm Sanctuary, "About Us: Position Statements," http://www.farmsanctuary.org/about/position.

[21] Farm Sanctuary, *Cultivating Compassion: Humane Education Resources for Teachers*, descriptive brochure.

[22] Farm Sanctuary, "Dear Teacher," distributed as part of Cultivating Compassion education kits.

[23] Farm Sanctuary, *Cultivating Compassion: Teachers' Guide and Student Activities*, Elementary Level (Watkins Glen, N.Y.: Farm Sanctuary, 2001).

[24] Ibid., p. 13.

[25] Ibid., p. 12.

[26] Ibid., p. 15.

[27] Ibid.

[28] Ibid., p. 10.

[29] Ibid.

[30] Ibid.

[31] Ibid.

[32] Ibid., p. 22.

33 Ibid., p. 24.

34 Ibid., p. 27.

35 In Defense of Animals, "Dissection Campaign: Resources," http://www.idausa.org/campaigns/dissection/resourcesdis.html.

36 In Defense of Animals website, Sample Letter to the Editor, http://www.idausa.org/campaigns/dissection/sampleletterd.html.

37 Debra J. Saunders, "Vegan Elementary," *San Francisco Chronicle*, October 26, 2003. (Saunders is married to the author.)

Chapter 9: Advocating Terror

1 Susie Steiner, "Security Alert as Protestor Nears Death," *Times* (London), December 7, 1998.

2 Barry Horne, "An Animal Passion with Murder in Its Heart," *Sunday Times* (London), December 6, 1998.

3 Ibid.

4 John Vidal, "Animal Rights Activist Buried," *Guardian*, November 17, 2001.

5 J. V. Chamry, "Another Day at the Office," BBC Focus, July 2008, p. 63.

6 Wesley J. Smith, *Fighting for Public Justice: Cases and Trial Lawyers That Made a Difference* (Washington, D.C., and Oakland: Trial Lawyers for Public Justice Foundation, 2001), pp. 98–105.

7 Ibid., pp. 179–80.

8 Ibid., pp. 358–59.

9 Southern Poverty Law Center, "From Push to Shove," *Intelligence Report*, Fall 2002, p. 21.

10 Ibid.

11 Ibid., p. 26.

12 Ibid., p. 27.

13 Terry Frieden, "FBI, ATF Address Domestic Terrorism," CNN, May 19, 2005, http://www.cnn.com/2005/US/05/19/domestic.terrorism.

14 Statement of John E. Lewis, Deputy Assistant Director, Counterterrorism Division, before the U.S. Senate Committee on Environment and Public Works, May 18, 2005.

15 Federal Bureau of Investigation, *Terrorism 2002–2005*, pp. 32–34, http://www.fbi.gov/publications/terror/terrorism2002_2005.htm.

16 Adrian Morrison, interview with author, January 12, 1999.

17 P. Michael Conn and James V. Parker, *The Animal Research War* (New York: Palgrave Macmillan, 2008), p. 103.

18 Screaming Wolf, "A Declaration of War: Killing People to Save the Animals and the Environment," no named publisher, no copyright, 1991, p. 10.

19 Ibid., p. 44.

20 Ibid., p. 60.

21 Anonymous authors, *Arson-Around with Auntie ALF: Your Guide to Putting the Heat on Animal Abusers Everywhere*, no copyright, no year of publication available, p. 2.

22 Ibid.

23 Ibid., pp. 6–7.

24 Ibid., p. 20.

25 Anonymous author(s), *The ALF Primer: As Darkness Falls*, no copyright, distributed by the North American Animal Liberation Front Support Group and online.

26 Ibid., p. 4.

27 Ibid., pp. 10–11.

28 Ibid.

Chapter 10: Tertiary Targeting

1 Editorial, "Beastly Behavior," *USA Today*, December 9, 1999.

2 Federal Bureau of Investigation, *Terrorism 2002–2005*, p. 16, http://www.fbi.gov/publications/terror/terrorism2002_2005.htm.

3 Ibid.

4 "Animal Rights Activists Target Medical Field," MSNBC, May 18, 2005, http://www.msnbc.msn.com/id/7898194.

5 "Terrorizing Villaraigosa," *LA Weekly*, December 19, 2007.

6 "Developer Quits after Animal Activist Threat," *Dutch News*, January 7, 2008, http://www.dutchnews.nl/news/archives/print/008020.php.

7 Gareth Walsh and Jonathan Calvert, "Unmasked: Animal Extremist Waging War on Oxford," *Sunday Times* (London), February 19, 2006.

8 "Row Rages as Monkey Lab Shelved," BBC News, January 27, 2004.

9 "Willing to Maim in the Name of Animals," BBC News, December 7, 2006.

10 Greg Moran, "Animal Rights Activist Pleads Guilty to Charge Related to Arson," *San Diego Union Tribune*, December 15, 2007.

11 Amy Goodman, interview with Jonathan Paul, *Democracy Now!* NPR, October 31, 2007, http://www.democracynow.org/about.

12 Zoe Broughton, "Seeing Is Believing—Cruelty to Dogs at Huntingdon Life Sciences," *Ecologist*, March 2001.

13 SHAC has begun demonstrating against Staples, the office supply company, for selling supplies to HLS. http://www.shac.net/ ARCHIVES/ 2008/february/20.html.

14 Statement of William Trundley, Director, Vice President Corporate Security & Investigations, GlaxoSmithKline, before the U.S. House Judiciary Subcommittee on Crime, Terrorism and Homeland Security, May 23, 2006, http://judiciary.house.gov/HearingTestimony.aspx?ID= 413.

15 David Hartman, "Stock Market Trader Targeted," *Edmonton Sun*, August 30, 2002.

16 "Animal Groups Bomb Chiron HQ," DrugResearcher.com, September 2, 2003, http://www.drugresearcher.com/news/ng.asp?id=10799-animal-groups-bomb.

17 Sean Holstege, "Home of Chiron Exec Vandalized," *Oakland Tribune*, August 17, 2004, http://findarticles.com/p/articles/mi_qn4176/is_ 20040817/ai_n14580550.

18 Wesley J. Smith, "Wall Street Goes Wobbly," *Weekly Standard*, October 17, 2005.

19 Jo-Ann Goodwin, "The Animals of Hatred," *Daily Mail*, October 15, 2003.

20 Anonymous communiqué, *Bite Back Magazine*, December 7, 2007, http://www.directaction.info/news_dec10_07.htm.

21 Southern Poverty Law Center, "From Push to Shove," *Intelligence Report*, Fall 2002, p. 27.

22 Statement of Richard P. Bernard, Executive Vice President and General Counsel, New York Stock Exchange, before the U.S. Senate Committee on Environment and Public Works, October 26, 2005.

23 Life Sciences Research press release, "LSR to List on the New York Stock Exchange," August 22, 2005.

[24] Statement of Mark Bibi, General Counsel, Huntingdon Life Sciences, before the U.S. Senate Committee on Environment and Public Works, October 26, 2005.

[25] Statement of Richard P. Bernard.

[26] Aina Hunter, "Targeting the Testers," North American Animal Liberation Press Office, June 20, 2006, http://www.animalliberationfront. com/News/2006_06/WARTargettingTesters.htm.

[27] United Press International, "Animal Researchers Claim Victory with NYSE," December 28, 2006.

[28] http://www.shac.net/TARGETS/suppliers/suppliers.html.

[29] http://www.shac.net/ARCHIVES/2008/february/18.html, accessed on February 19, 2008.

[30] Telephone request for interview with Mr. Brockway, February 19, 2008.

Chapter 11: *Praising with Faint Condemnation*

[1] Gary L. Francione, interview with author, March 21, 2008.

[2] Steven Best, "Agent Wayne Pacelle, the Hypocrisy Society of the United States, and the Thrill Kill Cult," Institute for Critical Animal Studies Blog, August 25, 2008, http://criticalanimalstudies.blogspot.com/ 2008/08/agent-wayne-pacelle-hypocrisy-society.html.

[3] Carla Bennett, "Ask Carla," http://www.askcarla.com/answers.asp? QuestionandanswerID=282.

[4] David T. Hardy, *America's New Extremists: What You Need to Know about the Animal Rights Movement* (Washington Legal Foundation, 1990), p. 32.

[5] Center for Consumer Freedom, "Blackeye," ActivistCash.com, http://www.activistcash.com/organization_blackeye.cfm/oid/21.

[6] "A Serious Case of Puppy Love," *Time*, November 28, 1988.

[7] David Martosko, interview with author, February 20, 2008.

[8] Government's Sentencing Memorandum, *United States of America v. Rodney Adam Coronado*, No 1:93-CXR-116, July 31, 1995.

[9] Ibid., p. 6.

[10] Ibid., pp. 6–7.

[11] Ibid., p. 9, emphasis within the text.

[12] It is worth reiterating that Newkirk refused my request to interview her about these and other matters.

[13] Sentencing Memorandum, *United States v. Coronado*, pp. 9–10.

[14] People for the Ethical Treatment of Animals, Form 990, Tax Return of Organization Exempt from Income Tax, 2000, http://www.undueinfluence.com/PETA%20990%202001.pdf.

[15] Center for Consumer Freedom, "Joshua Harper Biography," Activist-Cash.com, http://www.activistcash.com/biography.cfm/bid/3249.

[16] PETA, 2000 Tax Return.

[17] Southern Poverty Law Center, "From Push to Shove," *Intelligence Report,* Fall 2002, p. 24.

[18] Ibid.

[19] Ibid.

[20] Steven Best and Anthony J. Nocella II, eds., *Terrorists or Freedom Fighters?* (New York: Lantern Books, 2004).

[21] David Kocieniewski, "Six Animal Rights Advocates Are Convicted of Terrorism," *New York Times,* March 3, 2006.

[22] Berny Morson, "CU Regents Fire Ward Churchill," *Rocky Mountain News,* July 25, 2007.

[23] Rod Coronado, "Direct Actions Speak Louder Than Words," in *Terrorists or Freedom Fighters?* pp. 183–84.

[24] Gary Yourofsky, "Abolition, Liberation, Freedom: Coming to a Fur Farm Near You," in *Terrorists or Freedom Fighters?* p. 130.

[25] Quoted from "Animal Rights 2002" convention in "Pattrice Jones," ActivistCash.com, http://www.activistcash.com/biography.cfm/bid/3372.

[26] Pattrice Jones, "Mothers with Monkeywrenches: Feminist Imperatives and the ALF," in *Terrorists or Freedom Fighters?* p. 151.

[27] Ingrid Newkirk, "The ALF: Who, Why, and What?" in *Terrorists or Freedom Fighters?* p. 341.

[28] Ibid., p. 343.

[29] Ibid., p. 342.

[30] Bruce G. Friedrich, "Defending Agitation and the ALF," in *Terrorists or Freedom Fighters?* p. 254.

[31] Ibid., p. 262.

[32] Tom Regan, "How to Justify Violence," in *Terrorists or Freedom Fighters?* p. 235.

[33] Ibid., p. 234.

[34] Ibid., p. 236.

Chapter 12: Murder They Wrote?

[1] Rod Coronado, "Direct Actions Speak Louder than Words," in *Terrorists or Freedom Fighters?* ed. Steven Best and Anthony J. Nocella II (New York: Lantern Books, 2004), p. 183.

[2] Tim Luckhurst, "Professor Colin Blakemore: The Science of Defiance," *Independent*, December 28, 2003.

[3] Code of Federal Regulations, Title 28 (Judicial Administration), Part 0.85.

[4] Tom Ragan, "UCSC Researcher Targeted in Attack—Animal Rights Activists Believed to Be behind Home Invasion," *Santa Cruz Sentinel*, February 25, 2008.

[5] Lisa Amin, "Pamphlet Threatens UCSC Researchers," KGO-TV, July 30, 2008.

[6] Mary Anne Ostrom, "Firebombs Target UC-Santa Cruz Scientists Who Use Animals in Research," *San Jose Mercury News*, August 3, 2008.

[7] Peter Fimrite, "$50,000 Reward in Chiron Probe," *San Francisco Chronicle*, December 5, 2003.

[8] United States Department of Justice press release, January 25, 2006.

[9] "Smash the State, Crush the Cage" conference Web page, http://hala-conference.blogspot.com/search/label/Saturday%20Workshops.

[10] For an excellent biography of John Brown, see David S. Reynolds, *John Brown, Abolitionist* (New York: Alfred A. Knopf, 2004).

[11] Rod Coronado, "In the Spirit of Solidarity," *No Compromise!*, www.nocompromise.org/issues/22solidarity.html.

[12] Gary Yourofsky, "Animal Rights and Ethical Veganism," *The Shield*, University of Southern Indiana, January 24, 2008, http://media.www.usishield.com/media/storage/paper605/news/2008/01/24/Opinion/Special.Editorial.Animal.Rights.Ethical.Veganism-3164767.shtm.

[13] Sophie Goodchild and Steve Bloomfield, "Revealed: Animal Rights Extremists Set Up Combat Skills Training Camp in Britain," *Independent*, July 25, 2004.

[14] Rosie Murray-West, "Animal Rights Camp to Export Terror," *Telegraph*, May 5, 2006.

[15] Steven Best, "It's War! The Escalating Battle between Activists and the Corporate-State Complex," in *Terrorists or Freedom Fighters?* p. 301.

[16] Ibid., pp. 336–37.

[17] Gareth Walsh, "Clarke Bars U.S. Animal Activist," *Times* (London), August 28, 2005.

[18] "Banned Activist Resorts to Video," BBC News, September 4, 2004.

[19] Center for Consumer Freedom, "Dr. Jerry Vlasak Biography," Activist-Cash.com, http://www.activistcash.com/biography.cfm/bid/3437.

[20] http://www.animalliberationpressoffice.org/

[21] Jamie Doward, "Kill Scientists, Says Animal Rights Chief," *Observer*, July 25, 2004.

[22] Jerry Vlasak, "Dr. Jerry Vlasak Replies to Media Libel," Indymedia UK, July 25, 2005, http://www.indymedia.org.uk/en/2004/07/295293.html.

[23] U.S. Senate Committee on Environment and Public Works, transcript, "A Second Hearing on Eco-Terrorism Specifically Examining Stop Huntingdon Animal Cruelty (SHAC)," October 26, 2005, http://www.naiaonline.org/pdfs/Oct.%2026,%202005%20eco-terrorism%20transcript.pdf.

[24] Southern Poverty Law Center, "From Push to Shove," *Intelligence Report*, Fall 2002, p. 23.

[25] "David Blenkinsop Receives Prison for Animal Rights Bombing Campaign," AnimalRights.Net, http://www.animalrights.net/archives/year/2002/000385.html.

[26] Andrew Alderson, "This Is the Front Line in the Animal Rights War—and the Doorstep Is the Battlefield," *Telegraph*, July 27, 2007.

[27] Stephanie van den Berg, "Fortuyn's Suspected Killer Silent on Eve of First Hearing," Agence France-Presse, August 8, 2002.

[28] Justin Sparks, "Fortuyn Killer Linked to Earlier Death," *Sunday Times* (London), May 12, 2002.

[29] Ibid.

[30] Adam Sage, "I Had to Do What I Did, Claims Fortuyn's Assassin," *Times* (London), March 28, 2003.

[31] Southern Poverty Law Center, "From Push to Shove," p. 29.

[32] S. 3880: Animal Enterprise Terrorism Act, 109th Congress, 2nd Session, http://thomas.loc.gov/cgi-bin/query/D?c109:4:./temp/~c109SqIqkL.

[33] Humane Society of the United States, Fact Sheet, "Oppose the Animal Enterprise Terrorism Act (AETA)," http://www.hsus.org/webfiles/PDF/109_AETA_factsheet.pdf.

[34] Steven Best, "The Animal Enterprise Protection Act: New, Improved, and ACLU Approved," posted on Animal Liberation Front.com, http://www.animalliberationfront.com/ALFront/AgainstALF/AETA New.htm.

[35] S. 3880: Animal Enterprise Terrorism Act.

[36] Kevin Jonas, "Bricks and Bullhorns," in *Terrorists or Freedom Fighters?* p. 269.

[37] United States Attorney's Office, District of New Jersey, "Militant Animal Rights Group Convicted in Campaign to Terrorize Company, Employees, Others," press release, March 2, 2006, http://www.usdoj.gov/usao/nj/press/files/shac0302_r.htm.

[38] "SHAC 7 Defendants Sentenced This Week," Indymedia, September 14, 2006, http://rochester.indymedia.org/newswire/display/19013/index.php.

Chapter 13: *Animal Rights vs. Medical Research*

[1] As quoted in, "How Ingrid Broke Her Wrist," *The PETA Files*, http://blog.peta.org/archives/2007/10/how_ingrid_brok.php.

[2] For a really good general history of pain control, see Thomas Dormandy, *The Worst of Evils: The Fight against Pain* (New Haven: Yale University Press, 2006).

[3] Eric Chevlen, interview with author, March 23, 2008.

[4] Leonard Grumbach, "The Prediction of Analgesic Activity in Man by Animal Testing," in *Pain: Henry Ford Hospital International Symposium*, ed. Robert S. Knighton and Paul R. Dumke (Boston: Little Brown & Co., 1966), p. 164.

[5] Ronald Melzack and Patrick D. Wall, "Pain Mechanisms: A New Theory," *Science*, vol. 150 (1965), pp. 971–79.

[6] Marcia L. Meldrum, "A Capsule History of Pain Management," *Journal of the American Medical Association*, vol. 290, no. 18 (November 12, 2003), pp. 2470–75.

[7] "The History of Smallpox," About.com, http://dermatology.about.com/cs/smallpox/a/smallpoxhx.htm.

[8] Wolfgang Weyers, *Death of Medicine in Nazi Germany: Dermatology and Dermatopathology under the Swastika* (Philadelphia: Ardor Scribendi, 1998), p. 293.

⁹ Hartmut M. Hanauske-Abel, "Not a Slippery Slope or Sudden Subversion: German Medicine and National Socialism," *British Medical Journal*, vol. 313, no. 7070 (December 7, 1996), Internet version, p. 16.

¹⁰ Jochen Vollmann and Rolf Winau, "Informed Consent in Human Experimentation before the Nuremberg Code," *British Medical Journal*, vol. 313, no. 7070 (December 7, 1996), Internet version, p. 3.

¹¹ Hanauske-Abel, "Not a Slippery Slope or Sudden Subversion."

¹² Robert Jay Lifton, *The Nazi Doctors* (New York: Basic Books, 1986).

¹³ Ibid., pp. 267–414.

¹⁴ For the full text of the Nuremberg Code, please see Supplement.

¹⁵ The Nuremberg Code, as published in Vollman and Winau, "Informed Consent in Human Experimentation," pp. 7–8.

¹⁶ Tom Regan, *The Case for Animal Rights*, paperback ed. (Berkeley: University of California Press, 1985), p. 393.

¹⁷ Gary L. Francione, "The Use of Nonhuman Animals in Biomedical Research: Necessity and Justification," *Journal of Law, Medicine & Ethics*, vol. 35, no. 2 (Summer 2007), pp. 247–48.

¹⁸ Ibid., p. 247.

¹⁹ Mary Carmichael, "Atkins under Attack," *Newsweek*, February 23, 2004.

²⁰ For example, PETA's 1999 federal tax return revealed that the organization gave a "cash grant" in the amount of $432,524 to the PCRM. See also, ActivistCash.com, http://www.activistcash.com/organization_overview.cfm/oid/23.

²¹ Carmichael, "Atkins under Attack."

²² Jamie Doward and Mark Townsend, "Beauty and the Beasts," *Observer*, August 1, 2004.

²³ Neal D. Barnard and Stephen R. Kaufman, "Animal Research Is Wasteful and Misleading," *Scientific American*, February 1997, p. 80.

²⁴ Ibid., p. 82.

²⁵ PETA, "Not Ours to Experiment On," at StopAnimalTests.com, http://www.stopanimaltests.com/index.aspx.

²⁶ P. Michael Conn and James V. Parker, *The Animal Research War* (New York: Palgrave Macmillan, 2008), p. 94.

²⁷ Ingrid Newkirk, "Ms. Bea and Other Beings," sidebar, *Animal Times*, Spring 1999, http://www.peta.org/Living/AT-Spring1999/bea.html.

[28] Jack H. Botting and Adrian R. Morrison, "Unscientific American: Animal Rights or Wrongs," *HMS Beagle*, February 20, 1998.

[29] Ibid.

[30] Associated Press, "WHO Polio Eradication Drive in Home Stretch," *New York Times*, July 8, 1999.

[31] Steven L. Teitelbaum, "Animal Rights Pressure on Scientists," *Science*, vol. 298, no. 5598 (November 22, 2002), p. 1515.

[32] Anne Underwood, "How the Plague Began," *Newsweek*, February 8, 1999, p. 53.

[33] John L. VandeBerg and Stuart M. Zola, "A Unique Medical Resource at Risk," *Nature*, vol. 437 (September 1, 2005), p. 31.

[34] *Vogue*, September 1999, and quoted widely ever since, including at PETA's website.

[35] Jon Cohen, "Drug Development: Protease Inhibitors: A Tale of Two Companies," *Science*, vol. 272, no. 5270 (June 28, 1996), pp. 1882–83.

[36] Peter Tatchell, "Why Animal Research Is Bad Science," Abolitionist-Online, http://www.abolitionist-online.com/article-issue05_why.animal.research.peter-tatchell.shtml.

[37] I learned about this controversy in Brian Carnell, "Did Animal Research Delay Protease Inhibitors?" AnimalRights.net, August 4, 2004.

[38] Richard Gray, "Breakthrough in Animal Spare Parts for Humans," *Telegraph*, July 20, 2008.

[39] Elliot Katz, "President's Message," In Defense of Animals website, http://www.idausa.org/about/welcome.html.

[40] Gary Yourofsky, "Empathy, Education and Animal Rights," Abolitionist-Online, 2005, http://www.abolitionist-online.com/article-issue05_empathy.education.violence_gary.yourofsky.shtml.

[41] Peter Singer, *Animal Liberation*, rev. ed. (New York: Avon Books, 1990), p. 94.

[42] Matthew Scully, *Dominion: The Power of Man, the Suffering of Animals, and the Call to Mercy*, paperback ed. (New York: St. Martin's Griffin, 2002), p. 381.

Chapter 14: Our System of Animal Research

1 World Health Organization, *Severe Acute Respiratory Syndrome (SARS): Status of the Outbreak and Lessons for the Immediate Future*, May 20, 2003, http://www.who.int/csr/media/sars_wha.pdf.

2 National Institutes of Health, press release, "First U.S. SARS Vaccine Trial Opens at NIH," December 13, 2004.

3 Centers for Disease Control and Prevention, Fact Sheet, "Basic Information About SARS," May 3, 2005.

4 Benedict Carey, "Monkeys Think, Moving Artificial Arm as Own," *New York Times*, May 29, 2008.

5 Dr. Edward Taub, interview with author, November 16, 2007.

6 Sabin Russell, "Stanford Nanotech Project May Find Tumors," *San Francisco Chronicle*, April 3, 2008.

7 National Institutes of Health, Fact Sheet, "Regenerative Medicine," http://www.nih.gov/about/researchresultsforthepublic/Regen.pdf.

8 In other work, on ethical grounds, I have supported President George W. Bush's federal funding restrictions on embryonic stem cell research and supported outlawing all forms of human cloning, one purpose of which would be to obtain cloned embryonic stem cells. For more information about my views in this area, see Wesley J. Smith, *Consumer's Guide to a Brave New World* (San Francisco: Encounter Books, 2004).

9 James Fallon et al., "*In Vivo* Induction of Massive Proliferation, Directed Migration, and Differentiation of Neural Cells in the Adult Mammalian Brain," *Proceedings of the National Academy of Sciences*, vol. 97, no. 26 (December 19, 2000), pp. 14686–91.

10 "Adult Stem Cell Findings Offer New Hope for Parkinson's Cure," Physorg.com, June 6, 2008, http://physorg.com/news131968438.html.

11 Kazutoshi Takahashi and Shinya Yamanaka, "Induction of Pluripotent Stem Cells from Mouse Embryonic and Adult Fibroblast Cultures by Defined Factors," *Cell*, vol. 126, no. 4 (August 25, 2006), pp. 663–676.

12 Junying Yu, James A. Thomson et al., "Induced Pluripotent Stem Cell Lines Derived from Human Somatic Cells," *Science Express*, November 22, 2007.

13 Thomson Financial News, "Stem Cell Therapy in Rats Improves Parkinson's: Study," *Forbes*, April 7, 2008, http://www.forbes.com/markets/feeds/afx/2008/04/07/afx4859467.html.

[14] Code of Federal Regulations, Title 21 (Food and Drugs), Part 312.

[15] These are generally governed by the rules and policies of the Center for Drug Evaluation and Research and the Center for Biologics Evaluation and Research.

[16] United States Food and Drug Administration, "FDA and the Drug Development Process: How the Agency Ensures That Drugs Are Safe and Effective," http://www.fda.gov/opacom/factsheets/justthefacts/17drgdev.html.

[17] PETA, *The PETA Guide to Compassionate Living,* http://www.peta2.com/college/pdf/CompassionateLiving.pdf.

[18] 3R Research Foundation Switzerland, "Three R Training," http://3r-training.tierversuch.ch/en/module_3r/draize_test_replacement/eye_irritation.

[19] Research Defense Society, "Animal Welfare: Eye Irritancy," http://www.rds-online.org.uk/pages/page.asp?i_ToolbarID=4&i_PageID=149#eye.

[20] Board on Environmental Studies and Toxicology, National Academy of Sciences, *Toxicity Testing for Assessment of Environmental Agents: Interim Report* (Washington, D.C.: National Academy of Sciences Press, 2006), p. 29.

[21] Ibid., p. 30.

[22] Ibid., p. 33.

[23] Ibid.

Chapter 15: Ensuring the Proper Care of Lab Animals

[1] Some of this material first appeared in Wesley J. Smith, *Culture of Death: The Assault on Medical Ethics in America* (San Francisco: Encounter Books, 2001).

[2] National Research Council, Commission on Life Sciences, et al., *Use of Laboratory Animals in Biomedical and Behavioral Research* (Washington, D.C.: National Academies Press, 1988), pp. 49–50.

[3] Sally Satel, "You Dirty Rats: Activists Jeopardize Biomedical Research," TCS Daily, December 11, 2001, http://www.tcsdaily.com/article.aspx?id=121101E.

[4] Source: Association for Assessment and Accreditation of Laboratory Animal Care International (AAALAC).

[5] John G. Miller, executive director of AAALAC, interview with author, April 7, 2008.

[6] Carl Cohen, "The Case for the Use of Animals in Biomedical Research," *New England Journal of Medicine*, vol. 315, n. 14 (October 2, 1986), p. 869.

[7] Allison Abbott, "Swiss Court Bans Work on Macaque Brains," *Nature*, vol. 453 (June 12, 2008), p. 833.

[8] Frankie Trull, interview with author, June 10, 2008.

[9] Gilbert M. Gaul, "In U.S., Few Alternatives to Testing on Animals," *Washington Post*, April 12, 2008.

Chapter 16: Meat Is Not Murder

[1] The "meat is murder" slogan is used ubiquitously throughout the animal rights movement. Indeed, PETA sells T-shirts and lapel buttons carrying the slogan on its website.

[2] Dan Piraro, "Are Humans Carnivores?" Bizarro website, http://www.bizarro.com/vegan/vegan_carnivores.htm (accessed June 16, 2008).

[3] "Humans Are Omnivores," adapted from a talk by John McArdle, Ph.D., Vegetarian Resource Group, http://www.vrg.org/nutshell/omni.htm.

[4] Natalie Angier, "Cooking and How It Slew the Beast," *New York Times*, May 28, 2002.

[5] "Humans Are Omnivores."

[6] PETA, "Factory Farming: Mechanized Madness," http://www.peta.org/mc/factsheet_display.asp?ID=103.

[7] Animal Agriculture Alliance, "A Few Common Myths and Facts," http://www.animalagalliance.org/main/home.cfm?Section=Main&Category=PressReleases.

[8] Michael Pollan, *The Omnivore's Dilemma: A Natural History of Four Meals* (New York: Penguin Books, 2006).

[9] Ibid., p. 316.

[10] Ibid., p. 326.

[11] Ibid., p. 317.

[12] Ibid., p. 231.

[13] Ibid., p. 363.

[14] Humane Society of the United States, "Humane Eating and the Three Rs," http://www.hsus.org/farm/humaneeating/rrr.html.

[15] Farm Sanctuary, "Humane Meat," http://www.farmsanctuary.org/about/humane_meat_position.htm.

[16] Pollan, *The Omnivore's Dilemma*, p. 411.

[17] These were the price differentials at my local Safeway supermarket in June 2008.

[18] Matthew Scully, *Dominion: The Power of Man, the Suffering of Animals, and the Call to Mercy* (New York: St. Martin's Press, 2002), p. 393.

[19] PETA Media Center, Factsheets, "Factory Farming: Mechanized Madness," http://peta.org/mc/factsheet_display.asp?ID=103.

[20] Temple Grandin and Catherine Johnson, *Animals in Translation: Using the Mysteries of Autism to Decode Animal Behavior* (New York: Scribner, 2005), p. 17.

[21] Ibid., p. 23.

[22] Ibid.

[23] Ibid., p. 268.

[24] Stephanie Simon, "Killing Them Softly," *Los Angeles Times*, April 29, 2003.

[25] Arnold Bender, *Meat and Meat Products in Human Nutrition in Developing Countries* (Rome: Food and Agricultural Organization of the United Nations, 1992), http://www.fao.org/docrep/t0562e/t0562e00.htm.

[26] For example, see Matthew Hill, "Vegetarian Diet Linked to Genital Birth Defects," BBC News, July 2, 1999.

[27] Alison McCook, "Babies' Mental Delay Tied to Moms' Vegan Diet," Reuters, January 30, 2003.

[28] Vegetarian Society, Information Sheet, "Vitamin B12," http://www.vegsoc.org/info/b12.html .The Vegetarian Society defines "a vegetarian as someone living on a diet of grains, pulses, nuts, seeds, vegetables and fruits, with or without the use of dairy products and eggs. A vegetarian does not eat any meat, poultry, game, fish, shellfish or crustacea, or slaughter by-products."

[29] Source: United States Department of Agriculture, MyPyramid.Gov, http://www.mypyramid.gov/index.html.

[30] Rachel Shields, "Animal Rights Group Turns Its Fire on Celebrity Meat-Eaters," *Independent*, June 29, 2008.

[31] Gary L. Francione, interview with author, June 28, 2008.

[32] S. L. Davis, "The Least Harm Principle Suggests That Humans Should Eat Beef, Lamb, Dairy, Not a Vegan Diet," *Proceedings of the Third Congress of the European Society for Agriculture and Food Ethics*, 2001, pp. 449–50, as reprinted in *Free Republic*, August 29, 2003, http://www.freerepublic.com/focus/f-news/972951/posts.

Chapter 17: Fur, Hunting, and Zoos

[1] PETA, "Down and Silk: Bird and Insects Exploited for Fabric," http://www.peta.org/mc/factsheet_display.asp?ID=121.

[2] PETA, "Animals Used for Clothing," www.peta.org/actioncenter/clothing.asp.

[3] American Veterinary Medical Association, *AVMA Guidelines on Euthanasia*, June 2007, p. 28. The AVMA says, "For smaller species, CO appears to be an adequate method for euthanasia." Ibid., p. 10.

[4] PETA Media Center, "Inside the Fur Industry: Animal Factories," http://www.peta.org/mc/factsheet_display.asp?ID=56.

[5] *AVMA Guidelines on Euthanasia*, p. 28.

[6] Ibid., p. 15.

[7] Paul Westwood, interview with author, June 30, 2008.

[8] United States Department of Agriculture, National Agricultural Statistics Service, "Mink," 2007 Report.

[9] PETA, FurIsDeadCom, www.furisdead.com.

[10] PETA, "Inside the Fur Industry: Trapping Maims and Kills Animals," http://www.peta.org/mc/factsheet_display.asp?ID=57.

[11] Herb Bergquist, interview with author, June 29, 2008.

[12] David W. Kuehn et al., "Trap-Related Injuries to Gray Wolves in Minnesota," *Journal of Wildlife Management*, vol. 50, no. 1 (January 1986), pp. 90–91.

[13] Bergquist interview.

[14] Donnie MacLeod, interview with author, June 28, 2008.

[15] Bergquist interview. For more information on fur trapping, see for example http://www.macrwm.org/highly.htm.

[16] Clifford Krauss, "The War against the Fur Trade Backfires, Endangering a Way of Life," *New York Times*, February 4, 2003.

[17] The Wildlife Society, "Final TWS Position Statement: Traps, Trapping, and Furbearer Management," http://joomla.wildlife.org/documents/positionstatements/09-Trapping.pdf.

[18] "In New Twist on Animal Rights, Hunter Is Prey," *New York Times*, November 23, 1990.

[19] *Full Cry*, October 1990, as quoted at ActivistCash.com, http://www.activistcash.com/biography_quotes.cfm/bid/3366, and many other sources.

[20] Humane Society of the United States, "Wildlife Abuse Campaign," http://www.hsus.org/hunt.

[21] Jim Amrhein, "Right to Hunt vs. Animal Rights," *Daily Reckoning*, www.dailyreckoning.com/rpt/LegendsOfTheFall.html.

[22] PETA, "Zoos: Pitiful Prisons," http://www.peta.org/factsheet/files/FactsheetDisplay.asp?ID=67.

[23] Bridget M. Kuehn, "Is It Ethical to Keep Animals in Zoos?" *Journal of the American Veterinary Medical Association*, December 1, 2002.

[24] Association of Zoos and Aquariums, *The Guide to Accreditation of Zoological Parks and Aquariums*, 2008 edition (Silver Spring, Md., 2008), p. 6.

[25] John H. Falk et al., *Why Zoos and Aquariums Matter: Assessing the Impact of a Visit to a Zoo or Aquarium* (Silver Spring, Md.: Association of Zoos and Aquariums, 2007), p. 4, http://www.aza.org/ConEd/Documents/Why_Zoos_Matter.pdf.

[26] Association of Zoos and Aquariums, "Numbers, Numbers, Numbers," http://www.aza.org/Newsroom/CurrentStatistics/index.html. A list of all the AZA-accredited institutions may be found at: http://www.aza.org/Accreditation/AccreditList/index.html#M.

Chapter 18: The Importance of Being Human

[1] Ilana Mercer, "In Defense of Michael Vick," WorldNetDaily, August 17, 2007, http://worldnetdaily.com/news/article.asp?ARTICLE_ID=57192.

[2] Ilana Mercer, "In Defense of Michael Vick, Part 2," WorldNetDaily, August 24, 2007, http://worldnetdaily.com/news/article.asp?ARTICLE_ID=57295.

[3] Carl Cohen, "Rights and Interests," in *The Animal Rights Debate*, by Carl Cohen and Tom Regan (Lanham, Md.: Rowman & Littlefield, 2001), p. 17.

[4] Carl Cohen, "Why Animals Do Not Have Rights," in *The Animal Rights Debate*, pp. 30–31.

[5] David S. Oderberg, "The Illusion of Animal Rights," *Human Life Review*, Spring–Summer 2000, p. 42.

[6] Robert P. George and Christopher Tollefsen, *Embryo: A Defense of Human Life* (New York: Doubleday, 2008), p. 112.

[7] Matthew Scully, *Dominion: The Power of Man, the Suffering of Animals, and the Call to Mercy* (New York: St. Martin's Griffin, 2002), p. 287.

[8] Allen C. Guelzo, *Abraham Lincoln: Redeemer President* (Grand Rapids, Mich.: William B. Eerdmans, 1999), p. 367.

[9] David Grumett, "Vegetarian or Franciscan? Flexible Dietary Choices Past and Present," *Journal for the Study of Religion, Nature and Culture*, vol. 1, no. 4 (2007).

[10] For more particulars on Peter Singer's philosophy as it relates to the treatment of human beings, see Wesley J. Smith, *Culture of Death: The Assault on Medical Ethics in America* (San Francisco: Encounter Books, 2001).

[11] Oderberg, "The Illusion of Animal Rights," p. 43.

[12] Declaration of Independence, 1776.

[13] Hans Jonas, *The Phenomenon of Life: Toward a Philosophical Biology* (Evanston, Ill.: Northwestern University Press, 1966), p. 283.

[14] Charles S. Nicoll, "A Physiologist's Views on the Animal Rights/Liberation Movement," *Physiologist*, vol. 34, no. 6 (1991), p. 307.

[15] Ibid., pp. 307–8.

[16] Carl Cohen, "Do Animals Have Rights?" *Ethics and Behavior*, vol. 7, no. 2 (1997), p. 95.

[17] Peter Singer, "All Animals Are Equal," in *Animal Rights and Human Obligations*, ed. Tom Regan and Peter Singer (Englewood Cliffs, N.J.: Prentice-Hall, 1989), p. 169.

[18] Cohen, "Do Animals Have Rights?" p. 97.

[19] Ibid., p. 98.

[20] Mortimer J. Adler, *The Difference of Man and the Difference It Makes* (New York: Fordham University Press, 1993), p. 264.

[21] Ibid., p. 265.

[22] Michael Specter, "The Extremist," *New Yorker*, April 14, 2003, p. 58.

[23] Animal Liberation Front, "Anthropocentrism," http://www.animalliberationfront.com/Philosophy/Morality/Speciesism/Anthropocentrism.htm.

[24] Scully, *Dominion*, p. 359, p. 77.

[25] Ibid., p. 389.

[26] Ibid., p. 298.

[27] See my review of *Dominion*, titled "Man and Beast," *Weekly Standard*, October 28, 2002.

[28] Swiss Federal Ethics Committee on Non-Human Biotechnology, "The Dignity of Living Beings with Regard to Plants: Moral Consideration of Plants for Their Own Sake," 2008.

[29] Ibid., p. 12.

[30] Ibid., p. 5.

[31] Ibid., p. 10.

[32] Ibid., p. 9.

[33] Gautam Naik, "Switzerland's Green Power Revolution: Ethicists Ponder Plants' Rights," *Wall Street Journal*, October 10, 2008.

[34] For more information on the "rights of nature" in Ecuador, see Wesley J. Smith, "Why We Call Them Human Rights," *Weekly Standard*, November 24, 2008.

[35] Frans de Waal, *Good Natured: The Origins of Right and Wrong in Humans and Other Animals* (Cambridge, Mass.: Harvard University Press, 1996), p. 218.

[36] Ibid., p. 215.

[37] Ibid., pp. 215–16.

Index